History of Education
Volume 1
1972

History of Education
Volume 1

Volume 1 of the journal *History of Education*

Editor: Malcolm Seaborne

 DAVID & CHARLES: NEWTON ABBOT

ISBN 0 7153 5889 8

Set in Imprint
and printed in Great Britain by
Latimer Trend & Company Limited Plymouth
for David & Charles (Publishers) Limited
South Devon House   Newton Abbot   Devon

Number 1   Volume 1   1972   January

Contents

Contents

History of Education Society

The aim of the Society, founded in 1967, is to further the study of the History of Education by providing opportunities for discussion among those engaged in its study and teaching.

Conferences and meetings are organised, a Bulletin is published twice a year in Spring and Autumn and other publications pertaining to the History of Education are sponsored.

Membership is open to all connected in a professional capacity with education, or engaged in the study or teaching of the History of Education. Overseas members are welcomed and are offered a specially reduced subscription rate. Libraries are invited to subscribe to the Bulletin only; otherwise Society membership is individual not institutional.

Annual Subscriptions Members £2
Overseas Members
  (surface mail) £1
Student Members 50p
Libraries £1
Life Membership £25

Journal subscription

Members of the Society may subscribe to the Journal at the reduced rate of £1.50 pa, provided that they pay their subscription, made out to the History of Education Society, direct to the Treasurer at St Paul's College, Cheltenham. (This concession applies to individual members and not to libraries and other institutional members.)

Editor's Foreword

THE decision to establish this new journal was taken at a general meeting of the History of Education Society,* which was formed in 1967 to further the study of the history of education by providing opportunities for discussion among those engaged in its study and teaching. Already the society organises conferences and meetings on a regular basis and a *Bulletin* is published twice a year for the information of its members. Now, however, by starting this new journal, it is hoped that a wider audience will be reached and that original work in this field of historical study will be promoted still further.

While there are certainly a number of existing journals which include articles on the history of education, there is no one journal in Britain devoted entirely to this subject. The history of education is already studied in university departments and colleges of education, and the number of books and higher degree theses bearing on the subject is considerable and seems to be increasing. Our hope, however, is that this new journal will promote a much wider conception of the history of education than has been usual in the past. Asa Briggs, in the opening article of this first issue, suggests some of the lines along which the study of the subject might develop, and other approaches are being explored in the conferences of the society which have taken themes which help to widen the scope of the subject and to suggest inter-relationships with other disciplines—eg 'The government and control of education' (1968), 'The changing curriculum' (1969), 'History, sociology and education' (1970), and 'Local history and education' (1971).

It is hoped that the publication of this journal will encourage further work in these and other areas. The editorial board, half of whose

---

* The Secretary of the History of Education Society, from whom details of membership may be obtained, is Ian Taylor, St John's College, York YO3 7EX.

3

members are on the committee of the History of Education Society, will not merely act as a body of referees (with outside help where needed) but will seek to pursue an active policy of development. In addition to publishing individual articles arising from current work in the history of education, surveys of the state of research and published work in particular fields are being planned and we hope to have contributions dealing with the history of education in other countries. There will be a separate book review section, in which we propose to concentrate on giving detailed reviews of a limited number of books, together with review articles which deal with books on major or related themes. We also hope to provide brief notices of articles and books in the whole field of the history of education. The Editor will be glad to receive not only articles for consideration but also ideas for discussion or contributions on specific points, which can be included in a separate 'Communications' section.

This first issue of the journal includes articles relating mainly to the nineteenth and twentieth centuries. Articles covering earlier periods will, however, be included in future issues and it is hoped that the proposals outlined above will result in such other regular features as reviews of research, notices of periodical literature and a 'Communications' section.

Malcolm Seaborne

Articles and other contributions should be addressed to the Editor, and books for review to the Reviews Editor, at the addresses given on the inside cover. Articles should normally be between 3,000 and 5,000 words, and should not in any case exceed 8,000 words without prior agreement with the Editor. To facilitate the refereeing of articles, two copies should be submitted (ie original typescript plus carbon or photostat copy). Intending contributors should obtain from the Editor the leaflet 'Information for Contributors'.

ASA BRIGGS

The Study of the History of Education*

I

THE study of the history of education is best considered as part of the wider study of the history of society, social history broadly interpreted with the politics, the economics and, it is necessary to add, the religion put in. Yet for long the study was either neglected or left to a small and scattered group of specialists, some of whom were unaware of the broad trends of historical scholarship. During recent years changes both in education and in the study of history have altered the picture. Education has once more become a major social, political and economic issue; it is natural in such circumstances that there should be a re-interpretation of old issues and the struggles surrounding them. We are already far removed, in consequence, from the attitudes eloquently expressed by J. L. Garvin in his biography of Joseph Chamberlain. 'No Ezekiel's wind,' Garvin exclaimed, 'can make dry bones live in some valleys. Nothing seems more dead and gone today than the educational battles of the early seventies in the Victorian age.'[1] A year after the centenary of the Education Act of 1870, which itself stimu-lated the production of large numbers of local studies based on the examination of source materials which had long been buried and forgotten, the mood of the times is a very different one. It is easy to understand why the 'battles' were so fiercely contested. As for changes in the study of history, they have been sufficiently comprehensive for slogans like 'the new history' to be bandied around in academic circles. Several of these are of special interest and importance to historians of education, and this paper is particularly concerned with six of them.

The first is a new approach to local history, a far more sophisticated version of local history than that common in the past. The study has

* This note is based on a talk to the History of Education Society, given at the London Institute of Education on 22 May 1971.

5

cast off the shackles of antiquarianism, has moved from a rural to an urban ambiance, and has begun to take account not only of institutions or of personalities but of structures and processes.[2] At its best, such study does not divide the past into convenient periods: it searches across the centuries for continuities and discontinuities. Moreover, as it broadens out, it ceases to involve an exercise in illustrating what is already known about national history from local examples and becomes a means of reconstructing national history afresh from local materials. We can already trace the breaking down of set interpretations of national history and the building up of new interpretations in their place.[3]

The second is a new approach to comparative history, a natural sequel to the rediscovery of the variety of experience embedded in local, regional and national sub-cultures. Comparative studies pivot on the discovery of what was common between and what was distinctive to different societies. 'When an analyst cannot experiment with his subject matter through replication, establishment of controls and the manipulation of variables,' an American historian has observed recently, 'then he resorts to the comparative method in the hope of achieving the same explanatory results.'[4] Whatever the difficulties in establishing categories and definitions—and to establish them is essential if historians are to ask similar questions of similar materials—the approach implies both greater care for methodology in research and greater analytical power.

The third is the study of quantitative history, 'Cliometrics', as some Americans have christened it. What began with 'new' economic history has subsequently been paralleled in the writing of social history, with historical demography playing a strategic part in the development of scholarship.[5] There are dangers in a commitment to quantitative approaches which excludes other approaches and in a multiplication of quantitative studies at a low level of argument, but given a critical frame of mind and the ability to ask relevant questions on the part of the historian, quantitative studies, assisted by statistical techniques and supported when necessary by computers, can point to fascinating and sometimes unexpected conclusions. In one respect they are particularly important. 'A quantitative discrepancy between theory and observation,' Professor Kuhn has written, 'is obtrusive. No crisis is so hard to suppress as that which derives from a quantitative anomaly that has resisted all the usual efforts at reconciliation.'[6] Moreover, the analysis of bodies of data which were often collected for strictly limited immediate purposes, very different from the purposes of the historian, can in itself stimulate the asking of new questions. As Schumpeter put it, 'we need statistics not only for explaining things but in order to know precisely what there is to be explained'.[7]

Quantitative history has attracted many able, pioneering minds. So too has the 'new social history', 'history from below', which is still in the process of articulation and development. This, indeed, is the fourth approach which deserves to be identified. Such history makes use of concepts derived from sociology, anthropology and psychology without (when it is at its best) being imprisoned in borrowed social science categories. It also directs attention to people whose names never figured in the older history books, the people who were deprived or neglected in their own time and whose participation in government was minimal or non-existent, whose attitudes towards 'authority' could be deferential or resentful, passive or hostile. The study of 'history from below' often creates a greater sense of understanding along with a recovery of immediacy. It quickens the curiosity of the historian and leads him into the examination of related patterns of work and 'leisure', participation and 'apathy'.[8]

The fifth change in the study of history—at the opposite end of the spectrum—has been the development of a more analytical kind of political history, with attention moving from particular pieces of legislation, though these are still studied within a different frame, to cumulative administrative processes, to the making of critical decisions, to the changing scale and role of organisation. A re-scrutiny of nineteenth-century administrative history is in process, carrying with it useful controversy. It involves less concentration on the 'landmarks' and more on the interplay of people and problems. It will eventually produce a new synthesis, particularly in relation, perhaps, to the forging of social policies.[9]

The sixth change relates to intellectual and cultural history. The history of ideas is beginning to come into its own, not merely the history of the ideas of 'great thinkers' but the history of chains of ideas and their mode of communication through different 'media', the shifting relationships between 'minority' and 'mass' communication, the significance of 'language' and the forms of 'control'. The new history of ideas has been associated with a re-examination of such crucial changes as the invention and development of printing and the subsequent history of literacy and the more recent 'communications revolution'.[10] Yet it has encouraged new tendencies within political and social history also. The kind of interpretation advanced by A. V. Dicey in his still influential *Law and Public Opinion in the Nineteenth Century*, first published in 1905, has been challenged without so far being fully replaced.[11] Although Dicey had very little specifically to say about education, his approach to the broad subject of the making of social policy has done much to influence writers of every kind, many of whom have sharply questioned his assumptions and conclusions.

It is the main argument of this paper that each of these new approaches—and they are related to each other—needs to be studied carefully by historians of education. To some extent they all reflect, as most historiographical change has always reflected, current preoccupations. To some extent they are made possible by the availability of new materials and techniques, although techniques (including oral interview) are, of course, instrumental and depend for their success on the quality of the questions asked. Most important of all, the new approaches represent a somewhat new balance between specialisation and generalisation. Historical study must involve specialisation if it is to advance, but the old barriers between the different sub-branches of history are breaking down and new efforts at synthesis are being made.

The study of the history of education will not, in my view, be adequately furthered if there is to be new departmentalisation with a new sub-branch of history, 'the history of education', being increasingly separated out from the rest. There may be something to learn in this connection from recent developments in the study of labour history and of urban history. In both of these cases groups of interested historians have been created in this country in recent years, each with its own meetings and its own system of scholarly communication.[12] Unfortunately there are always historians who are more aware of their separate identity as specialists, even of their status, than of the potential contribution which they can make to the study of history as a whole. Yet the wisest among the labour and urban historians have recognised that critical issues in the history of labour and of cities cannot be studied in isolation from other branches of history. Against this background the History of Education Society, founded in 1967, is poised at a particularly interesting moment in its short life.[13] There are so many questions to ask about educational history (curriculum as well as policy) that it is essential that they should be placed in their general context and that the answers should be related, when possible, to the kind of answers which social historians are seeking to provide.

Although the six developments outlined in this paper are 'new', less new perhaps than some of their practitioners realise, there are old guides in the history of education who point in the same direction. One of the most stimulating of them was R. H. Tawney, who was always looking for a synthesis. In an essay written as long ago as 1914 he argued that 'educational problems cannot be considered in isolation' and that in every period of history—he himself was mainly concerned with pre-industrial periods—'educational policy reflects its conceptions of human society'.[14] Much of the later Tawney is forecast in this early statement. In one of the key passages in *Equality* (1931) he emphasised that in considering the place of education in English society it is always necessary to bear in mind that the English social system has been shaped by pre-industrial as well as industrial influences, that it is marked not by a single set of class relations but by two. 'It is at once as businesslike as Manchester and as gentlemanly as Eton; if its hands can be as rough as those of Esau, its voice is as mellifluous as that of Jacob.'[15] The remark has often been overlooked by those who have generalised too simply about English experience, and it reminds us that historians of education must concern themselves not only with 'crises' or 'struggles' of a dramatic kind but with long-term influences and trends. Tawney also reminds us perpetually that society in the

last resort must be looked at not in terms of categories, however
valuable they may be, but in terms of people. He was willing to look
for evidence in every kind of place from 'high literature' to 'common
experience'.

II

Each of the six approaches outlined above is relevant to the study of
the history of education in this country. The first, indeed, is basic. The
new approach to local history and its relationship to national history
must be grasped because of the 'localism' of the English educational
pattern. It was from the periphery not from the centre that English
education developed. As Sir Joshua Fitch, for thirty-six years a leading
HMI, put it in a magisterial article in the *Encyclopedia Britannica*
which deserves to be reprinted, educational provision in England was

> not the product of any theory or plan formulated beforehand by statesmen or
> philosophers. It has come into existence through a long course of experiments,
> compromises, traditions, successes, failures and religious controversies. What
> has been done in this department of public policy is the resultant of many
> diverse forces, and of slow evolution and growth rather than of clear purpose
> and well-defined national aims.[16]

If it is necessary to turn to foreign writers, like de Tocqueville, to
grasp the significance of 'localism' and 'de-centralisation' when viewed
in international terms,[17] it is equally necessary to explore local
economic, social (including religious) and political structures, to understand why initiatives and activities in education varied as much as they
did before the passing of the Education Act of 1870; and it is necessary
to examine in this way a body like the Lancashire Public School
Association which, like the Anti-Corn Law League, to which it owed
much, professed itself a 'national' body in 1850. The contrast between
Manchester and Birmingham, about which so much has recently been
written in relation to nineteenth-century history as a whole, has its
significance in relation to the history of education. The point was clear
enough, indeed, to Francis Adams, the Birmingham-born and based
secretary of the National Education League, founded in 1869. After

directing attention to the Manchester Education Aid Society, established in 1864, he went on to quote the words of George Dixon, the chairman of the league:

> Had my suggestions been favourably received by the gentlemen [in Manchester] to whom they were made, Birmingham would not have originated the League, but would have followed Manchester, which, in my opinion, ought to have headed and was entitled to lead a national movement.[18]

Given comments of this kind and what we already know of the contrasting profiles of England's two largest cities,[19] it is obviously not sufficient in discussing what happened in English education before 1870 to talk in simple terms of differences between 'rural' and 'urban' areas. A far more intensive survey and analysis of particular places is necessary.

After 1870, though the framework changed, the same kind of survey and analysis remains necessary, with the additional point to consider— the relationship between 'national' pressures and local provision. The fact that between 1870 and 1902 the first development of a deliberately organised pattern of national primary education was left to locally based 'school boards' is of major importance, as is, of course, the role of local education authorities since 1902. Several histories of individual boards have been written, often in the form of theses,[20] but few of them move into the kind of comparative local history which is most rewarding. There were more than 2,000 boards in 1902, and there are some interesting aspects of their distribution. Yorkshire, for example, had 280 boards; Lancashire with a population nearly a million larger had only around 50. The contrast here is worth studying, as is the contrast between Lancashire and Yorkshire in other matters of education, including technical education.[21] Within Yorkshire it would be interesting to compare Leeds and Bradford. Turning to comparative national histories, we still lack studies of the way in which primary education was developed 'on the ground' say in one British and one French or German city or in two agricultural areas.[22] The next stage in our understanding of nineteenth-century English history as a whole may well be to follow up the local breakdown of structures and processes within England by comparing across national boundaries.

In this connection it is useful to turn back again to Fitch's *Encyclopedia Britannica* article which was written at the time of the debate on the Education Act of 1902 and remains a good starting point for further exploration. Fitch went out of his way to outline developments in other countries, drawing out what seemed to him the relevant comparisons and contrasts. The same approach had been followed in a more limited way by Francis Adams in the last decades of the nineteenth century when he preceded his important book on *The Elementary School Contest* (1882) with an earlier study of *The Free School System of the United States* (1875). Such 'anatomisation' had been pursued even earlier by Bulwer Lytton in his still valuable book (one of the first nineteenth-century examples of a *genre* which has led up to Anthony Sampson), *England and the English* (1834, reprinted in 1874 in the aftermath of the Education Act).[23] Books of this kind have been used far too little by historians of education, yet backed by contemporary evidence they help us to understand (i) the place of 'voluntarism' within the English context, (ii) the lateness of 'national development' (G. M. Young rightly called education 'the great Victorian omission'), and (iii) the lack of 'system'. It is important to note that none of these points can be explored adequately in terms of the history of education narrowly interpreted.

There is a further way in which comparative approaches are useful. It is interesting to compare the successive *Encyclopedia Britannica* articles on education with each other, going back to James Mill's famous essay for the fifth edition. Fitch, perceptive as always, showed how the approach had changed. In particular, he drew attention to the contrast between his own article and that of Oscar Browning, the famous Eton master, which had been printed in the main volumes of the ninth edition. Browning, writing very much in dilettante style, had been concerned with 'the ideals which have prevailed from time to time' in education (going back to the ancient world); Fitch concentrated on tracing 'the gradual growth of what may be called the English system, the forces which have controlled it, and the results it effected during the last quarter of the nineteenth century'.[24]

At this point, the third new approach to the writing of history becomes directly relevant—the use of quantitative techniques. It was always evident in the nineteenth century, at least from the time of the foundation of the local statistical societies in the 1830s, that the case for educational reform was buttressed by if not grounded in the exposition of statistics. The Act of 1870 was itself preceded by the major local statistical inquiries of the 1860s, some of which were deliberately comparative in character. The mass of nineteenth-century material is worth sifting as it stands, yet it is worth noting that far more can be done with it than was done in the nineteenth century itself. Increased statistical sophistication has already influenced the way in which educational issues are being presented in the twentieth century,[25] and more attention is being paid in current debate to the 'economics of education' (claims on national resources; shares of national income devoted to education; modes of financing numbers, buildings and equipment) than has ever been the case before.[26] The reason has doubtless been the growing volume of public educational expenditure and the need to formulate policies. At the same time, quantitative methods have been applied to educational sociology also, with reference both to class differentials and mobility.[27]

So far these increasingly fashionable approaches have had little impact on historical studies, although one interesting article by E. G. West, who has been actively involved in current debate, is of a pioneering kind, and on the basis of rigorous quantitative analysis questions a number of accepted assumptions about relative educational provision in England and Scotland in the early nineteenth century. The contrast between England and Scotland is one which must be explored by all students of British educational history, and this article is far more than a gloss.[28] There is as much scope for assessing quantitatively the economic limitations to the expansion of voluntary primary education in the nineteenth century (and its social limitations) as there is for examining comparable aspects of public provision in the 1970s. We know far too little about the economics of voluntary effort in every field of social policy and the financial and manpower 'crises' which were a feature of the 'system' both locally and nationally. It is perhaps important to bear in mind also that the Education Act of 1870 which shifted the locus of finance was passed in a year of exceptional business prosperity.

The fourth of the new approaches to the study of history—the emergence of a new kind of social history—has such obvious bearings on the study of educational history that it is not necessary to do more than identify a number of key issues. As far as the relationship between social history and sociology is concerned (terminology, methodologies, boundary questions), there has already been one paper in the *Bulletin* of the History of Education Society,[29] and one textbook, P. W. Musgrave's *Society and Education in England since 1800* (1968), draws fully on sociological analysis.[30] It is important to bear in mind that in any partnership between historian and sociologist (even the most manageable of partnerships, that where historian and sociologist are the same person), the role of the historian is not simply to supply facts and to correct errors.

> History has always been a borrower from other disciplines, and in that sense social-scientific history is just another example of a time-honoured process; but history has always been a lender, and all the social sciences would be immeasurably poorer without knowledge of the historical record. The social sciences are not a self-contained system, one of whose boundaries lies in some fringe area of the historical sciences. Rather the study of man is a continuum, and social-scientific history is a bridge between the social sciences and the humanities.[31]

It would be unfortunate if there were to be boundary disputes in relation to the history and sociology of education, given the need of both for each other. Musgrave has rightly related the history of education to changes within the family, the economy and the social-class system, and the historian of education must be interested in such matters as 'education' through agencies outside the school and relative 'mobility' through education and other routes or agencies in society (a basic problem in nineteenth-century social history), even if these are not his primary focus of interest. It is absurdly restrictive to argue that the history of education is primarily the history of teaching.[32]

At every point in the history of education institutions and motivations, facts and values must be considered together. Take any key passage from the past relating to educational provision and it immediately provokes questions. In 1851, for example, Nathaniel Woodard, founder of the Woodard schools, had this to say:

> It is the glory of a Christian State that it regards all its children with an eye of equal love and our institutions place no impassable barrier between the cottage and the front of the throne; but still parity of rights does not imply equality of power or capacities, of natural or accidental advantages. Common sense forbids that we should lavish our care on those least able to profit from it while we withhold it from those by whom it would be largely repaid. The class compelled to give the greater part of each day to the toilsome earning of its daily bread may be as richly endowed as that which is exempt from this necessity but it is manifest that those who are subject to such a pressure must, as a body, enjoy less opportunities of cultivating their natural endowments.[33]

Whenever the historian of education comes across terms like 'common sense' or 'it is manifest that' he must begin to probe deeply. Indeed, he must be sensitive at every stage to the language of the past (vocabulary, tone, rhetoric). It is important to bear in mind that in the middle years of the nineteenth century, to which this passage belongs, the relationship between education and social class was posed most frequently within the context of relations between the 'middle classes' and the aristocracy and gentry. The leading voices were Tawney's two voices of Eton and Manchester, not those to whom we have become accustomed in twentieth-century dialogue. The Taunton Commission, which does not figure in Eric Midwinter's useful booklet in 'seminar studies on history' called *Nineteenth-Century Education*, is an essential source.[34] It needed an unorthodox thinker like Lytton to get away from mid-Victorian 'common sense' about education and society. 'One great advantage of diffusing knowledge among the lower classes,' he wrote provocatively, 'is the necessity thus imposed on the higher of increasing knowledge among themselves. I suspect that the new modes and systems of education which succeed the most among the people will ultimately be adopted by the gentry.'[35] During the last two decades of the nineteenth century attitudes towards education and society changed as much as attitudes towards other aspects of organisation and policy, with H. G. Wells playing a prominent part in shifting the terms of the debate about education and class to the middle-class/working-class matrix. The Education Act of 1870 was for him 'an act to educate the lower classes for employment on lower class lines, and with specially trained inferior teachers'.[36]

At this point 'history from below' comes into its own. Since the Act of 1870 owed little to working-class pressure and aspects of its implementation were often bitterly resented in working-class areas—the 'school bobby' was never a popular figure[37]—it is essential to examine what happened after 1870 from the vantage point of those who were 'receiving' education as well as from the vantage point of those who were 'supplying' it or causing it to be supplied.[38] Recently it has been clearly realised also that the same kind of examination is necessary even in the period of voluntary provision before 1870 when education was thought of as an instrument of social control, not least by Kay-Shuttleworth.[39] It was difficult for those engaged in promoting education fully to understand the attitudes of those *for* whom they were promoting it, as was frankly recognised by Henry Moseley (a scientist as well as a clergyman), one of the first HMIs. 'The fact is,' he wrote in a minute of 1845, 'that the inner life of the classes below us in society is never penetrated by us. We are profoundly ignorant of the springs of public opinion, the elements of thought and the principles of action among them—those things which we recognise at once as constituting our own social life, in all the moral features which give it thought and substance.'[40] The same kind of point has been made about social policy as a whole in the nineteenth and early twentieth centuries by R. M. Titmuss:

> The poor law, with its quasi-disciplinary functions, rested on assumptions about how people ought to behave. . . . Valuations about the nature of man were written into the social legislation of the day. They informed the means of policy. Derived, as they commonly were, from the norms of behaviour expected by one class from another, and founded on outer rather than inner observation . . . their application to social questions led the new services to treat manifestations of disorder in the individual rather than the underlying causes in the family or social group.[41]

In examining the detailed history of schools it is essential, therefore, to look critically at 'behaviour' and 'discipline' as well as at curricula and methods of teaching. What can we make of such comments as that of the Rotherham School Board Inspector who wrote in a log book of

1890 'found boys and girls in the same playground. Witnessed much indecent behaviour'?[42] The relationship between discipline and 'drill' is well brought out in many late nineteenth-century logbooks, including that of the head teacher of another infant school in Rotherham who hired a drill sergeant to visit school every Tuesday afternoon after being criticised by an inspector.[43] Logbooks and diaries are particularly useful sources, but we have to penetrate beneath the surface to some of the fundamental problems of language and communication which were as crucial in the nineteenth century as they are today.[44] To understand what was 'going on' in a school it is necessary to take account of complex systems of personal and social interaction, involving complex relationships between the experience, language and values which children brought into the school from their own (sometimes contrasting) neighbourhoods and those imparted by their teachers. Questions of curriculum and methods of teaching are best examined when these complexities are properly understood. The sixth new approach to the study of history identified earlier in this paper depends, like the fourth, on insights as much as techniques, although there is much to be gained from the work of anthropologists and of social psychologists.

III

The fifth approach is worth very full consideration in relation to the whole field of educational policy-making, since too often the history of educational legislation is treated in functional terms of a general kind as a necessary adaptation to new sets of economic or political circumstances. The difficulty is that similar circumstances produced different kinds of results in a different order in other societies. To understand what happened in each case we have to look at the intricate interplay of individuals and groups, ideas and interests, and pressures and restraints. The point was well made by John Rex in his *Key Problems of Sociological Theory* when, after urging 'the reshaping of sociological theory so that it is built around the notions of conflict, imperative coordination and balance of power', he went on to take the Education Act of 1902 as his example:

Some sections of the ruling classes were opposed to the ideas of secondary
education altogether. Those who were in favour of it vied with each other
about controlling it because they had different ideas about the content of
education. And the working classes demanded it either in the hope that their
children would 'get on' in the existing order, or because they recognised that
such education would help them in the establishment of a new social system.
The resulting educational system was the outcome of a compromise between
these competing pressures. It is not a system which can in any way be
explained in terms of orthodox functionalist theory. But the manner of its
development and the eventual compromise is exactly what we would have
expected from a conflict model.[45]

Yet whereas Rex dwelt on 'conflict', the historian must always take
account also of 'consensus'. Unlike many other countries, notably the
United States, England has never been a society where there was a
powerful built-in pressure either in the society (or in Parliament) for
the extension of education. It was a fitting prelude to the story of state
intervention that when Roebuck first raised the issue of a grant in 1833
he apologised for taking up the time of the House of Commons on so
uninteresting a topic, and it is interesting to note that in 1891 during
the debate on free education the House had to be counted to make sure
that forty members were present. There have been long periods when
little has happened, and these must be explained along with the
'emergencies', 'campaigns' and 'crises' when conflict was always apparent, as it was in 1869 and 1870 and again in 1902. When Butler
raised the question of education with Churchill in 1941 he was told by
the Prime Minister that instead of thinking of new legislation, which
would create a row, he should get on with his main task of getting the
schools working as well as possible under all the difficulties of wartime.[46]

MacDonagh's emphasis on cumulative administrative processes of a
self-generating kind is directly relevant, therefore, to the historian of
education, but attention must be paid also to what created the sense of
emergency at particular times, how opinion was mobilised, and what
were the practical results. Educational change has come in fits and
starts, and we have to look at moments of crisis as well as at administrative processes or social trends. This means going further, of course,
than examining particular pieces of legislation, and there is truth in

Midwinter's observation that educational history, when it is not written in crude functionalist terms, 'is often studied as a series of legislative enactments, with its students jumping from one Act of Parliament to the next, like mountain goats from peak to peak'. We need amongst other monographs a comprehensive modern study of the activities of the National Education League—explaining clearly why it lost influence as well as why it emerged as a national force. Francis Adams still remains the best source.[47]

Given that England accepted the notion of an educational 'system' imperfectly and falteringly—even Rex's use of the term in relation to the Act of 1902 must be qualified—we have to find a different kind of driving force during many periods of history to that of system-building. The most interesting suggestion for such an alternative was made by John Morley who was profoundly suspicious of 'systems' and at the same time wary about leaving everything to local initiative. As early as 1867 he was writing of the need to develop a 'collective national impulse'; by 1873 he had formulated the idea of reform through the identification of single great 'national issues', among which education was then paramount. His biographer speaks of Morley 'focalising'.[48] It may well be that the interpretation of the history of education in this country during the nineteenth and twentieth centuries would be strengthened if this concept were incorporated within the analysis.

University of Sussex

References

1 J. L. Garvin, *The Life of Joseph Chamberlain*, vol I (1932), 102.
2 See, for example, H. J. Dyos (ed), *The Study of Urban History* (1968) for the variety of approaches as represented by work in progress.
3 See, for example, the volume of essays which I edited called *Chartist Studies* (1958). Compare S. D. Chapman (ed), *The History of Working-Class Housing* (1971) which includes essays on housing in London, Glasgow, Leeds, Nottingham, Liverpool, Birmingham, South-East Lancashire and Ebbw Vale.
4 R. F. Berkhofer, *A Behavioral Approach to Historical Analysis* (1969), 252-3.
5 See R. W. Fogel and S. L. Engerman (eds), *The Reinterpretation of American Economic History* (1971); E. A. Wrigley (ed), *English Historical Demography* (1966).

6   T. S. Kuhn, 'The Function of Measurement in Modern Physical Science' in
    H. Woolf (ed), *Quantification: A History of the Meaning of Measurement in the
    Natural and Social Sciences* (1960), 50, 52.
7   Quoted by S. Thernstrom in the book of essays edited by himself and R. Sennett,
    Nineteenth-Century Cities (1969), 159. For further discussions of quantification,
    see W. O. Aydelotte, *Quantification in History* (1971) and D. S. Landes and
    C. Tilly (eds), *History as a Social Science* (1971).
8   Some of the main aspects and slants of the new social history are set out in the
    preface and postscript to E. P. Thompson, *The Making of the English Working
    Class* (Pelican edn, 1968).
9   See, for example, O. MacDonagh, 'The Nineteenth-Century Revolution in
    Government' in *Historical Journal* (1958), and his reappraisal reappraised by
    H. Parris in ibid (1960). There are useful articles on the same theme in *Victorian
    Studies*, notably V. Cromwell, 'Interpretations of Nineteenth-Century Administra-
    tion: An Analysis' (1966) and G. Sutherland, 'Recent Trends in Administrative
    History' (1970).
10 See, for example, L. Stone, 'Literacy and Education in England, 1640–1900' in
    Journal of Modern History (1968) and E. L. Eisenstein, 'Some Conjectures about
    the Impact of Printing on Western Society and Thought' in *Past and Present*
    (1969). I have dealt with some of the themes of the 'communications revolution'
    in a lecture with that title, printed by the University of Leeds (1965).
11 See the very valuable collection of articles edited by M. Ginsberg, *Law and
    Opinion in England in the Twentieth Century* (1959). For continued reliance on
    Dicey, despite all that has been written recently, see E. E. Rich, *The Education
    Act 1870* (1970).
12 The Society for the Study of Labour History was founded in 1960, and it publishes
    two *Bulletins* each year. There are parallel societies and bulletins in other parts of
    the world. The Urban History Group came into existence a little later, originating
    from 'a desire to exchange information on the scope and progress of research and
    published work'; it publishes an *Urban History Newsletter*. There is a parallel body
    in the United States.
13 The History of Education Society, which now has 410 members, published its
    first *Bulletin* in spring 1968. It provides an invaluable record of work in progress.
14 This important essay, originally published in the *Political Quarterly*, was dismissed
    by a critic as 'pert'. It remains pertinent. It has been reprinted in R. Hinden (ed),
    The Radical Tradition (1964), 70–81. It traces the history of the ideas of 'status'
    and 'the career open to the talents' in education.
15 R. H. Tawney, *Equality* (1952 edn), 58. The whole of this chapter on 'inequality
    and social structure' is essential reading. It should be compared with W. G.
    Runciman, *Relative Deprivation and Social Justice* (1966).
16 J. Fitch, 'Education' in the 'new volumes' of the *Encyclopedia Britannica*, vol
    XXVII (1902).
17 See, for example, A. de Tocqueville, *Journeys to England and Ireland* (ed by
    J. P. Mayer, 1958), passim.
18 F. Adams, *History of the Elementary School Contest in England* (1882), 195.
19 See, for example, my article on 'The Background of the Parliamentary Reform
    Movement in Three English Cities' in the *Cambridge Historical Journal* (1948), and
    The Victoria History of the County of Warwick, vol VII (1964).
20 One of the most quoted of them is J. H. Bingham's on the Sheffield Board (1949).
    The centenary of the 1870 Act has led to the unearthing and publication of
    material about many boards, and it is to be hoped that this work is being collated.

For an interesting story which should be compared with the story in neighbouring Sheffield, see *A Survey of Education in Rotherham* (1970). For the rural background in East Yorkshire, see J. Lawson, 'Primary Education in East Yorkshire, 1560–1902', a pamphlet published by the East Yorkshire Local History Society (1959). A 'Table of Yorkshire School Boards' was compiled in 1959. It includes some odd local evidence. Thus, a board was established at Startforth in 1874 and dissolved in 1887/8 on the petition of the ratepayers. At that date it had no school or site, and it was acknowledged by the board that there was sufficient elementary school accommodation in its districts. The best contemporary national source for the work of the boards was the *School Board Chronicle*, and there is a valuable summary of their achievements by Fitch in the *Nineteenth Century* (1902), which was reprinted in the journal of the Social Democratic Federation, the *Social Democrat*. (See B. Simon, *Education and the Labour Movement, 1870–1918* (1965), 214, and for Fitch's career J. Leese, *Personalities and Power in English Education* (1950), 165–71.) There is a useful account of the pattern of activities of the boards in M. Sturt, *The Education of the People* (1967). A recent History of Education Society discussion on the subject is reported in *Bulletin No 3* of the society (1969), 3–6.

21 See, for example, ibid, 6–8, for an account of a discussion on the work of the Technical Instruction Committees in the two areas.

22 For a possible approach, see my article 'Social Structure and Politics in Birmingham and Lyons' in the *British Journal of Sociology* (1950).

23 Lytton had chapters on 'the education of the higher classes', 'the state of education among the middling classes' and 'popular education'. His main international comparison was that with Prussia.

24 The phrase 'what may be called the English system' recurs in many later commentaries. The Robbins Committee on Higher Education used the phrase, 'if it may be called a system'. It is interesting that the parallel article to that of Fitch in the *Encyclopedia Britannica* on the United States was written by Nicholas Murray Butler, President of Columbia University.

25 See, for example, R. Layard et al, *Impact of Robbins* (1969).

26 See M. Blaug, *An Introduction to the Economics of Education* (1971); M. E. Leite, P. Lynch, K. Norris, J. Sheehan and J. Vaizey, *The Economics of Educational Costing*; and an interesting critical review of this approach by T. Barna in *Universities Quarterly* (Summer 1971).

27 See, for example, A. Little and J. Westergaard, 'The Trend of Class Differentials in Educational Opportunity in England and Wales' in the *British Journal of Sociology* (1964). The pioneering work in this field was D. Glass (ed), *Social Mobility in England* (1954).

28 E. G. West, 'Resource Allocation and Growth in Early Nineteenth-Century British Education' in the *Economic History Review* (1970). See also his article 'Private versus Public Education: A Classical Economic Dispute' in *The Journal of Political Economy* (1964).

29 P. Szreter, 'History and Sociology: Rivals or Partners in the Field of Education?' in History of Education Society *Bulletin* (Spring 1969).

30 See also J. Ryder and H. Silver, *Modern English Society: History and Structure* (1970) which gives education a prominent place in its 'sociological account of some of the more distinctive features of the contemporary English social structure' and its historical base. For an interesting exploratory article, see M. Sanderson, 'Education and the Factory in Industrial Lancashire, 1780–1840' in the *Economic History Review* (1964).

31 D. S. Landes et al, *History as Social Science* (1971), 142–3. See also A. Briggs 'Sociology and History' in A. T. Welford (ed), *Society, Problems and Methods of Study* (1962), 91–9.

32 D. Hopkinson, 'Teachers and the History of Education' in *Trends in Education* (1968).

33 N. Woodard, *Public Schools and the Middle Classes* (1851), quoted in W. L. Burn, *The Age of Equipoise* (1964), 266.

34 For the Commission, see *inter alia* H. Perkin, *The Origins of Modern English Society* (1969), 300–2, and Burn, op cit, 199–201. In both cases the work of the Commission is related to its social as well as to its educational context. See also B. Simon, 'Education: Owen, Mill, Arnold and the Woodard Schools' in *Victorian Studies* (1970).

35 Lytton, op cit, 149.

36 H. G. Wells in his *Experiment in Autobiography* (1934), quoted in G. A. N. Lowndes, *The Silent Social Revolution* (1937), 5.

37 For an interesting, if somewhat one-sided, account of working-class dislike of certain forms of state interventionism, see H. Pelling, 'The Working Class and the Origins of the Welfare State' in *Popular Politics and Society* (1968), 1–19.

38 The teachers have been dealt with more adequately than the pupils, but there is more to be said than has already been said by A. Tropp in *The School Teachers* (1957) or in his article on 'The Changing Status of Teachers in England and Wales' in *The Yearbook of Education* (1953). See also R. Bourne and B. Macarthur, *The Struggle for Education, 1870–1970: A Pictorial History*, a by-product of the centenary, and the report of the discussion at a History of Education Society meeting on 'School Boards and their Teachers' in the society's *Bulletin* (Spring 1969).

39 See the interesting article by R. Johnson on 'Educational Policy and Social Control in Early Victorian England' in *Past and Present* (1970).

40 Quoted in ibid, 104.

41 R. M. Titmuss, 'Social Administration in a Changing Society', in *Essays on 'The Welfare State'* (1958), 19.

42 *A Survey of Education in Rotherham*, 3.

43 Ibid, 4.

44 See D. Lawton, *Social Class, Language and Education* (1968) and B. Bernstein and D. Henderson, 'Social Class Differences in the Relevance of Language to Socialisation' in *Sociology* (1969).

45 J. Rex, *Key Problems in Sociological Theory* (1962), ch 4.

46 R. A. Butler, *The Art of the Possible* (1971), 94.

47 The comments on education, brief though they are, in J. Vincent, *The Formation of the Liberal Party* (1966) are particularly useful. He had studied an unpublished Oxford thesis by D. Roland, 'The Struggle for the Elementary Education Act and Its Implementation'.

48 D. A. Hamer, *John Morley* (1968), esp ch 6, a particularly illuminating analysis.

NORMAN MORRIS

1870: the Rating Option

I

THE year 1870 is in many ways the 1066 of English education. It is the date which all students know. It lurks in the memory as both a climax and a new beginning. Like 1066, it has its own peculiar Bayeux tapestry, telling a story that is more folklore than fact.

According to orthodox assumption, the key question at issue was religion; certainly the longest and most acrimonious debates during the passage of the Act centred on its religious sections which generated two areas of real difficulty.

Firstly, if it was to be mandatory for a school board to give rate aid to all denominations without discrimination, nonconformists might well resent having to foster the development of church schools; this was visibly demonstrated much later when something like this section of the Bill did, indeed, become law in 1902 and dissenters refused to support Canterbury and Rome with local money. On the other hand, if school boards were given permissive powers only and could decide for themselves whether to assist voluntary schools or not, the church had every right to fear what might happen to it in areas of non-conformist predominance; these fears were shown to be abundantly justified after 1870 when nonconformist school boards declined to implement section 25, refusing to make even a slight and indirect subsidy to the church by paying the school fees of voluntary school children whose parents could not otherwise afford them.

The second and more prolonged controversy took place over the religious complexion of schools to be provided by school boards themselves. Should a school board, as managers, be allowed the same rights as voluntary school managers to determine the type of religion to be taught in its own schools? Should it be allowed to abandon religion altogether and run wholly secular schools? Or should religious teaching in board schools be undenominational, whatever that might mean? Here were nice questions on which the establishment classes could fasten, which they could debate, heatedly and perhaps happily, in an endless series of sittings until the guillotine came down. And debate they did—so much so that the historian can be forgiven for thinking that these were the main points at issue. Nor, indeed, should they be minimised. But they were not *prime* issues. Religious questions only arose as a result of a prior decision to establish local authorities for education, with rating powers. Having taken that decision the government had necessarily to sort out its religious implications. But without such a decision there would have been no rates to apply to voluntary schools; without board schools there would have been no reason to consider the form of religious teaching in them. Although interest has centred on the religious compromise the major innovation of 1870 was not the Cowper-Temple clause for schools supplied by local agency but the actual establishment of public local agencies with powers to use local taxation for purposes which had hitherto been the prerogative of private and voluntary enterprise.

It is the intention of this article to look more closely at this fundamental proposition. Why did the Gladstone government set out to create school boards, both to complete gaps in provision and also to aid existing schools? What pressures were at work and what problems was the proposal intended to solve? Lastly, why did the government, at the committee stage, distort its own intentions by abandoning the application of rates to voluntary schools, creating instead an emasculated authority which, after thirty precarious years, was in the end replaced by a system far more akin to the First Reading proposal than was the Act itself?

II

The overt design of the Act was to fill the gaps in elementary school provision, so that every child who needed a place could find one within easy reach. This was not a point of vital controversy. The general principle had been conceded before 1870, nor had it awaited the Franchise Act of 1867 before finding acceptance. The Newcastle Commission had been set up in 1858 to consider the *means* of accomplishing universal, or near-universal, education; the *principle* was already assumed. Indeed, the area of common ground between the main interests involved had been quite extensive for at least the decade preceding 1870; even Edward Baines, the educational spokesman of the manufacturers—the power group least enthusiastic about providing schools for the working class—had been won over by 1867.

The defects of the 1833 grant system had been apparent to the observant from the outset. Government had no powers to promote schools; it could only assist projects already initiated by private action. This was spelled out by Robert Lowe in evidence to the Select Committee of 1865. Speaking with five years' experience as Minister of Education behind him, he emphasised that education was a voluntary service, provided by charity; the Education Department existed only to help voluntary schemes, wherever they arose.[1] Forster was only re-playing a familiar theme when he said, in the course of his speech on the First Reading:

> . . . we have done well in assisting the benevolent gentlemen who have established schools, yet the results of the State leaving the initiative to volunteers is, that where State help has been most wanted, State help has been least given, and that where it was most desirable that State power should be most felt it was not felt at all. In helping those only who help themselves, or can get others to help them, we have left unhelped those who most need help . . .[2]

If gaps in provision were to be closed it was essential that there should be some sort of authority with teeth, to assess the needs of an area, to determine where additional school places were needed and to ensure that the places were provided.

This was what the 1870 Bill set out to create but it is a mistake to suppose that the Gladstone government was the first to make the attempt; the previous Conservative government had ploughed the same field. Prior to the 1868 parliamentary session the Disraeli administration announced its determination to deal, once and for all, with the elementary school question and spent several months considering alternative plans. In February 1868, Forster reminded the Prime Minister of his promise and asked if there was any serious intention to honour it, adding (perhaps tongue in cheek) that Conservatives were in the most favourable position to legislate on education since they commanded the support of the church. Disraeli was able to reassure members and a month later the Lord President introduced a Bill in the House of Lords. This choice of location was probably due to the fact that the Lord President, the Duke of Marlborough, regarded the Bill as a most serious piece of legislation and preferred to handle it himself rather than leave it to his Vice-President who had originally favoured a different version. In brief, the Marlborough plan was to divide the country into school districts, to establish a Secretary of State for Education (not only for elementary education) who would be head of a state department, and to order an educational census of each district. The code under which grants were made was to become statutory and some increases were envisaged. Religious freedom was to be safeguarded by imposition of a statutory conscience clause. Where the census revealed deficiencies, the Secretary of State would take the initiative; if he failed to persuade or incite local voluntary bodies to meet needs he could apply to Parliament for any fresh powers which he felt the situation warranted. In essence, education was to continue to be a voluntary service, fed from the centre. But where voluntaryism clearly showed itself unable to deliver, there was to be a minister and a ministry with legal right to intervene and initiate schemes.

It became apparent that there would be insufficient parliamentary time to carry this Bill through all its stages before the forthcoming general election and it was withdrawn after its second reading in May. Whether it should be regarded as the serious solution which Marlborough thought it was, or not, can be debated. The very existence of such a Conservative move has become one of the more famous forgotten facts of history. It is important to recall it, however, because it indicates that both parties were united on a policy of a school place for every child, that where places were lacking there should be a public authority to ensure their provision and that elementary education was an appropriate subject for legislation. Politically, when Forster moved the Liberal version two years later he was knocking on a door that already stood open; Conservatives were ready to accept a reasonable solution.

Nor was this the only area of consensus. The memorandum incorporating suggestions from Lowe, which Forster submitted to Gladstone in October 1869, as a basis for a possible Bill, specified three major principles. Despite state intervention there should be the least possible encouragement to parents to neglect their responsibility, the least possible expenditure of public money and the least possible injury to existing denominational schools.[3] Between February and August 1870, the Bill underwent many changes but these basic principles remained inviolate. As Forster said in his opening address, he spoke for both sides of the House when he asserted that free education would sap the moral fibre of parents, that politicians owed a particular duty to taxpayers to spend as little as possible and that existing schools must be safeguarded; this implied the preservation of publicly aided denominational schools, with a conscience clause.

Why, then, with so much common ground between the parties, was it difficult to get an agreed measure on to the statute book? The answer clearly lies not in areas of agreement but in points of difference. Where the 1868 and 1870 Bills parted company was over the use of local authorities for education, with rating powers.

III

Forster's thesis was straightforward and challenging. It was agreed that present gaps had to be filled and that future population growth had to be matched by school growth. But, he said, the voluntary system had already been outpaced. It had not only fallen behind in the provision of places to match needs but was manifestly incapable of catching up; hence, some new machinery was required. In Forster's words: 'Voluntary local agency has failed, therefore our hope is to invoke the help of municipal organisation.'[4]

After a hundred years it is difficult to regard local government of education, in some form or another, as anything but an act of nature.

In 1870, however, when the first step was taken, a choice of routes was still open. Was Forster's argument for taking the local government road as logical and as reasonable as he made it sound?

Crucial to his case was the assumption that a sufficiency of school places could not be supplied by voluntary means; this was the simple pragmatic argument for another form of agency and its validity clearly turned on a question of statistics, on what was the true size of the gap to be filled. Strangely, no reliable count existed and neither the Liberals who were at pains to emphasise the massive nature of the deficiency, nor the Conservatives who seemed equally intent to play it down, had any hard evidence to support their respective claims. The Newcastle Commissioners, whose report was only nine years old in 1870, had carried through a large-scale exercise, comparing numbers already in weekday attendance with the total child population, concluding that only about 120,000 children were unaccounted for in one type of school or another. This is not the place to consider the dubious techniques which produced this complacent result; the fact is that Conservatives regarded the Newcastle figures with the utmost deference. In his opening speech on the 1868 Bill, the Duke of Marlborough rehearsed them at length, as showing how little really needed to be done. He was also clearly impressed by a recent National Society survey which demonstrated that although half of all ecclesiastical parishes were without their own church day-school, nevertheless almost every child was within one or two miles of a school in one parish or another. But if Conservatives saw the situation as being under control, the Liberal government was just as keen to assert the opposite. It commissioned the reports of Fitch and Fearon on four major industrial towns as a counter to previous reports and in his own opening speech on the 1870 Bill Forster followed Marlborough's example in reverse, mounting a devastating exposure of educational destitution. Unfortunately, Fitch and Fearon had repeated one of the errors of the Newcastle inquiry; instead of counting the number of school places available they had made a rough guess at the number of children in school, and calculated the number not in attendance, rather than the number of additional places required.

Worse still, instead of stating a mathematical deficit, Forster himself mixed up the question of lack of places with that of the efficiency of teaching. The difference of approach between the two political parties is seen most clearly in their treatment of the large group of uninspected voluntary schools, catering for some 650,000 pupils. Marlborough had agreed that some of them were below standard and needed an increased income to enable them to reach the level of inspected schools, but he included them in his count of available places. Forster simply dismissed them as too inefficient to be classed as schools at all and used their exclusion to swell the size of the gap. This helped the emotive appeal of his speech and has coloured the views of later generations. But to say, by implication, that all the places which those schools supplied would have to be replaced rather than improved was not only misleading but also irrelevant to the very Bill which he was proposing. The Bill contained no stipulation that all schools had to reach the standard demanded for receipt of parliamentary grant; on the contrary, any school—assisted, unassisted or private—could be accepted as satisfactory on the basis of quite minimal criteria and it is disconcerting to realise that almost all the unassisted schools which Forster dismissed out of hand in February were considered as efficient after the Act had passed in August.

The creation of a public local agency to supplement the efforts of private benefactors was therefore not a simple pragmatic response to established facts. Was the Liberal evaluation of the situation an act of inspired foresight and were the Conservatives burying their heads in sand in thinking that voluntary enterprise could fill the gaps?

The only reasonably precise assessment of school requirements was made by the Education Department as part of its duty after the 1870 Act had been put into operation.[5] It was reckoned that in 1871 there were 2 million places in acceptable schools and 4 million children to be placed. Thus if every child was to have his own place there was a deficiency of 2 million places; on the basis of 75 per cent attendance the deficiency was 1 million. Between 1871 and 1876 voluntary enterprise created 1 million new places—the amount required to satisfy 75 per cent attendance; in the same period, school boards added a further

500,000 places, so that when attendance was made compulsory in 1876 there were probably enough places for between 80 per cent and 90 per cent of the child population. The voluntary places were erected at a cost of at least £3 million, most of it raised by the churches themselves, since building grants ceased after the end of 1870. Had voluntary promoters received a grant of 50 per cent towards the cost of all their building they could have gone on to complete the extra 500,000 places without any additional cost to themselves and without the intervention of a local agency. It can be argued that the churches only produced their big effort by 1876 under threat of school board competition; development by negotiation on Marlborough lines might have been slower than progress by compulsion under the Liberals. But this was quite hypothetical in 1870; what was factual was that if the purpose of legislation was only to provide an adequate number of places there were two methods of procedure, either of which could have been adopted, and that there was no firm objective evidence pointing to one choice rather than the other.

IV

The rating movement was as old as the century. Individuals and organisations (of which the Central Society, the National Public Schools Association and, much later, the Birmingham Education League are well-known examples) kept up the pressure through publications, meetings and Bills in parliament (there were seven between 1850 and 1858 alone). Bills differed in points of detail and interest centred, as in 1870, on the question of how religious instruction should be arranged in schools provided out of rates. This has always attracted the easy headlines and led historians to try to identify the various protagonists with particular denominational, or even undenominational, interests. But it is difficult to find any neat fit. Many churchmen favoured rating and it was never in doubt, as the National Society was aware,[6] that if voluntary schools were to be assisted from rates the church, which had the greatest number of schools to be assisted, would be the greatest beneficiary. It is tempting, but contrary to the facts, to suppose that the Bills were a dissenters' conspiracy to counter church influence by creating undenominational schools. For most of the period many dissenters remained purely voluntaryist or totally disinterested; many of the Bills had Anglican sponsors and schemes were just as likely to favour denominational teaching in rate-provided schools as to exclude it. It is at least worth considering that there may have been a quite separate ideological conflict between centralisers and localisers and that the cleavage between the two existed in its own right, obscured by religious implications but separate from them. Nor did pressure for rates await the bankruptcy of exchequer aid as a means of supplementing school income; it grew and flourished parallel with the growth of the exchequer system.

Argument and counter-argument for and against the employment of rates were probably evenly matched. The greatest need for elementary schools, said the Duke of Marlborough, was in the boroughs where rates were inevitably heaviest. Urban ratepayers were already faced with poor rates, borough rates, lighting and watching rates, general district rates, rates levied by Improvement Commissioners, burial rates, water rates and, in some instances, church rates. Rates were already high—in Blackburn, 3s 2d in the pound; Devonport, 5s 3d; Plymouth, 6s 11¼d; Gateshead, 7s 0¼d. Loan debt was continuously rising; in Bolton it had increased from £188,000 to £270,000 between 1857 and 1866. How, then, could ratepayers face the immense additional burden of an educational rate?[7] To this, the typical reply was the argument used by Canon Richson of Manchester in 1851; to levy a rate for education would actually reduce rates by forestalling crime and pauperism, thus cutting the intolerable cost to the community of police, prisons and relief. The average cost of fourteen juvenile offenders, held in prison on several occasions, had exceeded 60 guineas each. Ten of them were ultimately transported at a cost of upwards of 100 guineas each, exclusive of shipping charge. Mr Neal, Chief Constable of Salford, had calculated that the average cost per head of the 6,311 offenders in his district was £10 6s per annum, as against the estimated cost of 16s per head for educating the entire juvenile population between four and fourteen years of age. In the light of this arithmetic an educational rate was a cut-price bargain.[8]

It was a favourite charge that the well of voluntary contributions would dry up if rates were levied. 'The day you sanction compulsory rating for the purpose of education you sign the death warrant of voluntary exertion.' This was said by no less a person than Gladstone in 1856, and several speakers in the 1870 debates were loath to let him forget it,[9] but the pro-rating party was unmoved. The real problem, Earl Russell pointed out, was that in those areas where income was most needed voluntary contributions had already disappeared; if local money was to be obtained, a compulsory rate was the only way of providing it.[10]

The Newcastle Commission, which examined the question at considerable length, totally rejected existing parochial rating areas as school districts on the grounds that their rateable value was frequently too low to provide sufficient resources. This was flatly denied by Kay-Shuttleworth who assured the commissioners that although some districts lacked the will, none was so destitute that it could not provide the means. He clearly failed to foresee the results of Forster's Act which set up numerous ineffective school boards in areas in which a penny rate brought in no more than ten pounds. The Newcastle Commission was probably justified in believing that local efficiency required large local areas.

It also took the view, with which the Duke of Marlborough concurred, that local management at parish level would lower educational standards, and quoted the experience of workhouse schools:

> The experience of the majority of workhouse schools leads us to fear that the consequence of putting the management of the schools into the hands of the parochial bodies would be that trained teachers and pupil teachers would in a great measure cease to be employed, and that the whole standard of elementary education would be lowered. . . . Though there are special difficulties connected with pauper education, the way in which it has been generally managed by the Boards of Guardians is certainly not encouraging as evidence of the fitness of similar bodies to undertake the management of elementary schools.[11]

To this, Frederick Temple rejoined that ratepayers had to be compelled to do their duty[12] and in any case as Kay-Shuttleworth had pointed out, standards of secular education were a national responsibility; the function of a local authority was to administer; educational levels should be set and secured by central government.[13]

Many convinced churchmen were uneasily aware that continued increase in child population might jeopardise the capacity of the church to maintain a proper supply of schools and that rate-provided schools, of necessity undenominational, might eventually out-compete them— as, indeed, happened; they preferred, therefore, an incomplete school system to opening the door to a flood of paganism.[14] Other churchmen, equally zealous, took the line which was later adopted in the 1870 Bill. The main function of rates was to provide additional income for the improvement of denominational schools and rate money would only be used to build new schools when voluntary effort had palpably failed to supply an acknowledged need, after sufficient time and notice had been given. Such occasions, Canon Richson thought in 1851, would be rare and manifestly justified:

> It is not believed that Diocesan and other educational societies, co-operating with local efforts, will be unable or slack to provide for the erection of schools in destitute districts; but if so, neither the Church nor any body of Dissent can justly complain, that schools should be created at the public cost, without the recognition of such distinctive principles as they respectively maintain.[15]

It is worth noting that the 1870 Bill, as first introduced, was not so uncompromisingly neutral as this and permitted schools boards to determine for themselves the religious complexion of their own schools. At the beginning of 1870 the cabinet saw no reason why board schools should not also be denominational schools, if that was what local opinion desired.

But perhaps the most unassailable argument in favour of local authorities for education was that used, precisely and pragmatically, by the civil servants in the Education Department. The system of ad hoc specific grants, commenced in 1833 but considerably elaborated since then, particularly as a result of the Minutes of 1846, grew so complex that by 1860 the machinery at central office was in danger of grinding to a standstill. 'The distribution of nine-tenths of the education grant', Lingen told the Newcastle Commission, 'is essentially a question of detail.'[16] Further growth in the number of schools would necessitate an alarming increase of Whitehall staff and it was urgently necessary to simplify the system. Instead of communicating individually with each school the Education Department would save time and labour by corresponding with a 'body' which represented all the schools in a parish.[17] Lingen and his successors were to hammer at this major point for the next thirty years.[18] Devolutionary policy gained nothing in 1870 and the civil service had to wait for the 1890s and Sir John Gorst before it found a politician who was ready to act upon its advice.

V

These were the intellectual arguments, with seemingly little between them to indicate why two different methods of providing schools for the working class should become causes to be fought over for two generations. It is always easier to recount the superficialities of debate —the ammunition of political exchange—than to discover what really moves men to take sides. As so often happens in public argument, it is clear that those who wanted local governmental intervention in elementary education and those who resisted it were each declaiming from prepared positions without listening to the other side. What lay behind the speeches?

The context of the elementary education question was essentially urban. Industrialisation had massed large concentrations of children into expanding areas of instant putrescence. Changes in the form and scale of industrial production made child labour progressively less economic; unemployment amongst the young was exacerbated by factory legislation which, by 1867, excluded almost all children under ten from full-time work. This left them literally on the streets without occupation or discipline, a present danger to law and order and an ominous reminder of things to come if they grew up untamed. This was the case for large-scale provision of elementary schools, preferably under the supervision of those who could command a heavenly as well as a civil sanction.

The urban situation was serious and those who had to live with the teeming hordes were likely to feel deeply about it. But this does not mean that there was an upsurge of demand for local powers. Rating is never popular and local action could take other forms. The civil service demand for agencies through which Whitehall might operate could have been satisfied by the creation of decentralised bureaucratic offices dealing with voluntary schools on the spot, instead of from the centre. Voluntary bodies themselves resented the imputation that they were not locally concerned; the schools which they provided were tangible monuments to their identification with the community. Although municipal authorities were firmly entrenched by 1870 as bourgeois pockets of independence from the old power structure of land, church and state and were creating their own empires, their own symbols and their own vested interests, there was one great difference between education and other local government functions; whereas street paving and lighting, sewerage and other services were created from the outset by collective municipal action in the absence of any other satisfactory means of supplying and controlling them, a system of privately provided but publicly supervised elementary schools already existed and was theoretically capable of extension. If lack of schools, like uncarted night soil, was an urban abuse which needed rectifying it was one which was already mollified under the aegis of professionals in the work of character training. To bring municipal organisation into education in 1870 would have been at best interference with established private institutions; at worst it threatened to supersede them.

Despite the vigour with which the cause was pursued by a minority it is unlikely that rating for education ever had broad appeal. It drew its support from three sources: from those who wanted to limit national taxation (it made some sense to argue that areas which benefited most from school provision should bear the largest share of the cost); from a minority of dissenters who saw local control over education as a means of blocking the influence of church and state (a thesis unlikely to command the sympathy of party leaders); and from doctrinaire radicals, of whom John Stuart Mill was the prime philosopher, who simply believed in the social and formative value of local democracy; their aim was to create an integrated education service in each area, under the control of elected representatives, not necessarily because this was the only way in which the education problem could be solved but because this was what they wanted.

Added together, these three sources of support came to relatively little; the movement, such as it was, had no common platform. Its greatest moments came in 1869 and 1870 when Joseph Chamberlain and others attempted to weld the three parts into a political weapon. The resulting fusion produced internal conflict and provoked its own opposition. If only to avoid expense, existing voluntary schools could not be dispensed with; some sort of two-fold category of school was therefore inevitable from the beginning, seriously infringing the pure radical concept. The most that radicals could hope for was that provided and non-provided schools should be conducted by local government as a unified whole and for this reason the league's initial statement of aims stipulated that voluntary schools accepting rate aid should be managed by local education committees.[19] On the other hand, since this was likely to antagonise existing managers who would lose control of their own schools, a specimen league Bill prepared by Collings in December 1869 was careful to say that managers would not be removed if they accepted the conditions which the education committee laid down.[20] In a bid for nonconformist support, the chief but quite impossible condition was that rate-aided schools had to be unsectarian. None of these difficulties and contradictions was new. That they came to the surface again in 1870 merely emphasises the incohesive nature of the rating alliance and the impracticability of winning broad-based support for local control of education at that point of time.

On the other hand, those who aided and supplied the voluntary schools were a positive and well-entrenched counter-force. Managers, backed by the church and supported by large sections of influential opinion, knew that their schools had to be used. Outright expropriation was never a matter of practical politics. As for taking rate aid, private bodies rarely refuse public money if they can acquire it on their own terms. Managers were probably less concerned with the principle of local grants than with the conditions attached to them. Conservatives, the self-appointed protectors of the independent voluntary schools, could sit back. They were quite happy to perpetuate the existing direct grant system, with such improvements as occasion might demand; but if the Liberal Party forced the use of rates to supplement income it was only necessary to examine the terms. It was the Liberal Party, arriving in office with some commitment to the rating cause, which was likely to find itself in difficulty; extended use of local taxation and encroachment upon the property rights of managers were radical rather than Liberal measures and although some Liberal spokesmen, such as Russell, Bruce, Forster and even Lowe, had given encouragement to those who wanted to see education in the hands of the people's representatives, Liberals as a whole had no great desire to disturb the status quo.

VI

In framing a Bill in the latter part of 1869 the government had three main political objectives. It had to provide for the establishment of statutory local education authorities with defined powers; this had become the *sine qua non* of a Liberal Bill; the account which Liberals had run up over years of mild flirtation with radicalism and dissent had to be paid. Since any system would continue to make major use of existing schools, means had to be found for bringing them up to a satisfactory standard of efficiency; this implied priming them with public money. Lastly, the powers given to local authorities and the conditions attached to this extra money had to be such as would not alarm the managers and would, in fact, earn their goodwill.

Forster's opening speech on 17 February was carefully compiled. The voluntary system, which in practice meant the Anglican church, had failed; the extent of educational destitution was so great that only municipal action could save the day; the people's children should be educated by the people. The country would therefore be divided into school districts and a new agency, the people's school board, would come into being. So far, this was the language of dogmatic radicalism. When the embroidery ended and he came to proposals the story was different.

School boards were only to be set up if it could be objectively shown

that voluntary bodies had really failed and had no reasonable chance
of succeeding; or, alternatively, if there was a strong demand for a
board from the local inhabitants. By limiting the incidence of school
boards in this manner much anti-radical opposition was disarmed;
whatever their private feelings, it was difficult for voluntaryists to
argue publicly against the establishment of school boards in either of
the situations specified.

Additional money for voluntary schools was to come from rates but
opportunity for school boards to use the purse as a means of encroach-
ing on voluntary liberties was carefully circumscribed and there was no
possibility of a public take-over. Section 22 (headed 'Assistance by
School Board to Existing Schools') was cautiously drafted:

> A school board may, in their discretion, grant pecuniary assistance, of such
> amount, and for such purposes as they think fit, to such public elementary
> schools in their district not provided by them as are willing to receive it,
> provided that such assistance is granted on equal terms to all such schools
> upon conditions to be approved by the Education Department.

At the discretion of a school board, therefore, voluntary schools could
receive a rate supplement to their income; each board was at liberty to
prescribe the purposes for which the grant might be earmarked but if
a grant was offered it had to be available to all voluntary schools in the
district on the same conditions. As a safeguard against unreasonable
terms conditions of aid required central government approval; even
so, a voluntary school which found itself unable to accept the conditions offered was under no obligation; it could decline to receive rate
aid, just as many schools had refused parliamentary grants. Such a
school could continue to operate as a recognised elementary school,
independent of outside authority.

The purpose of this section was to pump money into existing schools
without impairing the rights of managers. Most Conservatives, no
doubt, still preferred the direct grant system, which made money
available on equal terms in all parts of the country; Forster's proposal
had the weakness that there would be no additional income in just
those areas of voluntary strength where no school board was established, or in districts where a local board chose not to exercise its

powers. Nevertheless, the circumstances in which a school board would be created were so limited, and section 22 so closely drawn, that it was difficult to claim that existing voluntary interests were jeopardised. Believing that a radical measure might have been far worse, the Conservative opposition decided to support the Bill. Many of the school boards, it was thought, would come under church influence. Even if fewer schools were aided than under the Marlborough plan, those which were offered rate aid could accept it without having to make undue concessions to community demands.

By the end of the second reading, therefore, the main features of the Bill commanded a majority in the House; the chief unresolved problem was board school religion. This was the issue which Gladstone and his cabinet settled down to discuss in the interval between the second reading and the committee stage. Why, then, on the resumption of debate did the Prime Minister suddenly and quite unexpectedly take back so much that was already acceptable and go out of his way to rescue voluntary schools from even the remotest shadow of school board influence, leaving them to be fed by direct grant from the central authority?

This last-minute reversal of policy appears to have emanated from Robert Lowe who wrote briefly to Gladstone on the eve of the committee stage setting out the new proposal. As it stood, the Bill involved him in personal electoral difficulties. Gladstone immediately circulated Lowe's message to key cabinet members who just as quickly, and apparently without discussion, endorsed the change.[21] The minority radical dream of an integrated education service under local government control had already taken a beating; now it crashed in ruin. Henceforth there were to be two categories of elementary school, each insulated from the other and guaranteed by statute law. Where they operated, school boards would manage only their own schools; although they could compel children to attend school and even pay their fees, large numbers of pupils would use schools in which the accommodation, equipment and standards might be far below board school level; nevertheless, school boards would have no authority over them and would be unable to stimulate improvement by means of local subsidy.

The speed with which this policy switch was engineered and the privacy in which the decision was taken make it difficult to read the minds of those responsible for it. Without fuller documentation it is only possible to surmise the reasoning behind it.

It is likely that Gladstone and his principal ministers saw the education question in much the same way as did their Conservative counterparts. They wanted a public body which could take the initiative in supplying schools where gaps existed and they wanted to raise standards by increasing school income. Given the powers which Marlborough had proposed, the central government could have performed both functions. Under Forster's system there could have been areas without the means of aiding voluntary schools. There is also little doubt that the government was impressed by the vigour and venom which many dissenters exhibited during the debates; so far from compromising with them, Liberal leaders were just as anxious as Conservatives to protect voluntary schools from possible nonconformist erosion. Their difficulty was that they led a party with a minority commitment to urban radicals. Lowe himself, in a notorious speech, had declared his conversion to the use of rates for education.[22] Having introduced and defended a Bill which promised rate aid to voluntary schools the government no doubt felt itself compelled to stand by its own scheme. It was at this point that Lowe intervened. As he saw it, rates were probably needed in order to fill gaps but school boards were not appropriate bodies for dealing with voluntary managers; therefore there should be two systems. Radicals could have their local management for rate-provided schools but voluntary managers would continue to be served by exchequer grant, central government and gentlemen. With some sardonic quips at governmental embarrassment, Conservatives readily accepted the new proposals which were so much a part of their own thinking and the Bill was duly passed, in the face of radical opposition, with the help of Conservative support.

It is probable that the day of the hard line was already over in 1870 and that, except for dogmatic radicals, feeling on the rates question was not particularly high. The case for the use of rates to assist private benefaction was greater in the earlier part of the century, before voluntary effort had had time to cover the country with schools. During the period of growth managers had resolutely opposed the use of rates for fear of local interference with what was, after all, their property. By 1870, some of the bitterness had been lost. The 1870 proposals had a relatively easy passage not, as Forster suggested, because so much remained to be done but because leaders of both political parties believed that there was relatively little to do; the main task was to consolidate and improve. Twenty thousand boards of independent trustees, providing almost the whole of the school service at that time, could feel confident in their capacity to absorb public money from any quarter without giving too much away. Nevertheless, there is no doubt that managers, like some grammar school heads today, preferred a direct grant, with relatively remote supervision, to assistance from a group of locally elected dignitaries. Rightly or wrongly, independent bodies have always felt that association with local authorities is the kiss of death. This managerial sentiment could no doubt have been ignored if there had been any overriding need to do so. But given a voluntary system, it had been a prime consideration of policy, since 1833, to secure and retain the co-operation of the managers who not only provided the schools but also ran them. From the standpoint of political and administrative realism it made more sense to Gladstone to conciliate the managers than to satisfy a demonstrative minority group of ideologues, even if they sat on his own benches. When Lowe, the Chancellor of the Exchequer, came out clearly for increased exchequer grant, there was no reason for the rest of the cabinet to hold back.

University of Manchester

References

1   *Proceedings of the Select Committee on Education*, 1865, vol 1, 36–7.
2   *Hansard*, vol 199, 17 Feb 1870, col 442.
3   PRO Ed 24/2, 21/10/1869.
4   *Hansard*, ut sup, col 451.
5   The figures given here are those in Craik, H. C., *The state in its relation to education*

(1884), ch vi. The details from which these rounded figures are made up are contained in PRO files Ed 2 and Ed 16 for 1870–2.

6 The National Society was always apprehensive of possible competition from rate-provided schools but was quick to claim its share of rates when they appeared inevitable towards the end of 1869. See Burgess, H. J., *Enterprise in Education* (1958), ch 13.

7 *Proceedings of the House of Lords*, 24 March 1868, col 115.

8 Richson, Rev C., *A sketch of some of the causes which, in Manchester, induced the abandonment of the voluntary system in the support of schools and the introduction of the Manchester and Salford Education Bill* (1851), 86–7. See also Richson, Rev C., *Manchester and Salford Education* (1853), paper no 4.

9 *Hansard*, 1870, vol 199, col 473, quoted in Cruikshank, M., *Church and state in English education* (1963), 27.

10 *Proceedings of the House of Lords*, ut sup, col 135.

11 *Report of the Newcastle Commission*, vol 1, 303–4.

12 Ibid, vol 6, 346, Temple's reply to q 2767.

13 Memorandum from Kay to Russell, 11 Oct 1839 (Kay-Shuttleworth papers). See Smith, F., *The Life and Work of Sir James Kay-Shuttleworth* (1923), 92–3.

14 Archdeacon Denison, 'A reply to the committee of the promoters of the Manchester and Salford education scheme', in *Manchester and Salford Education*, ut sup.

15 Richson, Rev C., ut sup, 1851, 81–2.

16 *Report of the Newcastle Commission*, vol VI, 78.

17 Ibid, 60.

18 See Lingen's evidence in the *Report of the Select Committee on Education*, 1865, vol 1, 11, and in the *Report of the Cross Commission*, 1885, 534.

19 Maltby, S. E., *Manchester and the movement for national elementary education*, Manchester (1918), 110.

20 Education Cuttings, 1869, Birmingham Public Reference Library, 62285.

21 This version of events is narrated in Roland, D., 'The struggle for the Elementary Education Act and its implementation, 1870–73', unpublished BLitt thesis, Oxford (1955).

22 *Hansard*, vol 188, 15 July 1867, col 1549.

R. A. LOWE

Some Forerunners of R. H. Tawney's Longton Tutorial Class

ON Tuesday, 9 October 1900, at the Toynbee Hall in the East End of London, R. E. S. Hart initiated the first University Tutorial Class, his subject being 'The Dissolution of the Monasteries'. This was one of three classes set up during the term by the University of London Extension Board, which, varying the pattern usually followed in extension lecturing, prescribed that 'the instruction, instead of consisting of lecture and class is tutorial throughout'.[1] Subsequently the board was to undertake more experiments to diversify its extension work. In 1903, for example, Senate agreed that the first three-year course should be offered on a 'Humanities' syllabus drawn up by R. D. Roberts, registrar of the London Extension Board and one of the early historians of the extension movement.[2] This course involved the usual extension lectures and 'attendance at supplementary lectures or Tutorial Classes'.[3] A central course was taught at South Kensington, and classes established in outlying centres.[4] London persisted with this experiment; by 1907 there were five tutorial classes operating, at Toynbee Hall, Battersea, Smithfield and two at Gresham College.[5]

This work did not anticipate in character the courses begun by Oxford University, under R. H. Tawney, at Longton and Rochdale in January 1908, which are generally considered to be the first tutorial classes. Under Oxford's arrangements, a group was recognised as a tutorial class only if the number of students was limited to forty, and if they pledged themselves to regular attendance and written work. Further, the standard of an honours degree was aimed at, in the hope that some students would go on to study at Oxford (as two Longtonians, Albert Emery and Maud Griffiths, did in 1913). None of these characteristics was shared by the first London classes, and this contrast allowed Albert Mansbridge to claim that the Battersea class, which

43

studied 'Civics' under Professor Patrick Geddes, although serious in intention, 'was not a University Tutorial Class, and did not become one for some two or three years'.[6] Not surprisingly, Mansbridge, who had himself studied at Toynbee Hall,[7] was anxious to show that the Oxford classes he helped to initiate were truly pioneer. Tawney's first two Oxford classes, designed to point the way towards new developments in extension teaching, were certainly quickly and widely imitated, for, following on the recommendations of the famous report of 1908 on *Oxford and Working Class Education*, there were, by 1912, 117 such classes at work.[8] This, too, was in contrast to the experience of the London board. But the existence of the London classes must throw some doubt on Mansbridge's claim, which has never been challenged, that 'the first University Tutorial Class . . . in England was held at Longton'.[9]

This early experimentation by the London Extension Board stands, too, as an interesting example of the fact that extension lectures were by no means as inflexible, and limited in their effectiveness, as has sometimes been implied, and this fact offers a key to resolving a problem which hangs over some of the first Oxford tutorial classes, particularly those in the North Staffordshire area. The problem is to reconcile their enormous success with the difficulties which extension lecturers had faced only a few years earlier in the same centres.

Longton offers a good example of this. Within three years of Tawney's appearance in the Potteries, the members of the Longton tutorial class had determined to communicate their enthusiasm for learning to the outlying villages of the district. Under the auspices of the North Staffordshire Miners' Higher Education Movement, which they founded and for which they taught, Tawney's students had by 1913 established twenty-seven classes, run on tutorial lines,[10] and A. E. Zimmern, who lectured in the Potteries during the session, commented that if Erasmus were to come to England again he would visit North Staffordshire to find the new learning.[11] Longton students found their way to Oxford, and E. S. Cartwright, secretary of the Longton class, was chosen by Oxford as first secretary to the Tutorial Classes Committee. The achievement of Longton was exceptional, yet it was at this centre that Oxford lecturers had struggled with difficult audiences since the re-establishment of extension lecturing in 1901. A. W. Bateman-Brown called it 'the least intellectually inclined' of the centres of which he had experience,[12] and, although he reported a considerable improvement in both students' work and the general character of the audience in 1902, successive lecturers found difficulties at Longton. A. Hardcastle asked that the juvenile element might be excluded after his series on astronomy, and in 1903 A. H. Fison, who had lectured on 'The Electric Current', wrote caustically:

> this series of lectures cannot . . . appear satisfactory. The large proportion of young children, for whom University Extension lectures are not intended, and for whom my lectures are not at all adapted, was most trying both to the lecturer and the rest of the audience . . . further, the extraordinary numbers coming into the lecture room late would by itself have been fatal to the success of the lectures.[13]

E. L. S. Horsburgh, who lectured in the following year thought that 'some time [would] have to elapse before paper work and class work are up to the mark', and his examiner commented that the majority were small children, 'quite incapable of taking an examination'.[14] In 1905 Hudson Shaw found the attendance of eighty elementary schoolchildren a 'somewhat disturbing feature'.[15] While there is also evidence of a growing interest in classwork and essay writing in the reports of these lecturers, and some foresaw a bright future for Longton, the contrast between the experience of the extension lecturers before 1908, and of those who came into contact with the class later, remains marked.

North Staffordshire was traditionally a difficult area for extensionists: 'the people of the district are conspicuously lacking in any real interest in education', wrote A. W. Brown in 1902, and 'progress is bound to be slow'.[16] The first experiments in the district had been discontinued by the Cambridge Syndicate for local lectures after only two years' work. In 1874, at a time when Cambridge was beginning work in over one hundred centres, lecture courses were established at four Potteries towns.[17] Two local enthusiasts were made secretaries for this work. One was Bishop Lovelace Stamer, who was involved in the North Staffordshire Adult Education Society, founded in 1861 'to

foster the work of night schools and similar efforts',[18] and who became
chairman of the School of Art at Stoke, treasurer of the Stoke
Athenaeum, and, in 1871, chairman of the Stoke school board.[19] The
other, F. E. Kitchener, a cousin of the Field Marshal, had been
involved with Josephine Butler and Anne Clough in the early work of
the North of England Council for Promoting the Higher Education of
Women, and later, as the first director of education for Staffordshire,
was to play a large part in the experimentation which preceded
Tawney's work.[20] But, despite the work of these two, poor support
brought about the collapse of the Cambridge lectures in 1876. The
second attempt to establish extension work in North Staffordshire was
equally unsuccessful. In 1887 Oxford reopened the Newcastle-under-
Lyme centre, and until 1892 extension lecturers from both Oxford and
Cambridge attempted to re-establish the work locally. Despite lavish
support from the County Technical Instruction Committee (including
a renewable annual grant of up to £200),[21] and the establishment of the
North Midland Association for the Extension of University Teaching,[22] none of the lecture courses at Stoke, Newcastle, Tunstall, Hanley
or Burslem was continued after 1892. The average attendance at
Burslem had fallen from 420 to 76 in two years, and at Stoke from over
300 to 70.[23] There was very little in the reception offered to the first
university extension lecturers to suggest that North Staffordshire
might soon become an area famous for its work in adult education.

But the Longton Tutorial class was preceded, during the first years
of this century, by a vigorous experimentation with extension work,
which may help explain Tawney's success. This experimentation
originated in attempts to establish a university in North Staffordshire,
canvassed first by F. E. Kitchener while addressing a group of local
industrialists in 1890, and taken up in 1899 by T. Turner, director of
technical instruction to the Staffordshire County Council. A committee
of inquiry was set up, and its report called for 'special scientific
instruction' which would relate to the industries of the area, arguing
that 'no industry has any right to expect permanent prosperity which
is not constantly training experts to observe all the facts which bear
upon it and to interpret their significance'.[24] The North Staffordshire

College would also teach literature and classics 'such as would supply culture to the general public', and it was hoped, too, that a day-training department for elementary teachers might be affiliated.

This development coincided in time with the re-establishment of Oxford extension lectures in North Staffordshire, so it is hardly surprising that, when this committee of inquiry decided to become a permanent council to press for a local university college, it turned to an Oxford extension lecturer living at Stone, A. W. Bateman-Brown, to become its first secretary. This Council for the Extension of Higher Education in North Staffordshire was founded in 1900 in the hope that its links with Oxford would enable the Potteries to follow the example of Reading where, in 1892, a local college had developed from a university extension centre. In fact, one of the most significant results was that Brown was forced to mould extension lecturing in North Staffordshire to the demands of his council; in particular, he developed and enunciated the idea that extension work was preliminary to something more rigorous. At a council meeting in 1902, Brown referred to the extension lectures as a temporary expedient, although at this time they were beginning to prove very successful in the area, and he went on to call them 'a useful advertisement'.[25] In his first annual report, Brown pointed out that 'the chief direct educational work of the year has been the consolidation of university extension lectures in the district', but went on 'to express the hope that the time may not be far distant when the council may be able to provide education of a more systematic and continuous character than is possible under the extension lecture system alone: a system which is in its very nature preliminary, and the pioneer of more permanent work'.[26] F. E. Kitchener, who was by this time a member of the council, also looked forward to 'a more continuous system of education' since extension lectures could not be compared with 'a continuous and settled course in any one of the chief branches of education'.[27] These ideas were being expounded at a time when many saw the traditional pattern of teaching, through a lecture followed by a class, as sacrosanct. J. A. R. Marriott, a leading extension lecturer, wrote stiffly to Brown at this time warning him that he would 'exceedingly dislike anything

that bore the title Oxford University Extension lecture being vul-
garised in the way you describe',[28] in response to Brown's plea for
experimentation at the Hanley centre.

In the *University Extension Journal* a few months earlier, Brown had
given some indication of the way in which he saw extension work
developing in North Staffordshire. A main concern of the industrialists
who had set up the council was that the seven Potteries towns were
endeavouring, singly, to set up facilities for higher education. Part of
their task was to co-ordinate these efforts. For Brown, this meant
co-ordination of extension work:

> I have taken every possible opportunity of advocating the formation of
> University Extension societies. . . . Co-ordination has many advantages. The
> lecturer's physical powers are not taxed to so great an extent as when he is
> engaged in isolated centres, whilst, as he resides in the district for some days
> in each week or fortnight, he can be made use of for improving the class work
> and opportunities of individual study. It is hoped that experiments in this
> direction will be made in the coming session.[29]

In response, the Oxford Extension Delegacy recognised Brown as its
superintending lecturer in North Staffordshire 'for the purpose of
giving cohesion to the extension work in that district'[30] (an appointment which prefigured that of R. H. Tawney as resident tutor for
North Staffordshire by eighteen years), and by the end of 1902 he had
given extension courses at Stoke, Hanley, Longton, Newcastle, Burslem, Fenton and Tunstall. Living locally, he was to concentrate on the
development of effective classwork at the close of each lecture; at Longton in 1902, for example, he attracted only six students to his class, but
reported that they did 'earnest work' and submitted papers weekly.[31]

From the outset Brown sought opportunities to experiment. In 1901
he corresponded with Colchester,[32] where the extension college established in 1896 developed into a technical college, and with the registrar
of the university college at Reading. It may have been this correspondence which gave him the idea of developing more vigorous work
among the pupil-teachers of North Staffordshire, although he was
warned that the Reading pupil teacher centre had not been set up until
after the college had 'somewhat developed'. The registrar claimed it,
though, as 'one of the useful pieces of work we did in our early stage'.[33]

The training of teachers was a major problem in the small towns of the Potteries and as early as 1901 Brown arranged for his council to take over the certificate classes for teachers organised by the Hanley School Board.[34] These were to form the nucleus of the North Staffordshire Pupil-Teachers' Centre which, during the following years, became the first attempt to centralise this work in the Potteries. In April 1901 the local school boards agreed to Brown's proposal that a combined pupil-teacher centre should be established, and that, in due course, this would become part of the intended North Staffordshire College.[35] J. Liberty Tadd, visiting England in 1901, was invited to North Staffordshire to give three lectures on his educational methods,[36] and in the following year a sessional course was established under A. W. Andrews on 'The Influence of Geography on History'. Fifty-five pupil-teachers qualified for the examination, and the series was repeated in the following year.[37]

It was in this attempt to put into practice the intentions of those industrialists who had advocated in 1899 a local college incorporating a day-training department for teachers, that Brown began to use extension teaching in a way which foreshadowed Tawney's work. In March 1904 Brown submitted to his council a memorandum outlining his proposals for the development of classes for uncertificated assistant teachers in elementary schools. He intended to use two Oxford extension lecturers 'to combine lecturing with tutorial work, with a view to making the classes as educational as possible'. These classes, which would run over two years, would help the students prepare for the acting teachers' certificate, and might divert them from the correspondence courses 'and other cramming agencies' to which the majority succumbed. He proposed lecture courses to be offered on two nights of the week for thirty weeks each year, and tutorial classes on Sunday mornings or other evenings of the week. He emphasised that it was not intended to offer 'lectures of the University Extension type. *The lectures would be as informal and tutorial as circumstances would permit* [Brown's emphasis]. The purpose they are destined to serve must be kept steadily in view, viz., to arouse a real interest in the subjects of the examination, and to teach from as broad a standpoint as possible. . . .

The combination of lectures and classes seems specially adapted to this end'. What marked this scheme as different from similar ones operating in many areas under the local authorities was the insistence upon tutorial classes, which Brown considered 'a very important part of the scheme'. It is clear, too, that for the first time a tutorial class was intended to be limited in size, for he went on to specify that if many teachers enrolled and the classes became too large for tutorial work, the extra income would allow for 'extra tutorial teaching'.[38]

Brown's suggestion was taken up, and in October 1904 what was intended to be a two-year lecture and tutorial course was begun for the uncertificated assistant teachers of North Staffordshire. The two lecturers were provided by the Oxford Extension Delegacy; J. A. Dale gave lecture courses on English Literature and Education, and R. W. Jeffery taught History and Geography. The tutorial classes met on Saturday mornings. This experiment was an important precursor of Tawney's class in another sense, for it pioneered the financial co-operation of the county education committee, which guaranteed £250 annually to support this work, and of the local authorities, who also assisted with finance. A managing body was set up, representing the Council for the Extension of Higher Education in North Staffordshire, the Staffordshire and Hanley Education Committees, and the three pupil-teacher centres already operating in the locality. The Board of Education gave recognition to the work under its regulations for evening schools, and by June 1905 Brown, whose report mirrored his own enthusiasm rather than the real prospects of the experiment, was

> confident that the experiment will demonstrate the utility of the university extension system, and will open up in other places a new sphere for its activities. Here in North Staffordshire it can be only a temporary experiment. The formation of the North Staffordshire college cannot be long delayed, and when that day comes these classes will necessarily become part of the ordinary activities of the college.[39]

Although the experiment was to collapse as quickly as it began, it still seemed, in the summer of 1905, that there were good reasons for optimism. Francis Bolton, chairman of the council, was offering a plot of land in Stoke, which had been purchased by his father for this purpose, as a site for the new college, and in August the Duke of Sutherland offered his residence at Trentham. This was less altruistic than it appears, since the dukes of Sutherland had for several years been troubled by sewage from the Potteries towns which found its way into the Trent and made Trentham Hall 'unbearable as a residence'.[40] The duke's offer to enable 'a training college and technological institute in close connection—an institution for general higher education in the district',[41] was for Brown and his supporters 'the culmination of a definite social movement'.[42] For Sutherland it was but one of several attempts to get rid of the hall. It was, also, an important turning point for extension lecturing in North Staffordshire. This was the golden opportunity to implement the scheme which Brown had been faithfully canvassing since 1901 for a composite institute, including a mining department, a school of pottery, a joint pupil-teacher centre, and a university extension department and offices, 'the elements out of which a full university college could grow'.[43] Brown intended that the arts and day-training departments would be organised 'on the plan of a university extension college'.[44] Failure to accept Sutherland's offer was quickly followed by the collapse of the experimental teachers' classes, and of Brown's council, leaving a gap in extension work in the area, and in the provision made locally for teacher training, although, of course, the more usual extension lectures continued at several centres.

Despite sustained attempts during 1905 to push through the scheme for a local college, it foundered for want of financial support. The council submitted to the Staffordshire Education Committee a detailed scheme on the financing and operation of the college, and petitions went to Stafford from the North Staffordshire Institute of Mining and Mechanical Engineers, the Ceramic Society and the Chamber of Commerce. But the county officials refused to underwrite the scheme, perhaps because they sensed opposition from other quarters. G. Balfour, who in 1905 was director of education for the county, suggested subsequently that the North Staffordshire industrialists were not agreed as to the siting of the college, many of them opposing the scheme when it involved the college being set up at Trentham, some miles from the heart of the conurbation.[45] Morant wrote to Balfour at this time expressing similar reservations on the siting of a pupil-teacher centre at Trentham. He emphasised the policy 'which my Board consider wise and have adopted elsewhere, almost without exception . . ., that a Pupil-Teacher centre should be attached to a secondary school'. Ironically, he could find only 'the dignity and beauty of the surroundings' as an argument for accepting Trentham. Morant undermined the scheme further by expressing reservations on the staffing of a college such as Brown foresaw. He was afraid that the staff of the training college might be 'affected in character by proximity to a Technical Institute'.[46] With the failure of the county education committee and the local industrialists to finance either undertaking, both the scheme and the Council for the Extension of Higher Education in North Staffordshire collapsed. Brown claimed that the teachers' classes had proved a success, adding glumly in his report to the Oxford delegacy that there was little chance of the experiment being repeated 'in view of the withdrawal of recognition by the Board of Education of such lectures for Pupil Teachers'.[47] One of the two lecturers complained bitterly that the pupil teachers had too much to do already.[48]

The experiment had been made, and North Staffordshire given its first taste of intensive classwork under the auspices of Oxford University. It is significant that pupil-teachers and uncertificated teachers made up a large part of the audiences for extension lectures which continued in the Potteries during these years, and that Tawney's first class at Longton included eight elementary schoolteachers. When Hudson Shaw lectured at Longton during the autumn of 1905 he attracted 'a large number of schoolteachers' (their interest in the Longton centre may explain the strong juvenile element at Longton referred to above; for this series a whole class from the Higher Elementary School attended). 'Real students were few', Shaw reported, 'but very earnest, especially the teachers.'[49] It is reasonable to speculate that several schoolteachers from Brown's classes now turned to other forms of extension lecturing to provide the educational facilities they sought; since 1903 the county education committee had found the tram fares of pupil teachers who studied at some distance from home, so some of them were accustomed to travelling within the area for their education.[50] The nucleus of teachers at the Longton centre goes some way to explain the demand which arose for tutorial classwork. It is significant, too, that the two men who provided the organisation and administration which enabled extension classes to be established in Longton were both full-time officials of the local education office. W. T. Cope, first secretary of the Longton extension centre, was secretary also to the education committee. E. S. Cartwright worked under him at the education offices and was well known nationally as an administrator of adult education classes,[51] as well as being first secretary of the Longton tutorial class. It has been claimed that the Social Democratic Federation provided the 'organising nucleus' for the work at Longton,[52] but it seems that the local education office played at least as great a part.

The attempts of A. W. Brown to use extension lecturing in North Staffordshire to provide intensive coursework for schoolteachers were an important forerunner of R. H. Tawney's first tutorial class and, although conducted a few miles away, ensured that there was some familiarity within the district with tutorial teaching techniques. Brown's council helped, also, to establish the financial co-operation of local authorities, county administrators and Oxford, without which the first tutorial classes could not have prospered. Set alongside Hudson Shaw's intensification of the work in Longton, through his extension lectures there after 1905 (by July 1907 a semi-permanent reading circle had been set up to help students prepare for his lectures and classwork),[53] and the growing demand from within the Labour movement for involvement in extension lectures, A. W. Brown's experimentation may be seen as an important element in the success of Tawney's Longton tutorial class.

At the same time that this preparatory work was being undertaken in North Staffordshire, there was a growing feeling within Oxford that more needed to be done to meet the increasingly strenuous demands for workers' education. For some years Albert Mansbridge had been advocating a closer liaison between university extension and the trade unions.[54] When it became clear that Ruskin Hall was not producing workers 'educated in the image of the "reasonable" university man',[55] extensionists began to seek some remedy for its defects.

In response to developments at Ruskin, Hudson Shaw and Dr John Percival, Bishop of Hereford, arranged a private conference at Balliol in November 1905 'about the possibility of putting the work done for working men at Oxford in touch with [the Extension] Delegacy'.[56] Tawney, J. A. R. Marriott, Hudson Shaw, Percival, Canon Barnett, and Sidney Ball were among the extensionists present at what was to be the first of a series of meetings. Also present were Albert Mansbridge, Robert Young of the Amalgamated Society of Engineers (and formerly a Ruskin student) and Albert Taylor, representing the ASE executive and the Council of Ruskin College. This small informal group eventually passed a resolution that the Extension Delegacy should help to finance Ruskin's work, but its deliberations reflect a growing concern within Oxford that extension work was failing to reach trade unionists, and many of the ideas put forward at its first meeting anticipated the establishment of tutorial classes. Mansbridge argued, for example, that a new type of extension centre was needed if the movement was to avoid the charge that it had failed, and he advocated small classes in a defined scheme extending over not less than two years. These classes could become outposts of the university, from which students might come either to Ruskin or to an extension hostel which might be established. Hudson Shaw went further than this, arguing for a new Oxford college, or the surrender of an existing one to offer a two-year course in History and Economics for the leaders of the labour movement, and to allow working men to read for degrees. For Shaw the educational 'ladder' was already complete for the working classes, but he doubted whether Ruskin College could effectively provide for the worker without segregating him from the life of Oxford. Young opposed him firmly, and argued for the status quo. Any new college could only increase the hostility of the trade unions, who would also resist any tinkering with Ruskin by the government or the university. Although working men dreaded contact with Oxford, the feeling was being dissipated.

In conclusion, the Bishop of Hereford emphasised that closer contacts were needed between Oxford and the trade unions, and that a new type of extension centre, offering class teaching, might supply this want and provide a nursery for working-class students who might enter Oxford. This was an exact recipe for the tutorial classes begun by Tawney in 1908.[57] So, impelled by the growing demands of the trade unions, and by concern that Ruskin was working towards ends different from their own, Oxford extensionists were becoming increasingly prepared to accept changes in their work, along lines which men such as A. W. Brown were, in practice, already pioneering.

The negotiations which led to the establishment of the first Oxford tutorial classes are well documented. In August 1905, at a national conference of Mansbridge's Association to Promote the Higher Education of Working Men (later the WEA), he canvassed his scheme for class teaching under the auspices of the universities to establish 'a triple cord' between university extension, trade unionism and the co-operative movement.[58] In the following year the London conference led to the setting up of a small committee which 'definitely recommended the formation of a tutorial class for working people'.[59] The Battersea group, under Patrick Geddes, which began work in September 1907 with a small group of students (the average attendance was fourteen) was one attempt to implement these ideas.[60] Meanwhile, a tutorial class was planned for Rochdale, where for many years the co-operative movement had supported extension lectures,[61] and where both E. L. S. Horsburgh and Hudson Shaw had taught (these two were also responsible for the Oxford lectures given at Longton after 1904). At the 1907 Oxford conference, the North Staffordshire delegates requested a similar class, Tawney agreed to teach both, and they began work in January 1908.

Tawney's achievement as a tutor at Longton and Rochdale was a considerable one; working men produced work of a new standard, and the WEA was given a model for its teaching which was to be followed for half a century. It is clear, though, not only that tutorial classwork had been canvassed for several years, but that, in one area at least, experimentation with extension lecturing for teachers led to the establishment of classes which Tawney's were to resemble in many ways.

Much work remains to be done to discover whether extension lecturing in other areas was as flexible as that undertaken in the Potteries, and whether it demonstrated what A. W. Brown called 'the capacity of the university extension movement to adapt itself to any set of local conditions'.[62] The exact nature of the work done under London University at the start of this century also needs close investigation. Perhaps such work will confirm the suggestion underlying this article that R. H. Tawney's reputation as a pioneer may have been overstated.

University of Birmingham

References

1 *University Extension Journal*, VI, 46, October 1900, 15.
2 R. D. Roberts, *Eighteen Years of University Extension*, Cambridge (1891).
3 *University Extension Journal*, VII, 71, May 1903, 115.
4 Ibid, IX, 73, October 1903, 3.
5 *University Extension Bulletin*, I, Michaelmas 1907, 8.
6 A. Mansbridge, *An Adventure in Working Class Education* (1920), 36.
7 B. Simon, *Education and the Labour Movement* (1965), 305.
8 A. Mansbridge, *University Tutorial Classes* (1913), 6.
9 A. Mansbridge, *An Adventure in Working Class Education*, 37.
10 R. A. Lowe, 'The North Staffordshire Miners' Higher Education Movement', *Educational Review*, 22, 3 June 1970, 263–77.
11 A. E. Zimmern, 'Education and the Working Class', *The Round Table*, 14 March 1914, 255–79.
12 Oxford Extension Lecturers MS Reports, 1900–1 (Extra-Mural Delegacy, Oxford).
13 Ibid, 1903–4.   14 Ibid., 1904–5.   15 Ibid, 1905–6.
16 Oxford Extramural Delegacy Manuscript Minutes, 16 May 1902 (E-MD).
17 Historical list of lectures given by the Cambridge University Board of Extra-Mural Studies (Stuart House, Cambridge).
18 F. D. How, *Bishop Lovelace T. Stamer* (1910), 110.
19 *Keates' Gazetteer and Directory of the Staffordshire Potteries*, Hanley (1874), 336–7.
20 *Rendezvous with the Past: Sentinel Centenary, 1854–1954*, Stoke (1954), 50.
21 Minutes of the Staffordshire Technical Instruction Committee, 28 November 1891 (CRO, Stafford).
22 R. G. Moulton, *The University Extension Movement* (1886), 44.
23 Cambridge University Local Lecturers' Reports, 1890–2 (SH).
24 *A College for North Staffordshire: the Report of a Committee of Enquiry*, Hanley (1899), 18.
25 Council for the Extension of Higher Education in North Staffordshire, Manuscript Minutes, 21 January 1902 (CRO).
26 Ibid.   27 Ibid.
28 Letter: J. A. R. Marriott to A. W. Brown, 12 July 1901 (E-MD).
29 *University Extension Journal*, VI, 53, May 1901, 116.
30 *University Extension Journal*, VII, 58, January 1902, 56.
31 *Staffordshire Technical Instruction Committee Report, 1901–02*, Stafford (1902), 94.

32 Letter: J. A. R. Marriott to A. W. Brown, 1 June 1901 (E-MD).
33 Letter: F. H. Wright (Registrar, Reading University College) to A. W. Brown, 2 April 1901 (CRO).
34 A. W. Brown, Memorandum on the proposed classes for uncertificated assistant teachers in elementary schools, 8 March 1904 (CRO).
35 Report of a meeting between representatives of the Council for the Extension of Higher Education in North Staffordshire and the Stoke-on-Trent School Boards, 18 April 1901 (CRO).
36 *University Extension Journal*, VI, 53, May 1901, 116.
37 Oxford Extension Lecturers Manuscript Reports, 1902–3 (E-MD).
38 A. W. Brown, Memorandum on the proposed classes for uncertificated assistant teachers in elementary schools, 8 March 1904 (CRO).
39 A. W. Brown, 'University Extension and the training of teachers: some notes on an experiment', *University Extension*, 3 June 1905, 16.
40 Letter: G. Menzies (agent to the Duke of Sutherland) to F. Blackiston, 8 April 1903 (CRO).
41 G. Balfour, *Ten Years of Staffordshire Education, 1903–13*, Stafford (1913), 22.
42 *Staffordshire Sentinel*, 20 April 1914.
43 Oxford University Extension Delegacy Minutes, 16 May 1902 (E-MD).
44 A. W. Brown, Memorandum on a possible basis of agreement between the major local education authorities and my council for the building and maintenance of the proposed North Staffordshire college, 14 January 1905 (CRO).
45 G. Balfour, op cit, 22.
46 Letter: R. Morant to G. Balfour, 4 December 1905 (CRO).
47 Oxford Extension Lecturers Manuscript Reports, 1904–5 (E-MD).
48 Ibid.   49 Ibid, 1905–6.
50 Longton Education Committee, draft minutes, 30 August 1903 (Horace Barks Library, Hanley).
51 H. P. Smith, 'E. S. Cartwright', *Rewley House Papers*, III, I, 1949–50, 8–24.
52 H. P. Smith, *Labour and Learning*, Oxford (1956), 42.
53 Oxford Extension Lecturers' manuscript reports, 1907–8 (E-MD).
54 *University Extension Journal*, VIII, 67, January 1903, 53, and ibid, VIII, 69, March 1903, 85.
55 S. Rowbotham, 'The call to University Extension teaching 1873–1900', *Birmingham Historical Journal*, XII, I, 1969, 71.
56 Letter: J. Percival to J. A. R. Marriott, 24 October 1905 (E-MD).
57 These arguments are reconstructed from a pencilled note made at the conference found in the archives of the Delegacy for Extra-Mural Studies, Oxford.
58 A. Mansbridge, *An Adventure in Working Class Education* (1920), 11.
59 A. Mansbridge, *University Tutorial Classes* (1913), 17.
60 Ibid, 17.
61 *University Extension Journal*, VIII, 65, November 1902, 20.
62 Oxford University Extension Delegacy Minutes, 16 May 1902 (E-MD).

NB. A complete collection of the journals of the university extension movement is kept in the library of the University of London. Documents referred to in the archives of the Extra-Mural Delegacy, Oxford; Stuart House, Cambridge; the Horace Barks Library, Hanley; and the County Record Office, Stafford.

For plates, provided by the author, see p 73

DAVID A. TURNER

The Open Air School Movement in Sheffield

THE open air school is now dead—killed as much by success as anything else and overtaken by improvements in the general health of the nation. Its influence, however, still pervades our schools and many of the pioneering open air schools remain in use as special schools for delicate or maladjusted children. The open air school movement illustrates clearly some of the problems facing schools at the beginning of the century after some years of compulsory schooling and it was seen by many as a panacea for all ills. It illustrates, too, the immediate impact which the newly established health and welfare services had on the development of schools, as well as the rapid absorption of such ideas from Germany. Sheffield was a pioneer in the foundation of open air schools and the history of its schools reflects the development of the movement throughout the country.

Behind the development of the open air school was the increasing awareness of urban communities that compulsory education in itself was not sufficient, for the health and social conditions of the children made it impossible for them to benefit from the schooling provided. In the crowded classroom conditions of the time it was impossible to investigate causes of backwardness and many of the schools became clogged with dull children often classified as standard 'O'. The large school boards such as those in Bradford, Birmingham, Leicester, London, Nottingham and Sheffield had already in the 1890s set up classes for subnormal children following continental practice. Statutory provision had been made for the blind and deaf in the Act of 1893 and the Elementary Education Act (Defective and Epileptic Children) of 1899 made provision for ascertaining and establishing special schools so that in each area the size of the problem soon became apparent. It was under this Act that the first open air schools were maintained.

Another factor which led to their development was the growth of the school medical service, for only the doctors could establish the clear medical need for such schools and without them it is unlikely that teachers would have demanded these special schools. Attention had been focused on the physical condition of the nation's children by the Report of the Interdepartmental Committee on Physical Deterioration in 1904, and if the provision of school meals and the setting up of school medical services were the direct results of this report the open air school was an indirect one. A move in the direction of provision of medical and welfare services had already been made by a number of school boards in the 1890s, again following continental practice.

The open air school itself was a German idea, the first such school having been set up in the pinewoods of Charlottenburg outside Berlin in 1904, and the movement had quickly spread throughout Germany. Both there and in France and Switzerland (where schools were founded in 1906 and 1907) it was the medical profession which had advocated them.[1] The first open air school in England was set up by the LCC at Bostall Wood, Woolwich, in 1907 and in the following year was joined by open air schools at Bradford, Halifax and Norwich.[2] Sheffield opened the first of its three schools at Whiteley Woods in 1909 and this school still operates as a special school today. Whiteley Woods School and all the open air schools before it owed their existence not only to the strength of local feeling but also to the central support of the new school medical service. Sir John Gorst, a former Vice-President of the Board of Education, had spoken in favour of open air education as early as 1903:

> I think the practice of open air lessons should be enormously extended in our schools. In America every lesson they can give in the open air they do. They constantly turn children out of schools . . . even for history lessons. . . . I tried to encourage such practice . . . and I preached this open air doctrine to them [the schoolmasters]. They accepted the notion but they wrote to me afterwards that their managers would not agree to it. They had the schools, they liked to use them. They did not like the idea of children being put out of doors. . . . They ought to have a playground or covered shed in which the children can be exercised.[3]

It was Sir George Newman, Chief Medical Officer at the Board of

Education, in his annual reports on school health from 1907 who was the most persistent advocate of open air education. For twenty-five years he exhorted the LEAs and the government to give every assistance to these schools. He was ably supported in this campaign by his medical colleagues at the board: Dr Crowley, Dr Eichholz, Dr Janet Campbell and later Dr Williams from Sheffield. Dr Alfred Eichholz had drawn attention to the condition of schoolchildren and suggested methods of improving their health in his major contribution of evidence to the Physical Deterioration Committee.[4] This evidence had the endorsement of at least two hundred individuals or organisations throughout the country whom he had consulted. Both he and Dr Kerr (formerly of the Bradford School Board and with the LCC from 1902) had suggested a special type of school for semi-convalescent children who needed plenty of fresh air.[5] Dr Eichholz maintained regular contact with the Sheffield open air school and was always ready with helpful advice and encouragement. He continued to visit the school at least once a year almost until his retirement in 1930.

The condition of children in Sheffield was as bad if not worse than that of children in other large industrial cities. Sheffield was essentially a city of small homes and large families. As many as 15,000 houses were built on the back-to-back principle. Infant mortality was as high as 234 per 1,000 in parts of the city and throughout averaged 200. Young children were described as going to school 'in a most filthy condition . . . terribly verminous and neglected'.[6] In 1909 of all the schoolchildren examined 70 per cent were described as being in moderate condition only and 8 per cent in bad condition. In the poor districts 16 per cent of senior boys and 11 per cent of infants examined were badly nourished. Of the 4,000 children examined 36 per cent had verminous heads and 12 per cent dirty bodies. These figures would have been much higher if the schools had not had warning of the inspection.[7] The city had employed a part-time medical officer to inspect schoolchildren as early as 1905 and in the following year had appointed Dr Ralph Williams as its first full-time medical officer for schools. In 1908 he worked with Dr Crowley of the Board of Education in examining teachers and students following a course of lectures on health. Open air recovery schools were the subject of some of these lectures, so that it was not surprising that when the opportunity arose he persuaded the city to set up an open air school in Sheffield. Its organisation and routine followed closely that established at Charlottenburg and the schools in London and elsewhere.

Whiteley Woods village school had been established as a voluntary school in 1878 by Alderman and Mrs T. R. Gainsford of Whiteley Wood Hall, but had been taken over by the Sheffield School Board in 1893. It was situated on the very edge of the city, five miles from the centre, surrounded by fields and woodlands. The numbers attending the school had fallen below fifty so it had been closed in March 1909, but it reopened on 21 June 1909 as an open air school. The needs of the open air school were few, so that conversion of the building was quickly and easily accomplished. The old infants class became a kitchen and one other classroom was divided, with showers on one side with a new zinc floor covering and a medical inspection room on the other. Two sheds were provided—one facing south for the dining-room and one facing north used only in wet weather for resting. There were two classes of twenty-five children, standards II & III working together and IV, V & VI. In common with all existing open air schools the first session continued for only a limited period of nineteen weeks.

Recruitment of pupils had been limited to those within easy walking distance of the tramcar terminus in the city centre. Each headmaster had been asked to send four of the most anaemic and poorly nourished children from his senior pupils. The school medical department had examined a hundred of these and in making their final selection had had to exclude any children unable to walk the one and a half miles downhill through the woods to the tram every evening. The first pupils admitted suffered almost entirely from anaemia and malnutrition, with some tuberculosis or suspected tuberculosis of the lung. 'The majority of children are very backward owing to their long absence from school,' wrote the headmistress in the school log book.[8] During the first year, entry was restricted to the 9–13 year olds. The routine which developed in the school's first year was similar to that of open air schools elsewhere and there was very little deviation from this basic formula during the following two decades except that Dr Williams was in favour of rather more sleep than was normal—at least two hours daily.[9]

The routine was highly organised and the school day was a long one. Under the provisions of the 1899 Act the city was able to pay for the children's transport to school. They all gathered at the tramcar station near the education office at 8.45am and travelled by special car to the Ecclesall terminus, thereafter being taken by two wagonettes uphill to school (see plate, p 74). In the evening the children walked back to the terminus to catch the car at 6.20pm, arriving back in the city centre at 6.45pm. Only in winter, when the children left a little earlier, was there any modification of this routine. Occasionally in exceptionally bad weather a motor bus was sent to take them all the way from the school. The use of the wagonettes was discontinued in 1913 when their place was taken by a 'motor omnibus' (see plate, p 74).[10]

Feeding was an important part of the school routine and as soon as they arrived the children were given the traditional open air school breakfast of porridge, to which resistance was common.[11] 'Oatmeal porridge the first two mornings was a total failure . . . but they gradually acquired a liking for it.'[12] The children were given dinner at 1pm and tea at 5pm. These meals were carefully planned in consultation with the superintendent of the Domestic Science School and cost just under 2s 6d for each child weekly. Parents were expected to contribute from 6d to 2s 6d according to income. During the first year three children were forced to withdraw because their parents refused to contribute anything to their support.[13] The meals were cooked on the premises with the assistance of the lady caretaker. The city had had some experience of providing cheap school meals in 1909 as 372,924 free breakfasts and 99,786 free dinners had been provided in schools during the severe unemployment in the area.[14] The weekly menu for Summer 1914 is reproduced on page 63.

The recruitment of teachers for the first open air school was done by personal recommendation or invitation of the Chief Education Officer. The first heads and their assistants had had no experience in this field or in any special schools. They simply went up to London to see what was going on in the open air schools there.[15] The first five heads of the school between 1909 and 1929 had had no experience of such schools, thereafter the heads had been assistants in other open air schools. When Sheffield opened its second open air school in 1919, the head-mistress had been an assistant at the Whiteley Woods School. The first headmistress, Miss Lee, was the only one to leave for the headship of another open air school (The Lord Mayor Trelor Open Air School for Crippled Children at Alton, Hants),[16] the others being promoted to normal headships in Sheffield or leaving to marry. During the first two decades the school had one or two qualified assistant teachers and a number of uncertificated assistants. The one element of stability at the Whiteley Woods School over a very long period was the caretaker/cook, Mrs Hancox, who also bathed and looked after the children.

CITY OF SHEFFIELD.
WHITELEY WOOD OPEN AIR RECOVERY SCHOOL.
M E N U.

BREAKFAST. (daily)	Porridge with Treacle or Sugar and ½ pint Milk (boiled) Rusks.
DINNERS.	
Monday.	(1) Lentil or Split Pea Soup & Bread. Yorkshire Pudding.
	(2) Mutton Broth with Barley.
	(1 & 2 given on alternate Mondays.)
Tuesday.	Cheese Pie. Baked suet fruit pudding.
Wednesday.	Beef & Vegetable stew with suet pudding.
Thursday.	Haricot Beans & Meat in Brown Gravy. Fruit and/or Jam Pasties.
Friday.	Boiled Fish & Parsley Sauce *or* Baked Fish Pie. Potatoes in jackets. Milk Pudding. Rusks.
TEA.	½ Pint of Milk (boiled). Bread with Jam, Dripping or Margarine followed by Rusks. Plain Cake once a week.

This dietary works out at 2/6d. per head per week of five days.

It was in the keeping of records that the open air schools were most thoroughly organised. It was understandable that Dr Williams would wish to prove conclusively that this pioneering venture was successful.

(Form 68 M.I.)

Recommended by..
Previous Sessions at O.A.R.S.......................................
Passed by Dentist...

Diagnosis...

CITY OF SHEFFIELD.—EDUCATION COMMITTEE.

OPEN-AIR RECOVERY SCHOOL RECORD.

Name of Child...

(Surname first.)

Date of Examination.. Age...........................
Address ....
School.. Dept...................................Standard...................
Social Conditions :—Weekly Wage.................No. in Family (inc. Parents)....................Rent.................
Previous Illnesses :—Measles............Whooping Cough............Chicken Pox............Scarlet Fever................
          Diphtheria.................Rheumatism..................Pneumonia..................Pleurisy..................

Family History :—
   Father, if dead, cause...Age...........................
   Mother, if dead, cause...Age...........................
   No. of Children living.......................dead....................causes of death.......................

History of Illness : { ....
                          ....
                          ....
                          .... }

Present condition :

General :—Nutrition ....
   Anæmia ....
   Weight ....
   Av. Wt. for Age.....................
   Height ....
   Fever ....
   Tired ....
   Sweats ....

Glands :—Neck ....
   Mediastinal....................
   Tonsils.................. ...
   Adenoids....................
Respiratory :—Cough ....
      Sputum.........T.B. ...
      Hæmoptysis ....
      Pain....................
   Cleanliness :—Head......Body......

Alimentary :—Teeth....................
   Appetite ....
   Bowels...........................
Circulatory :—Heart.................
   Pulse ....
Mental Condition ....
Vision R..............L............
Ext. Eye Dis ....
Deafness.........Ear Dis. ....

Chest Measurements :—
         On ad.   On dis.
Greatest Ins..............................
   „ Exp. ....

Urine :—
   On ad......................
   On dis......................

Hæmoglobin :—
   On ad......................
   On dis. ....

Medical Officer's Initials...................................

DATE.	HEIGHT.	WEIGHT.	NOTES.

(BACK OF FORM).

He was a regular visitor along with the school nurse and they kept a systematic record of each pupil's progress long after he had left school. Homes were also visited by teachers and nurses so that the parents could ensure that treatment continued when the children were there. The senior dental surgeon at the Sheffield Royal Hospital examined the teeth of all the children on entry and later provided treatment for those who needed it. After 1912, on the appointment of the first school dentist by the city, it became standard practice to have full dental treatment at the school. Full medical records were kept of all the children, who were weighed every fortnight and chest and height measurements were also taken at intervals (see plate, p 75). Their eyesight was tested on arrival. During the last two weeks of the school year there was an intensive medical inspection of each child. Only by this means could the newly established medical service demonstrate to both teachers and the public that its methods worked. At the end of the school's first year seventeen children were pronounced cured and the rest, save one, had improved. Height, chest measurements and

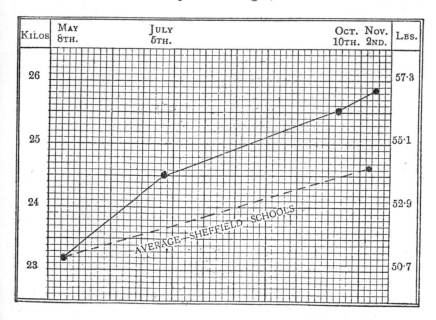

general appearance had all improved and graphs of this improvement were made to demonstrate this fact. Weights increased by an average of 5lb per child as the graph shows.

When the children left the open air school—and the whole purpose of the institution was to improve their condition so that they might attend a normal school—a close watch was kept on their health, even when they left school permanently, so that the medical department was able to establish that its success was a long-term rather than temporary one.

Much of the routine of the school was not concerned with a normal curriculum but with the special needs of its pupils. Rest was an important factor in the open air cure and all the children rested for at least two hours daily in the open in deck chairs. In later years they slept on canvas beds. There was, too, an emphasis on personal hygiene and each child had its own numbered blanket, rain cape for the long walk from school, toothbrush, mug and towels. All had at least two showers weekly with soap and loofahs provided by the school. This was all in keeping with the formula laid down by the French innovator of open air schools, Professor Grancher:

> Double ration d'air
> Double ration de nourriture
> Demi-ration de travail[17]

As far as normal school work was concerned, only just under four hours were devoted to this daily; a ratio which remained more or less constant for almost twenty years. Even within this limited time there was much more variety than in a normal school and extra emphasis was given to subjects such as gardening, housewifery and nature study. The girls took turns in setting the tables, serving and drying the dishes while the boys scraped potatoes, cleaned knives and boots.[18]

After the first nineteen-week experiment the medical service was in no doubt that

> the results of the school from the medical point of view are certainly very satisfactory. Educationally although many of the children will be found to have lost ground in their ordinary curriculum, they return to school much brighter, more alert, and more able to cope with their daily work. Their knowledge of nature and powers of observation are no doubt greatly increased

and all who were in contact with the children agree that their conduct at meals, during games and throughout their school work, improved immensely during their stay at the Open Air Recovery School.[19]

This improvement was also noted by the headmistress of the school, Miss Lee, and by the headmasters to whom the pupils were returned.

Dr Williams used the success of the school's first year as propaganda for the new methods. His detailed records, many photographs and invitations to the press all testify to this.[20] During its first year many visitors were taken to the school including Dr Eichholz and Dr Crowley from the Board of Education. Eichholz made a number of suggestions for minor changes such as using the neighbouring woods for rambles, and keeping accurate records of the exact amount of time spent indoors, which were accepted. The headmistress in her turn visited the London open air schools. Students from Sheffield University and from Sheffield and Lincoln training colleges made a number of visits, and this connection with several training colleges was maintained for many years with regular visits from students as far away as St Katherine's, Tottenham. Local students were to use the school both for teaching practice and observation. Parents expressed their thanks to the school in appreciative letters and the attitude of the general public became clear in 1910 when large numbers of children applied to attend the school. In spite of a twofold increase in numbers to a hundred many applicants had to be turned down.[21]

The procedure for enrolment was similar to that employed in the school's first year, namely that suitable applicants were recommended by headteachers in elementary schools. The decision to admit children was taken on medical grounds by the school medical officer who in 1910 gave a slight preference to younger children. Although over half the children again suffered from anaemia and malnutrition there was a wider range of disabilities including epilepsy and tuberculosis. The school in fact was specially recommended for the treatment of early stages of tuberculosis and in future thirty places were reserved annually for Dr Rennie's patients from the School Tuberculosis Dispensary.[22] The publicity given to the school during its first year had been responsible for the increase in demand for places there.

Further alterations were made to the school in 1910 to accommodate the extra children. A part of the school hall's southern window was cut away and replaced with folding doors so that when thrown open 'the hall was practically converted into an open air shed'.[23] A new resting shed was built and the dining shed remodelled. As it became well known, many gifts were received, including clothes and chocolate from Mr and Mrs Cadbury who visited the school. Lessons were as short, practical and interesting as possible and included arithmetic, reading, writing, singing, local geography and history. Manual instruction covered gardening, housewifery, plain and fancy needlework, clay modelling and general art work (see plates, p 76). Goldfish, rabbits, canaries and swallows were kept as pets. Extensive records were again kept and Dr Williams claimed once more that roughly the same proportion of children were cured or improved as a result of their stay.[24] Dr Williams based this claim upon the records he kept and upon general observation of the children. The records showed there had been an increase in height and weight for almost all the children beyond the average. Those considered completely ready to return to ordinary schools were categorised as cured, the others were thought of as improved. Only three were considered to have made no progress. It was the return of life and spirit to the children which really marked their improvement. Their total apathy both mental and physical on admission is difficult to imagine today, and the teachers really felt some success when the children began to be naughty and mischievous.[25] Publicity for the school remained intense and there were over 600 visitors, including delegates from the British Association and the TUC which had met in Sheffield in 1910. Dr Eichholz made further visits and offered more useful suggestions for improving the curriculum.[26]

At the end of the year Dr Williams felt able to recommend that 'another school should be established for 100 children' and that ordinary schools should make much more use of their playgrounds for teaching and that more lessons should be held in the open air of the parks.[27] This extension of open air methods into other schools was exactly what Sir George Newman was urging in his annual reports to the Board of Education.

The medical profession regarded the case for such schools as proven but the teachers and city officials were rather more cautious. Each year Dr Williams's annual report became more eloquent on the proven value of these schools, but the authorities after the first flush of enthusiasm were slow to respond. In 1912 he calculated that at least 2,000 Sheffield schoolchildren were in need of open air education. The children in the school were subjected to even more tests to prove the value of the new methods and he was able to claim that in addition to other benefits the haemoglobin content of the blood of anaemic children was increased by 11 per cent.[28] He felt too that the success of the open air school demonstrated that ordinary schools should now be designed with southern aspects and an efficient system of through ventilation. Dr Williams went to London in 1914 as a senior medical officer at the Board of Education, but by that time the Whiteley Woods school had been extended and developed several times so that it was open nearly forty weeks in the year and housed over a hundred children. Prominent visitors such as Sir George Newman, Dr Eichholz and Dr Hertz, the Chief Medical Officer of Danish schools, continued to visit the school. Its influence was being generally felt in the city for in 1913 open air classes were established in all the parks, 'the bandstands being available for shelter should the weather be unfavourable'.[29] In the same year the design of a new school, Whitby Road Infants, incorporated the medical officer's suggestions and was built as an 'E' shaped plan for maximum ventilation and sunshine.

The new medical officer for schools in Sheffield, Dr Chetwood, was equally fervent in his advocacy of the open air school and had equal support from the medical department in London. Although war made it impossible to extend the system, schools continued to use playgrounds and parks in the summer and (apart from brief interruptions because of Zeppelin raids in 1916) Whiteley Woods school functioned as normal. Visitors from London continued, including Dr Eichholz and H. A. L. Fisher, sometime Vice-Chancellor of Sheffield University. After the war Dr Chetwood recommended further development of the open air system and urged the city to buy suitable premises for a second school. Expensive and solidly built premises, he stressed, were not necessary; sheds especially of the temporary wartime variety were ideally suited to the needs of open air schools.[30] In 1918 a house was acquired in suitable grounds in a central position near a bus route. Arrangements were made to erect shelters and convert the house to cater for ninety children. In the meantime ordinary schools continued to hold classes in the city parks and arrangements were made to extend the system by taking groups of children to the seaside or the country for short residential visits. Sheffield's second school was opened in 1919 at Springvale House, Park Lane, and remained in session all the year round.

At the very moment when it seemed that the open air principle was penetrating into the general school system the Sheffield school management committee was having second thoughts. They had no doubt as to the medical value of open air education but they 'expressed the opinion that playgrounds and parks cannot usually be regarded as satisfactory classrooms'.[31] This was a preliminary warning and at that time the movement did not appear to be losing impetus for a massive extension of the system was in fact proposed in 1920. The city had acquired Redmires Camp with its wartime prisoners' hutments and land on a beautiful site on the edge of Derbyshire and had grandiose plans to develop it into an open air residential school for at least 600 children. Unfortunately in 1921 any further expenditure was forbidden by the government and after repeated attempts to begin work on the scheme it was finally dropped in 1926. The open air movement was caught up in the general postwar economic difficulties and expansion was therefore limited. Some extensions were made to the two existing schools so that by 1925 they contained between them nearly three hundred children. An ex-army hut was acquired for the Whiteley Woods school, rebuilt on one side, and fitted with double doors on the stable pattern on the other. However, by 1925 Dr Chetwood regretted that 'playground classes are not very much in favour here . . . and are not very commonly met with, and the holding of classes in the public parks has not been continued as the school management subcommittee has laid it down to the contrary'.[32] Though open air classes were no longer held in the parks they were still used extensively for the physical training of schoolchildren.

Interest in the movement was renewed in 1930 when a third open air school was opened with residential facilities at Bents Green, near the original Whiteley Woods school. Although open air education continued in the 1930s, some of the earlier pioneering spirit was disappearing. Throughout the country the numbers in such schools were either expanding very slowly or remaining static, though there was no actual fall in numbers. The schools themselves were changing as was the nature of some of the defects of the schoolchildren. Increasingly the term 'schools for the delicate' came into use and the 1944 Education Act gave statutory recognition to this category of child for the first time. The harsh spartan conditions of the early days were being modified. Miss Harbron, who became headmistress of Whiteley Woods school in 1928, after having served as an assistant at the Springvale House open air school since its opening in 1919, saw the end of the old days and the beginnings of many improvements in the physical condition of her school. She remained there until 1961 and so bridged the gap between the old and the new. Electricity, warm stoves, a telephone and improved cookers were all installed in the 1930s. Nevertheless, she maintained the open air tradition during the difficult wartime conditions and the Director of Education, W. P. Alexander, reported in 1943 that 'full use is made for teaching purposes in suitable weather of clear space outside and in the adjoining fields'.[33] Since 1934 the school had been open throughout the whole year.

What then has survived of the open air movement in Sheffield? Two of the three schools, Whiteley Woods and Bents Green are still in full operation as schools for the delicate. Miss J. M. Robson, headmistress of Whiteley Woods since 1961, has seen the nature and function of the school broadened considerably. The term 'open air school' is now seldom used throughout the country and since World War II there has been a decrease in the number of children requiring such education, from 16,000 in 1938 to 10,000 just after the war. The present schools are adapted to cater for children suffering from various forms of physical disability and in recent years have taken on an additional function of providing for maladjusted children. It is interesting to note that in the first school there were a number of children who also displayed maladjustment. 'Some little mites talk greatly in their sleep, others twitch their bodies and are very restless, though these signs of nervous disorder are diminishing after one month.'[34] The change in function seems to be universal since former open air schools in Denmark as well as in this country are also dealing increasingly with psychological rather than simply physical cases.[35] Whiteley Woods school still has just over a hundred pupils aged from five to almost seventeen; there is a hard core of 'chesty' children, especially asthmatic cases, but many others have physical handicaps, some of which are psychological in origin. These children benefit from the smaller classes and the closer community life the school can offer. The school continues to take advantage of its superb position out in the country, but the narrow emphasis on open air pursuits has disappeared and the curriculum is as wide as in any school, with courses which lead up to CSE. The school is still using all the original buildings, including the wooden huts dating from 1909 and 1910, but this year the school is undergoing another transformation of its buildings and is entering on yet another lease of life as it nears its centenary.

Some of the factors which brought about the demise of the open air school are quite clear. Foremost is the general improvement in the health of schoolchildren and the elimination of debilitating conditions such as anaemia, malnutrition and tuberculosis. Slum clearance programmes and the development of suburban housing estates have contributed to an improvement in home conditions for many children. Families today are much smaller. Health and welfare services have improved and expanded so that children in need today get attention before they begin school or having begun receive help in school or clinic, not merely in special schools.

Some of the methods employed by the open air schools were impracticable when transferred to ordinary schools. It was physically impossible to have all lessons in the open and much time was wasted moving classes and equipment in and out of schools and parks. Teachers were never wholeheartedly in favour of mass exodus of this kind. What is amazing is that this system of holding lessons out of doors ever had any success in the British climate, though one observer

Oxford Summer School, 1910. Albert Mansbridge (standing) and a tutorial class member demonstrate the capacity of the university extension movement to 'adapt itself to any set of local conditions' during the 1910 Oxford Summer School. (Courtesy: University of Oxford, Department for External Studies)

F. W. Cuthbertson, tutor of the Oxford classes at Burslem and Fenton, who took over the work at Longton from R. H. Tawney, leads a group on Balliol Lawn at the 1911 Oxford Summer School. (Courtesy: University of Oxford Department for External Studies)

See Lowe, 'Forerunners of Longton Tutorial Class', pp 43-57

Pupils taken to the Open Air School at Sheffield by wagonettes, 1909

The use of wagonettes was discontinued in 1913, when their place was taken by motor-buses
See Turner, 'Open Air School Movement', pp 58-80

Whiteley Woods Open Air School, Sheffield. Measuring a pupil, 1911
See Turner, 'Open Air School Movement', pp 58-80

Whiteley Woods Open Air School, Sheffield. An open air class making brackets, 1911

Whiteley Woods Open Air School, Sheffield. Gardening, 1910
See Turner, 'Open Air School Movement', pp 58-80

suggested that one reason why the English open air schools remained open throughout the year was that 'the cooler weather gave the best results'.[36] A glance at a few extracts from the Sheffield open air school records show that the real enemy was the weather.

> The children had to travel this morning through pouring rain and consequently arrived at school with very wet clothing—some wet through. We removed all wet clothing, gave some of the more delicate ones hot baths and put the children wrapped in blankets to rest, lessons being abandoned as impossible under the circumstances. (1912)[37]

> On cold days the children were either wrapped in their blankets or wore overcoats and all were busily employed in making woollen 'hug-me-tights' and felt slippers for the coming winter. (1913)[38]

> No artificial warming of an open air building is of any value, and consequently the onset of cold weather at once renders suitable warm clothing essential. (1915)[39]

> Rain screens have been provided for the main hall, dining shed and open air classrooms. These are light and portable, and can be readily fixed in position in wet weather. (1916)[40]

> This week has been intensely cold. It has been necessary to take the children for a short walk each morning and give plenty of breaks in their lessons in order to get them warm. (1936)[41]

> The classrooms have registered temperatures below freezing in spite of the stoves. The children have been taken out each morning for a good walk, and the work has been adjusted to whatever was possible in view of the weather. (1947)[42]

Such spartan conditions are clearly unacceptable today, indeed they would be illegal in factories. Even the present heating system in the former open air sheds at Whiteley Woods school does not really bring them up to modern standards.

The decline of the open air school cannot be attributed simply to the weather since there has been a similar decrease in open air education abroad. The movement also flourished on the continent and in the United States between the wars and was particularly widespread in France.[43] By 1937 sixteen nations had developed such schools and had held three international congresses in Paris, Brussels and Bielefeld to promote their further expansion.[44] Teaching courses designed specially for work in open air schools were officially recognised in France in

1939, yet after the war the movement never regained its former
influence. It was essentially the product of the social system of pre-war
Europe.

If the movement is now dead, its influence is not. Most schools
built in the 1920s and 1930s were designed with some open air classes
in mind as anyone who has suffered in such schools with their open
corridors, french windows and verandahs can testify. This influence
on school design has been noted in Sheffield as early as 1913. By 1929
it was claimed that 'slowly but gradually the value of the open air as
an educational medium is permeating the schools . . . the new schools
are so designed that every classroom can be opened on one side to the
air; the old school of rigid walls is passing'.[45] This view was so entrenched that the Hadow Report on *The Primary School* in 1931 stated
quite categorically that 'the more closely the design of the primary
school approaches that of the open air school the better'.[46] A number
of witnesses urged that all primary schools should in fact be planned
on the open air principle and the report made it clear that they felt that
the best modern designs for primary schools already incorporated a
number of features of the open air schools.[47]

The open air school pointed the way to smaller classes and to more
variety both in the curriculum and approach. The emphasis in the
present schools on physical training, games and hygiene owes something to the open air school. Even the general acceptance of sun-
bathing, showers and a varied diet may be indirectly attributed to the
open air school propaganda. The open air movement was even linked
with the development of the National Trust and the Youth Hostels
Association in the 1920s.[48] The open air school demonstrated the value
of co-operation between the different agencies which deal with children. These schools pioneered the provision of school meals, residential facilities in LEA schools and school transport. They also
directed attention to the needs of minorities in the schools and were
the most flourishing of the special schools which developed between
the wars. Post-war special schools have been able to build upon the
goodwill which they established. The open air school arose in Sheffield
and elsewhere as an organised response to a distinctive social and

medical need. That need is no longer so obvious and the schools have consequently changed their role to meet other needs.

Sheffield City College of Education

References

1 *Les Écoles de Plein Air en France*, published by L'Hygiène par L'Exemple, Paris (1943), 71 ff. Heck, A. O., *The education of exceptional children* (1940), 313, shows that the movement had crossed the Atlantic to the United States by 1908 and Canada by 1910.
2 Pritchard, D. G., *Education and the Handicapped* (1963), 171–5, gives a short, clear account of the open air schools in England though he does not mention the Sheffield movement.
3 *Interdepartmental Committee on Physical Deterioration: Report*, vol II, 432.
4 Dr Alfred Eichholz (1869–1933), born in Manchester, studied for a while in Berlin. He became an HMI in 1898 and Medical Officer at the Board of Education in 1907. He was appointed Chief Medical Officer in 1919 and retired in 1930. He was one of the early promoters of open air schools. He had given evidence to the 1903 Committee on Physical Deterioration and the 1908 Committee on the Feeble-Minded. He also had a lifelong interest in the welfare of the blind and deaf.
5 *Interdepartmental Committee on Physical Deterioration: Report*, vol I, 63, and vol II, 19 ff.
6 Ibid, vol II, 309 ff, evidence of Mrs F. J. Greenwood, Sheffield sanitary inspector.
7 *Sheffield Daily Independent*, 24 and 25 August 1909.
8 Whiteley Woods School Log Book, 22 June 1909.
9 *Sheffield Daily Independent*, 25 August 1909.
10 School Medical Officer, Sheffield, *Report*, 1913.
11 Porridge became the staple diet of Margaret MacMillan's open air nursery schools; see Stevinson, E., *The Open-Air Nursery School* (1923). Also in Danish open air schools today see *TES*, 12 June 1964, 1622–3.
12 School Medical Officer, Sheffield, *Special Report on the Open Air Recovery School*, 1909, 26.
13 Whiteley Woods School Log Book, 12 July 1909.
14 School Medical Officer, Sheffield, *Special Report*, 1909.
15 I am indebted to Miss M. V. Jolly who has given me some useful information about her first headship at Whiteley Woods Open Air School from 1924 to 1928. Miss Jolly went on from this headship to give much distinguished service to Sheffield both as a head and an inspector. She told me that Mr P. Sharp, the Director of Education, asked her if she would like to be head of the open air school and this was the first time she had thought about open air education. It was left to her, through visits to the school and to London, to make herself familiar with developments in this field. Her predecessors were appointed in a similar manner.
16 School Medical Officer, Sheffield, *Report*, 1913.
17 *Les Écoles de Plein Air en France*, 71.
18 *Sheffield Daily Independent*, 25 August 1909.
19 School Medical Officer, Sheffield, *Special Report*, 1909, 12.

20 See *Sheffield Daily Independent*, 25 August 1909. He also printed, during the first three years of its existence, separate supplements (referred to here as *Special Reports*) of his annual medical report to the city council devoted solely to the open air school.

21 School Medical Officer, *Special Report*, 1910.

22 Ibid.

23 Ibid.

24 Ibid.

25 Miss Jolly told me how delighted she was when headmasters reported that children from her open air school were being naughty on return to their former schools. On arrival at the open air school some children were unable to make any contact, cringing away from everyone—they could not even play—yet by the time they left they were joining in both work and games. These children were thought of as 'cured'. Others were so physically undernourished that the taste of fresh milk caused vomiting. These were gradually introduced to milk, beginning with a teaspoonful daily until by the end of the year they could cope with a normal diet.

26 Whiteley Woods School Log Book, 21 September 1910.

27 School Medical Officer, Sheffield, *Special Report*, 1910, 12.

28 *Special Report*, 1911.

29 *Special Report*, 1913.

30 *Special Report*, 1917.

31 *Special Report*, 1919.

32 *Special Report*, 1925.

33 W. P. Alexander, *LEA Inspection Report*, 27 October 1943.

34 *Sheffield Daily Independent*, 25 August 1909.

35 For the treatment of neurotic children in a Danish open air school see *TES*, 12 June 1964, 1622–3, and for a similar development in England see *Special Education*, 48, November 1959, 32 ff.

36 *TES*, 25 June 1932, 241.

37 Whiteley Woods School Log Book, 26 August 1912.

38 School Medical Officer, Sheffield, *Report*, 1913.

39 Ibid, *Report*, 1915, 41.

40 Ibid, *Report*, 1916.

41 Whiteley Woods School Log Book, 29 June 1936.

42 Ibid, 31 January 1947. Miss Jolly told me that on occasions the children could not write because the ink had frozen in the inkwells.

43 *Les Écoles de Plein Air en France*, Paris (1943), 73–4, gives details of development on the continent up to 1943. Heck, A. O., op cit, shows that in 1940 there was still a great deal of life in the open air movement in the United States.

44 *Les Écoles de Plein Air en France*, 74.

45 Editorial in the *TES*, 21 September 1929.

46 The Hadow Report on *The Primary School*, 1934 reprint, xx.

47 Ibid, 118.

48 Editorial in the *TES*, 21 September 1929, 411.

SIMON SCHAMA

The Rights of Ignorance: Dutch
Educational Policy in Belgium 1815-30*

THE right to remain ignorant has often been a jealously guarded
freedom. Disconcerting as this must be to all who share a view of
education as a universal ideal, the fact remains that historically, traditional priest-ridden teaching or even no teaching at all has frequently
been preferred over sound and modern teaching, most especially when
the latter has arrived under the auspices of foreign influence. However
benevolently intended, such gifts have gone spurned and their donors
reviled for their generosity. Such was the case in the southern half of
the United Kingdom of the Netherlands after 1815. As every schoolboy
knows, this was the state put together by the Vienna Congress from
the Dutch Republic, the 'Belgian' departments of the French Empire
and the Grand Duchy of Luxemburg. As he will also know, the
southern provinces of the Netherlands, separated from the Dutch since
the Eighty Years' War, were now presented to them as a reward for
having had the good sense and timing to defect from the French
Empire six months in advance of its capitulation, and in an attempt to
secure a viable buffer state on France's north-east frontier. In 1830 the
Flemish and Walloon subjects of King William I, after only fifteen
years of his suzerainty, rose in revolt and with some diplomatic
assistance from France and Britain succeeded in obtaining an independent Belgium.

Most textbook accounts follow liberal historiography in its automatic
sympathy for the national underdog and attribute to the Dutch regime
the besetting sins of cultural arrogance, linguistic imperialism and
religious intolerance. While their administration was doubtless no

* A review of *Van Schoolmeester tot Onderwijzer. De Opleiding van de Leerkracht in
België en Luxemburg van het Eind van de 18de Eeuw tot Omstreeks 1842*, by Dr Maurits
de Vroede, LEUVEN: UNIVERSITEITS BIBLIOTHEEK, 1970, pp 563, BFr 675.

paragon of even-handedness, neither was it quite the Calvinist tyranny of the conventional narrative. Modern Belgian historiography has gone a long way to redress the balance of historical bias but not surprisingly its results have been a long time in reaching a wider historical readership. Education and the language policy remain sensitive issues and have lost nothing of their controversial implications in contemporary Belgium. This may be one reason why a revisionist historiography has been slower to materialise than in other areas of study. Until Dr de Vroede's book, reviews of educational policy have either been tentative or else blatantly partisan in their approach. This has been a severe handicap to an overall revision of the period. For if the attitude of the Dutch regime towards their Flemish and Walloon co-subjects is to be clearly evaluated, then education should surely provide one of the most positive tests. The questions arising from this topic remain very taxing. How far did Dutch educational policy reflect a blinkered authoritarianism towards the differing needs of the south? How rigid were its rules on religion and language? And did its overall policy add up to a programme of enforced 'Netherlandisation' for the kingdom? Since such questions raise issues which go far beyond matters of education it is understandable, if much to be regretted, that Dr de Vroede has eschewed anything like a 'political' approach in his otherwise outstanding monograph. He has amassed an enormous amount of information, much of it new, and has offered this as a contribution to the debate. But excepting the admirably bold concluding chapter he has not so much ignored as delicately side-stepped the most provocative issues, devoting only a few pages to the language problem in teacher-training courses and merely a few more to the storm of reaction which burst about those responsible for the 'new' teaching of the 1820s.

Instead of a 'political' history of elementary education in the first half of the nineteenth century, Dr de Vroede has written a monumental account of the evolution of the elementary teacher 'from schoolmaster to educator' in the southern Netherlands with the emphasis, as his subtitle suggests, very much on the provision of training. His history makes clear that this transition was far from smooth. In common with much of eighteenth-century Europe the schoolmaster in the Netherlands was little more than a glorified sexton, the humble auxiliary of the local priest. Despised by his co-villagers and forced to subsist on the gleanings of the peasants, he combined drumming the catechism into the heads of his unruly charges with the duties of winding the town clock, ringing the church bells or digging its graves. His principal use to the community was to keep its boys out of mischief when there was no labour for them in the fields, or setting the destitute orphans of the town to the 'useful arts' of picking tow or spinning crude flax. As one would expect, standards in such an occupation were dismal. Dr de Vroede tells us that of ninety-six known teachers in Brabant at the end of the century, just sixty-nine had any inkling of the first rudiments of arithmetic and only seven more knew anything more advanced. In matters of literacy the distance between pupil and teacher was hardly greater. Indeed many teachers deliberately refrained from instructing their pupils in writing, holding the skill to be either useless or positively dangerous for young men of low station.

This society, *pace* Professor Kossman,[1] for the most part sluggish and culturally dormant, sandwiched between German, French and Dutch nations, was in the uniquely unfortunate situation of having to succumb in quick succession to the irruptive influence of all three. Added to this, revolution, war, occupation, and the beginnings of industrialisation all contributed to a profound disturbance of 'Belgian' society. But paradoxically it was the superficially least formidable of all these influences—that of the Dutch—which presented by far the greatest threat to its settled pattern of elementary teaching. The Josephist reforms which followed on from the Vienna *Schülordnung* of 1774, like much of the work of the 'revolutionary Emperor', were defeated by his early death and by the risings in Brabant and Flanders in 1789. After an initial flourish of good intentions by the Jacobins, the French Republic fell back on apathy and its traditional personnel—the *Frères*—to provide the bulk of primary education and failed to bring any novelties to its annexed departments. Napoleon's interest in the utility of secondary and higher education was matched only by his dismissal of elementary instruction as a mere social prophylactic and as Dr Gontard has made clear, if anything, set back its progress under the Empire by a decade or more.[2] In contrast the Dutch by 1815 had experienced twenty years of far-reaching change in their elementary education. Stealing a march on the Prussians, the Dutch school of law of 1806 enshrined in statute the 'modern' definition of the teacher as an 'educator for citizenship' and supplied the Netherlands with a thorough and sophisticated (if financially impoverished) establishment of inspectors, training courses, teacher-examinations and teaching societies.[3]

On the inception of the Kingdom of the United Netherlands those responsible for pioneering these advances were naturally interested in extending the benefits of their reforms to their new countrymen. Most enthusiastic of all was the 'Commissioner-General for Elementary Schools', Adriaan Van den Ende, the architect of primary education in Holland and one of the unsung heroes of modern education in Europe. For the most part Dr de Vroede acquits Van den Ende and his zealous disciples of any intended 'cultural imperialism'. They were by no means 'Greater Netherlanders', still less doctrinaire Calvinist evangelists. But there was something unmistakably condescending about their missionary dedication to bring illumination to the benighted. Their principal concern, as de Vroede stresses, was to try to narrow the distance between the two halves of the kingdom by introducing a common system of elementary education and giving equal opportunities to profit from it. This task was tackled with exemplary conscientiousness. Recognising the relative backwardness of the south, Van den Ende and his associates set about redressing the balance by creating a state-financed establishment of teacher training. Twinned with the famous college at Haarlem, a teacher-training school was established at Lier near Antwerp, primarily intended for pupils wishing to teach in the south. Appreciating that even with a generous system of scholarships the intake at Lier could only provide a very small proportion of the south's teaching needs, normal courses were provided, for teachers already practising, in the evenings and in the non-school months at a number of centres around the Kingdom, and grants were made available to suitable applicants. A network of 'model schools' was created in every province both to give the new graduates early practice in ideal conditions and to train new teachers concurrently with regular work in the classroom. As in the north, teachers' unions were encouraged to exchange ideas on the new methods and curricula, and with some assistance from public funds they flourished to the point where, according to de Vroede, on the eve of the Belgian revolution there were 165 scattered through the south.[4] Together with a number of teaching periodicals they made a significant contribution to the wider dissemination of the 'new education'. Perhaps the most remarkable aspect of this extensive programme was the financial responsibility undertaken by one of the smallest governments in Europe. In 1826 it was spending twelve times as much as its French counterpart on educating its citizens.

It is quite possible that in the consuming desire to transform the south Netherlands into model citizens of a constitutional monarchy, the Dutch were if anything a trifle over-zealous and under-sensitive. Gestures like insisting on a year's training at Lier over and above that prescribed for an identical course at Haarlem may have been intended generously but they looked suspiciously like an attempt to patronise the natives. More seriously the education provided by the new regime, however cosmopolitan in its intellectual content and approach, was, as put across to Flemings and Walloons, essentially shaped in the Dutch image and for that matter usually administered by Dutchmen. At the beginning, to be sure, it was difficult to find enough southerners sufficiently familiar with the methods of Pestalozzi and the standards of the northern schools committees to take a large share of the teacher-training work. Moreover the government was sufficiently mindful of the problems involved to appoint Dutch Catholics to nearly all the major posts in the south. But by the lights of the south, men like Schreuder, the able head of the college at Lier, were Dutch first and Catholic second. For that matter most of the pupils at Lier originated from the city and province of Antwerp which could be fairly said to be closer to the Dutch orbit of influence than elsewhere in the south, where the benefits of the 'new learning' were spread more unevenly. The Walloon provinces were of course worst off. While French was uniformly taught at training schools and automatically included in the

basic elementary school curriculum, officially it remained the secondary
language of the kingdom, tolerated rather than encouraged within a
system which set great store by uniformity. From the very decided
views of King William it was clear that whatever concessions would be
made in using French locally in the Walloon provinces, Dutch/Flemish
was to be the proper vehicle of the new schooling and a *sine qua non*
for all those who aspired to succeed within it. When a delegation of
Liège teachers petitioned Van den Ende for the establishment of a
French-language training college in that city, the project was swiftly
aborted by the firm opposition of the King. Such insensitivity on the
part of the rulers of the kingdom did nothing to soothe the fears and
suspicions of the vast majority of Flemings and Walloons that their
'new schools' were merely the instruments of an alien rule.

On the religious issue, similarly benevolent intentions, badly mis-
handled, appeared instead as arbitrary. In keeping with the strict
religious neutrality laid down by the law of 1806, and aware of the
delicacy of the situation, the local 'school juries' (boards) took pains to
forbid any doctrinal instruction in the elementary schools. Only 'Bible
studies' and a general treatment of Christian morality were to be permitted. While these scruples were intended in the north to spare the
feelings of minority denominations—like the Catholics—and to encourage their attendance at public schools, in the south their effect was
exactly the opposite. There the non-denominational, a-doctrinal lukewarm evangelism deeply offended the majority of Catholics accustomed to regard instruction in the catechism and the ritual of the
Church as one of (often the only) virtues of elementary schooling.
What they required of their children's upbringing was a respect for the
doctrine of the Church, not a familiarity with the wholesome social
ethics propagated under the guise of Christianity in the north. The
semantic distinction between *opvoeding* (signifying religious upbringing) and *onderwijs* (education) indicates the difference. In the Dutch
view only the latter was the teacher's proper job; for the Catholics of
the south, the two were indivisible. Dutch Catholics in fact adhered to
the ruling of 1806 and many of them had participated actively in the
earlier reforms. Indeed they were its principal missionaries in the

south. But as the major beneficiaries of a relaxation of the control of the established Church over education in the north, their years as a minority religion had imbued them with a certain doctrinal elasticity unknown in the much more strictly devout south. However ostensibly evangelical, it was undeniable that the more modern version of elementary education had been propagated with most success in the non-Catholic territories of North Germany, Switzerland and the Netherlands. Lip service to Christian ethics as prescribed by von Rochow, Basedow and Pestalozzi was, for those who remained faithful to the Catholic definition of education, no substitute at all for the imperishable and absolute right of the Church to transmit its fundamental doctrine to its children. From their standpoint, the very survival of the Church demanded it.

The Dutch teachers, Catholic or not, were thus separated from their southern pupils by more than methods and approaches to elementary education. Their very concepts of such an education were irreconcilable. On the one hand was the *onderwijs* which took the goal of such education to be a preparation of the child for his later development as an adolescent and to alert him to the rights and responsibilities of citizenship. On the other hand *opvoeding* required the inculcation of eternal truths to a passive and obedient flock. One teacher was the *'missionaire infatigable du bien public'*; the other a *'catecheet'*. Against this background it is hardly surprising that the Dutch initiatives were met at first with curiosity, then with apprehension and finally with fierce and unyielding hostility. As the reaction gathered force, Dutch authorities made little attempt to reconcile in any way the opposed views. Those teaching orders like the Brothers of the Christian Schools, which attempted to harness the newer methods of teaching to their more Catholic curriculum, were simply written off as the agents of fanaticism and denied the financial assistance lavished on the new 'model schools' and colleges. Yet the Brothers had two great advantages over their rivals: they automatically retained the trust and respect of the lay population, and in addition, grants or not, they offered *free* education to all their pupils. In the 1820s, according to figures provided by Dr de Vroede, they were, if anything, gaining in popularity. One order alone attracted nearly 8,000 pupils to its thirty-one schools. Publicity in the Catholic press and pulpits anathematised the new learning as 'godless' and the 'academies of the devil'. Parents withdrew their children and ostracised those unfortunate teachers who had gone through the mill of training, examination and licence only to find themselves at the end of it abused by their own countrymen. By the eve of the revolution the reaction had become so turbulent that it prompted Van den Ende to remark with some feeling that 'once again ignorance has become a title of recommendation'.

After the independence of the new state was secured, the Belgian authorities made some attempt to resume the interrupted momentum of reform. But as Dr de Vroede says, too much ground had been lost in the upheaval to be recovered in the 1830s and 1840s. Popular feeling continued to be hostile towards any reversion to the restoration of a system of education branded as 'Dutch', and the law of 1842 effectively defined its overthrow once and for all. Teacher-examinations and certificates were discontinued, the Lier school closed for a while and its place was taken by seven diocesan colleges which, while providing some substitute, were closer to the spirit of the seminary than that of the Dutch colleges. This situation was further aggravated by the fact that the Belgian revolution had been made in the name not only of national self-determination but also of the freedom of the local community against central government. So the chain of command from the Ministry of the Interior down to the 'school juries' was dismantled and arrangements for elementary education, along with their finance, left to local authorities. The paradoxical result was that the liberal supporters of 'free education' handed power for the overall control of education back to the Church, a situation which once again began to exercise their concern only in the 1860s. For the time being the moment of opportunity for great advances in Belgian elementary education had been lost. The traditional and clerical view had prevailed and the Dutch reforms became viewed historically as little more than a distasteful exercise in pedagogic imperialism. To be sure, the endeavours of Schreuder, Van den Ende and the rest were marked by a headstrong paternalism which did little to endear them to their fellow

Netherlanders, whom they required to swallow their modern catechism with as little protest as the pupil of any priest. But their efforts nevertheless have deserved a better memorial than either Belgian or even Dutch historiography has hitherto been willing to provide. It is greatly to Dr de Vroede's credit that his erudite and perceptive study will henceforth stand as a fitting and definitive history.

Christ's College, Cambridge

References

1   E. H. Kossman, 'België en Nederland, 1780–1830. Enkele Beschouwingen en Vragen', *Bijdragen en Mededelingen van het Historisch Genootschap te Utrecht*, 77 (1963), 27–49.
2   M. Gontard, *L'Enseignement primaire en France de l'ancien régime à la loi Guizot 1789–1833*, Paris (1959).
3   See Simon Schama, 'Schools and Politics in the Netherlands 1796–1814', *Historical Journal*, xiii, 4 (1970), 589–610.
4   See M. de. Vroede, 'De Onderwijzergezelschappen in Belgie, 1816–ca. 1846' in *Pedagogische Studiën*, 12 (December 1969), 650–86.

Book Reviews

Educational Documents in England and Wales, 1816–1968, edited by J. Stuart Maclure, METHUEN, 1965, second edition 1968, reprinted with additions 1969, pp x + 349, £2.50 hardback, £1.25 paperback.

Educational Documents 800–1816, edited by D. W. Sylvester, METHUEN, 1970, pp xii + 290, £3 hardback, £1.50 paperback.

'It would kindle a new spirit in the teacher if the history of education were more studied than it is; the teachers of the present day do not know enough of what has been done by the great teachers of past times, and they would learn much of the science of their profession by a study of its history.' These words have something of a topical ring about them; they are culled from the Majority Report of the Cross Commission, 1888. With the institution of the B Ed degree and the expanded provision for the M Ed and for advanced diplomas in Education, the teaching of the history of education is certain to enjoy a resurgence which invites comparison with the earlier popularity of the subject at the beginning of this century. It was in 1911 that Arthur F. Leach published his *Educational Charters and Documents, 598 to 1909.*

The emphases, however, will be very different from Leach's day; 544 of his 568 pages of documentary texts were devoted to the period before 1800. Even allowing for the fact that 228 of those pages may be discounted because he printed translations alongside the original texts of documents in Latin and other languages, and because he excluded material illustrative of the development of elementary and technical education, of education for girls and women, and of modern universities on the ground that 'these things are a matter of common knowledge, and perhaps do not require records at present' (p lii), this represents a very different balance from that to be found in Professor W. H. G. Armytage's *Four Hundred Years of English Education* (second edition 1970), where 77 pages out of 269 deal with the period 1563–1800, or in these companion volumes compiled by Messrs Maclure and Sylvester.

In the half-century which elapsed between the publication of Leach's *The Schools of Medieval England* and Maclure's collection of documents, students in colleges and departments of education were directed in the main to secondary works on the history of education. Indeed, since Leach's *Educational Charters* effectively finished at the Reformation and has in any case long been out of print, there was no suitable source-book available on education since the time of Robert Raikes, the period which increasingly commanded the attention and interest of tutors. Maclure's book, therefore, filled a very real gap when it appeared in 1965 and, moreover, happily coincided with the widespread acceptance of the importance of first-hand materials in historical studies at all levels from the primary school to the post-graduate course.

By any criterion, it is a good book. 'This is not a history of education,' Maclure tells us at the very opening of his introduction; it is not, nor should it have been. He confined his selection to extracts from the principal official documents. Consequently, the ideas of educationists do not emerge explicitly except when they happened to give testimony before committees or commissions of inquiry, and there is little mention of the actual working of the schools and universities. Concentration on the official reports, however, made it feasible within the space at his disposal to cover a wide spectrum without a loss of coherence and to provide extracts of an adequate length to convey the contemporary context of thought, from Brougham's Parliamentary Committee on the Education of the Lower Orders in the Metropolis to Newsom's first report of the Public Schools Commission. Each section is introduced by an editorial note providing a sufficient background for a meaningful examination of the quotation by the reader who may not have this command of fact.

The value of this deliberate restriction of purpose is seen to advantage in the refreshingly challenging sketch of educational development since 1816 which Maclure offers in his seventeen-page introduction.

One does not have to agree with Maclure's view of that development to benefit from the cogency of the argument and from the stimulation of his conclusions, which deserve careful comparison with those of Dr A. S. Bishop in his recent monograph, *The Rise of a Central Authority for English Education* (1971). For Maclure, 'the lack of an administrative machine is the key to much English educational history in the nineteenth century . . . there was no cheap alternative to the parochial system and the subsidization of voluntary bodies was, in that sense, inevitable' (p 4). The Act of 1870, by establishing elected local bodies in the school boards, provided a new source of initiative in English education, independent of both the voluntary bodies and the Education Department, but the success of the school boards only underlined the need for a similar expansion of secondary education, an expansion which could occur only after the administrative structure had been created in the county councils. The power of the central government, despite the recommendations of the Bryce Commission, remained largely indirect. Even when the ministry assumed responsibility under the 1944 Act, caution prevailed in the exercise of that authority and the ministry's power continued to be shared with the teachers on the one hand and the local authorities on the other. However, the 1960s saw a significant shift in the distribution of power within education in this country with the establishment of the Curriculum Study Group and the Schools Council, and the Robbins Report paved the way for higher education to be brought 'formally and unavoidably inside the arena of public responsibility' (p 16).

It is one of the fascinations of Maclure's collection that it affords ample ammunition for the discerning to demonstrate the relevance of the history of education to the decision-making of our own day. No one ever seems to have a realistic appreciation of the cost of educational development. In 1816 William Allen testified that an expenditure of £400,000 a year, or a much smaller sum probably, would 'leave not an uneducated person in the country' (p 22). In 1834 W. F. Lloyd, Secretary to the Sunday School Union, declared that 'if teachers are to have the wages of porters or ploughmen, you will never get fit persons for teachers' (p 34), but he would be content if 'every efficient teacher of a day school' had £100 a year (p 32). In 1870 W. E. Forster told Parliament that the government could not give up school fees in elementary education, which had amounted to £420,000 in the last year, since 'if this scheme works, as I have said we hope it will work, it will very soon cover the country, and that £420,000 per annum would have to be doubled, or even trebled' (p 102), but it would 'empower the school board to give free tickets to parents who they think really cannot afford to pay for the education of their children; and we take care that those free tickets shall have no stigma of pauperism attached to them' (p 103). In 1943 the Appendix to the White Paper on Educational Reconstruction quoted the estimated 'ultimate' extra cost of secondary education for all as £67.4 million, to make a total of £190.4 million (p 207), which seems incredible in retrospect.

Another of the fascinations to be derived from a detailed study of Maclure's collection is the antiquity of 'new' ideas in education. Thus the Report of the Royal Commission on the University of Oxford in 1852 has this to say:

> . . . as there have been, so there might still be men of genius who could adequately prepare themselves for the University even while pursuing mechanical or menial occupations, and who would confer honour on it as well as derive honour from it. The training institutions for masters of schools for the poor are likely to produce pupils of great powers, who would probably desire a University education if they considered it within their reach, and would submit to great privations in order to obtain it. The loss of one such person would be a serious loss. . . . What is needed is to place the best education within the reach of all qualified to receive it; not to offer some solace to those who are excluded [pp 66–7].

Or, again, Matthew Arnold remarks in his General Report for 1867 on payment by results, but in doing so enunciates a principle of wider applicability and decided relevance to the 1970s, '. . . the question is, not whether this idea, or this or that application of it suits ordinary public opinion and school managers; the question is whether it really suits the interests of schools and their instruction. In this country we are somewhat unduly liable to regard the latter suitableness too little, and the former too much' (p 82). In *The Art of the Possible* (1971), Lord Butler makes the point, and it is a point which has been very much overlooked in the polemics of debate, that the comprehensive idea, so far from being ruled out by the terms of the 1944 Act, was envisaged as a possibility, and even in some areas as a likelihood, at least as early as the White Paper of 1943. The extracts from the Spens Report of 1938 and the White Paper printed in Maclure bear Lord Butler's point out very well. 'There is in fact no clear line of demarcation, physical, psychological or social, between the pupils who attend Grammar Schools and those who attend Modern Schools, and all the evidence that we have heard on the existing methods of selection for one or other type of school confirms us in our opinion that the line as drawn at present is always artificial and often mistaken' (Spens, pp 195–6). The Spens Committee presented a reasoned argument against the general creation of multilateral schools 'even as the goal of a long range policy', but it also had this to say: 'The multilateral idea, though it may not be expressed by means of the multilateral school, should in effect permeate the system of secondary education as we conceive it' (p 198). The White Paper accepted the three main types of secondary school envisaged by the Spens Report but commented: 'It would be wrong to suppose that they will necessarily remain separate and apart. Different types may be combined in one building or on one site' (p 209).

Despite its relatively restricted purview, Maclure's collection is a rich resource for the study of the salient educational themes of the last century and a half. Equally good illustrations may be found in it of the changing roles of church and state in educational provision, of the constant raising of this country's educational sights, of the relative importance of financial, psychological, and social factors, and of the fundamental concern for the training of teachers. Sylvester's task, inherently more difficult because of the coverage of no less than a thousand years, was also conceived more comprehensively, 'to provide, as far as space would allow, a balanced selection of material on the curriculum and discipline of various educational institutions, and on the legal and constitutional framework in which they were founded' (p xi).

The attempt to cover so much fails and in the end result falls short in a number of important respects of the highest academic standards.

Commentaries are provided for each of the sections, which range from Anglo-Saxon to monitorial schools, but they frequently fail to indicate the provenance of the document, the position of the author, the implications for society, or to distinguish between material printed as in the original and material printed in translation or in modernised English. Further reading is suggested for each section but, again, no evaluation is attempted. For example, John Lawson's *Medieval Education and the Reformation* is quoted with Leach's *The Schools of Medieval England* for medieval grammar schools without any comment or a reference to the critiques of Leach by Joan Simon and W. E. Tate. Roger of Wendover's chronicle is used as a source on the dispersion from Oxford to Cambridge in 1209 without any comment whatever on the probable accuracy of the account. Many extracts are taken at second hand where the first-hand source is in fact accessible, and heavy reliance is placed upon Leach's *Educational Charters* for the earlier period.

The preface claims that: 'This book offers a selection of documentary material illustrative of the main themes of educational history from the Middle Ages to the beginning of the nineteenth century' (p xi). As Maclure comments, in a work of this kind, 'any selection must tend to be arbitrary and idiosyncratic' (p 1); it is a fair point. Yet there must be limits to a compiler's discretion. Sylvester's index contains, for instance, no reference to William Gilbert, Robert Recorde, Henry Billingsley, Richard Mulcaster, Sir Thomas Gresham, Thomas Sutton, Francis Bacon, or John Locke; Erasmus, surely influential in achieving changes in practice in the sixteenth century through his textbooks, is mentioned only incidentally and Brinsley, though quoted extensively, is not identified as a Puritan reformer of some consequence in bringing about changes in the seventeenth century. On the contrary, the statement is made, which is highly disputable, that 'the grammar schools of England during the sixteenth and seventeenth centuries were notable for the unchanging continuity with which they pursued their aims and practices' (p 91). Again, stress is laid in the section on the Clarendon Code on the difficulties experienced by teachers in securing a licence to teach and two extracts are printed from testimonials to the con-

formity of schoolmasters, taken from J. S. Purvis, *Educational Records*
(1959); but there is no qualification made to the point at all, no
mention, for instance, of the case of William Bates in 1670, who was
allowed to teach without a bishop's licence because he was appointed
by the founder of the school. Yet Canon Purvis himself commented in
his foreword (pp 3–4) that 'from many of these documents it is evident
that the schoolmaster had already been teaching for a time before the
Nomination or the Testimonial was sent in, so that there seems no
reason to suppose that the regulations were enforced with unreasonable
severity'.

It is difficult to escape the conclusion that it would have been better
to have confined the selection to a particular class of record, or to have
dealt with a limited number of identified themes chosen for their
importance. None the less, within its limitations, Sylvester's volume
will make a useful addition to the literature available in a convenient
form for the study of the earlier history of education in England and
Wales.

University of Sheffield   G. R. Batho

**The English School: Its architecture and organization, 1370–
1870,** by Malcolm Seaborne, ROUTLEDGE & KEGAN PAUL, 1971,
pp xxii + 317 + 112 pp plates, £7.50.

The growth of education in England has been studied from many
points of view, historical, sociological and philosophical. A book which
approaches the subject through the buildings in which teaching and
learning went on breaks new ground and is much to be welcomed.
Mr Seaborne's massive survey covers the period between the later
Middle Ages and 1870. He hopes to complete the study with another
volume on the last century. He has already been a pioneer in approach-
ing the study of education visually with his book in the Studio Vista
series. This book carries on a similar idea in much greater detail and
with much fuller elaboration. Each chapter has a full complement of
references. It would have been an advantage for this reader if the

references had been cited page by page rather than chapter by chapter, and if a complete bibliography had been given. There are valuable appendices, especially of school buildings illustrated in *The Builder* and *The Building News* before 1870, and 112 pages of plates, many of them from photographs taken by the author himself. The subject is so vast that Mr Seaborne has necessarily taken a large number of his examples from the East Midland area where he has been working in the University of Leicester School of Education, though there are many examples from other parts of the country as well.

The author is not, however, an architectural historian, and his purpose is, as he says, to offer 'a study of the development of educational ideas and practices over five centuries'. In one sense he carries on a tradition established by a classic of a former age, *The Architectural History of the University of Cambridge and of the Colleges of Cambridge and Eton*, by Robert Willis and John Willis Clark, published in 1886. Willis and Clark took as their subject a complex of buildings of national—indeed of international—importance, and it may seem fanciful to compare with the Cambridge colleges the somewhat scattered and fragmentary remains of our schools. Collectively, however, old school buildings provide an impressive body of evidence, and illustrate educational change in a very lucid way. Mr Seaborne is very skilful too in relating the ideas of writers like Brinsley in the seventeenth century or Lancaster in the nineteenth to the buildings in which they and their contemporaries taught.

Mr Seaborne's thesis, broadly speaking, is that curriculum change and the demands which society in different generations made upon the schools have always been closely linked with the material expression of these things in bricks and mortar. He naturally quotes Edward Thring: 'whatever men may say or think, the almighty wall is, after all, the supreme and final arbiter of schools. I mean, no living power in the world can overcome the dead, unfeeling, everlasting pressure of the permanent structure, of the permanent conditions under which work has to be done.' Mr Seaborne himself would not go as far as that; he points out, for instance, that in eighteenth-century Eton numbers grew and teaching methods were considerably modified without radical reconstruction of the buildings. Indeed Thring's statement may be truer of the century after 1870 than of the centuries before that date, which are the subject of this book.

The vital point here is that almost all school buildings until the middle of the last century were small and unpretentious, and in many cases not specifically designed for the educational purposes which they were made to serve. After the Reformation many buildings designed for other reasons were made into schools. Most of the private schools which provided such an important part of English secondary education in the last century were carried on in private houses, not in any way purpose-built. Even in the great foundations like Eton and Winchester, with their impressive mass of buildings, the amount of accommodation set aside for teaching was comparatively small. In both colleges there was originally a single schoolroom which 'occupied an architecturally subordinate position in the total complex'.

Mr Seaborne shows that the single schoolroom, alike in public and grammar schools and in elementary schools, had a very long life. Rugby among the public schools and City of London among the great town schools were distinctive in making provision for masters to teach, each in a separate classroom. In the elementary schools the monitorial system demanded a very large single space, and it was only slowly, as more teachers were trained, that class teaching became possible. As government grants became more important after 1839, central control over elementary school building became closer, and Mr Seaborne brings out the importance of directives like the Committee of Council's memorandum of 1851, which provided basically for a large room which could be divided by curtains, so that the pupil teachers could be to some degree on their own, but yet remain under the overall supervision of the master.

This is a book on a massive scale and is full of interest. Only a few particular topics can be mentioned here. School buildings in the sixteenth and seventeenth centuries were part of the vernacular architecture of their own regions, though slowly more formal planning was introduced. In the eighteenth century more and more schools came to provide teaching in subjects like English and writing. This in turn demanded more complex planning. One excellent example of this is the early nineteenth-century schools at Bedford, now occupied by Bedford Modern School, which originally contained a National school, rooms for the trustees, a hospital school, and a commercial school. Mr Seaborne's examination of these changes confirms the impression, gained from other sources, that the grammar schools of the eighteenth and early nineteenth centuries had done more to reform their teaching and curricula than the standard histories always allow. Another interesting sidelight on the same period is the growing involvement of professional architects in the design of elementary schools. After such a feast as this book provides, it is much to be hoped that Mr Seaborne will be able to make speedy progress with his second volume.

University of Sheffield   John Roach

Science and Education in the Seventeenth Century: The Webster-Ward Debate, edited by A. G. Debus, London: MAC-DONALD, New York: ELSEVIER, 1970, pp 307, £6.

Geschichte des naturwissenschaftlichen Unterrichts im 17. bis 19. Jahrhundert: Erziehungstheoretische Grundlegung und schulgeschichtliche Entwicklung, by Walter Schöler, WALTER DE GRUYTER & CO, Berlin, 1970, pp 373, DM58.

Both of these books are of considerable importance for historians of science education. In each case the scientific movement of the seventeenth century provides the initial standpoint for discussion. Debus examines its immediate relevance to the reform of university education in England, while Schöler traces the longer-term history of science education in German schools.

Debus takes us back to the educational ferment of the Puritan Revolution, reprinting the exchange of pamphlets between the army chaplain John Webster and the Oxford academics, Seth Ward and John Wilkins. These works are not literary classics to compare with Milton's tract on education, being rapidly composed and poorly

printed to join the explosion of controversial literature which charac-
terised this period. In this case absence of stylistic polish and literary
niceties is more than compensated for by historical interest. This
conflict is particularly interesting in exposing the dilemma over educational reform facing the advocates of the new science.

Reactions to this situation were largely determined by general ideological standpoints. Webster had strong sectarian sympathies. For him
it was desirable to sweep away the existing edifice of scholastic education and base university studies on the 'real' disciplines of science and
technology. Faced with such radical proposals, the ordained academic
natural philosophers found it necessary to defend current education,
even to the cost of denying any significant educational role to science.
It was asserted that science could be satisfactorily cultivated outside
normal academic work. Thus the founders of the Royal Society took
surprisingly little interest in educational reform, enabling traditionalists
to regain their hold on the universities in the period after the Puritan
Revolution.

In view of their association with the Royal Society, Wilkins and
Ward have received considerable attention from modern writers. Many
other minor authors supported them and this book reprints a pamphlet
by Thomas Hall as an appendix to the Webster-Ward controversy.
The most valuable Introduction gives an account of the scientific
affiliations of the disputants, providing a more sympathetic account of
Webster than hitherto available. The relevance of Paracelsianism to
social reform is strongly argued. Debus is one of the few authors to
give adequate recognition to the role of this iatrochemical movement
in the scientific revolution of the seventeenth century. Extensive anno-
tations give a good foundation for further reading on this subject.

The Puritan Revolution produced ambitious and sophisticated plans
for scientific education. However, the numerous advocates of a Bacon-
ian reconstruction of education had little immediate influence. If
science remained alive in English cultural life, it was not due to its
prominence in the classroom. When science again emerged as a
necessary and basic aspect of education, it was largely due to pressure
to follow the German example. For the scientists and their opponents,

German education provided the model for studies, both at the school and university levels.

Schöler's book provides one of the first comprehensive modern guides to the development of scientific education in German schools. It is precise, well documented and exhaustively annotated, providing an insight into educational debates and projects which had considerable influence on English reformers. As well as discussing the standpoint of such major thinkers as Pestalozzi, Stephani and Oken on scientific education, the author introduces the reader to a whole spectrum of local schemes and administrative developments. Many minor figures are introduced who must receive closer attention from English scholars before the full impact of German ideas on English reformers can be assessed.

The strongest sections of Schöler's book are on the first half of the nineteenth century, the period which will most interest English readers. The treatment of the period before 1800 is not adequate and it is extremely deficient for the seventeenth century. It is recognised that there is a strong international flavour about scientific reform in the seventeenth century. Indeed, the authors discussed by Debus received their basic inspiration from Germany and Bacon had a strong German following. However, German attitudes to educational reform during this seminal period are inadequately explored. Johann Valentin Andreae is not mentioned, while the German disciples of Comenius, Ratke and Joachim Jungius are not adequately understood. An equally deficient treatment is given of the pietists and their followers in the eighteenth century. Had this picture been fully revealed, a continuity in German attitudes would have been apparent which provides a striking contrast with England. Different responses of the two cultures to the educational potentialities of Baconianism and natural theology had great consequences for the development of their educational systems. Historians of education are becoming increasingly interested in comparative studies. Schöler and Debus provide many stimulating avenues for further research on Anglo-German interactions.

Corpus Christi College, Oxford   Charles Webster

Derbyshire Village Schools in the Nineteenth Century, by
Marion Johnson, DAVID & CHARLES, Newton Abbot, 1970, pp 224,
£2.50.

Two chapters in Flora Thompson's well-known *Lark Rise to Candle-
ford* describe an Oxfordshire village school at work in the 1880s. The
first chapter depicts the everyday routine; the second recounts the
climax of the school year, the dreaded day when Her Majesty's Inspector carried out his annual inspection. They are two excellently
executed miniatures. By comparison Marion Johnson's *Derbyshire Village Schools in the Nineteenth Century* is a much bigger picture, as full
of activity and incident as a Breughel village scene, or, more appropriately in time, such a painting as Frith's 'Derby Day'. Unlike Flora
Thompson, who wrote from childhood and family recollections,
Marion Johnson bases her book upon the firm foundation of information embedded in the detailed reports and inquiries that were so
characteristic of the nineteenth century, and which today provide
social historians with rich stores of evidence. Both kinds of source have
their place in historical research. Personal reminiscence frequently
contributes colour and liveliness, but the report of a commission or a
select committee's inquiry has far better perspective and judgement,
draws on a much wider experience, and often discloses incidents which
conjure up the scene as clearly as the well-written autobiography.

Marion Johnson has surveyed Derbyshire's village schools pretty
thoroughly. She begins with the charity schools founded mostly in the
eighteenth century, continues with the National, British, and other
denominational schools, and, in the second half of the book, examines
the work of the school boards. One gets the impression that she is
restricted by lack of space, but by summarising much information in
schedules of statistics, distribution maps, and tabulated lists, and by
keeping her narrative interesting and sprightly with selected examples,
she packs a lot of information into her pages without making her book
dull and heavy. Her interest is in no sense confined to the administrator's educational world—the Acts of Parliament, the regulations

received from Whitehall, the sectarian battles, teacher-pupil ratios, and the rest. She is just as frequently in the classroom, describing how the teachers, from the lowly monitors to the trained and certificated headmasters and mistresses, managed, or failed, to get satisfactory results from their serried benches of pupils. She quotes examples of self-opinionated and of lazy, inefficient teachers, but on the whole she sympathises with them, for the task the nineteenth-century parents, clergy, and authorities expected them to do was often made well-nigh impossible by classroom conditions, lack of money, and parental indifference to their children's education.

One of the academic values of a local study such as *Derbyshire Village Schools* is to examine what effect parliamentary decisions and Whitehall mandates had in the provinces. Most educational historians have concentrated upon the story of the provision of education—on what was being debated in the Commons, promulgated by the Committee of the Privy Council, published in the codes, or recommended by the commissions. In practical terms the results were never so neat as the planners designed. Local circumstances, outraged vested interests, and the support or opposition of powerful local personalities were always shaping, delaying, or distorting the outcome. Derbyshire illustrates this well for it is a county of contrast. In some villages most boys and girls could look forward to little but agricultural and domestic employment. In others the cotton mills were eager for child labour. In the eastern part of the county, coal, iron, and pottery industries offered children work, and in other villages children were early set to lace-making or stocking-knitting. One of the most interesting aspects of Marion Johnson's research is to reveal how these local employment factors influenced attitudes towards education in the different generations. For example, most of the mining communities were indifferent about educating their children, but there were several enthusiastic and efficient factory schools. Early in the century, villagers in the south-east of the county welcomed the possibility of both school education and adult education, but when changing conditions of work brought harder times, both forms of education quickly suffered.

David & Charles have already published a similar study of Devon village schools in the nineteenth century. Let us hope that these two books pioneer a line of research which scholars in other counties are ready to follow.

University of Liverpool   J. J. Bagley

History for their Masters: Opinion in the English History Text-book: 1800–1914, by Valerie E. Chancellor, ADAMS & DART, Bath, 1970, pp 153, £2.50.

Little Arthur's England was the only example of a pre-1914 children's history book to be mentioned by name in E. H. Dance's *History the Betrayer: A Study in Bias* (1960); now we have a pioneering study based on 150 such books. *History for their Masters* is a development of Valerie Chancellor's Birmingham University thesis, in which she studied 'how ideas are passed on to the rising generation, how these ideas are selected and what relation, if any, they bear to those current in contemporary society as a whole', with the aim of examining how far there was 'any attempt to use the history textbook to mould the opinions of a future electorate in a growingly democratic age'.

After an introductory chapter headed 'Censorship and Selection', Valerie Chancellor has divided her study of opinions into five main categories—those concerning social class, politics, morals, religion, and 'England and her Place in the World'—which she illustrates with examples of authors' attitudes to specific episodes in history taken from books meant to represent each decade of her chosen period. She had abandoned a statistically based analysis after failing to find sufficient books, since comparatively few children's history books appeared to have survived from the early 1800s compared with large numbers from 1870 onwards.

So her method of selecting the earlier books to be examined, though not stated, seems to have been mere availability: in which case, the usefulness of her bibliography would have been materially increased by the addition of a location for each scarce title and of a chronological list showing not only when the textbooks were first published but also their life-span. As it is, asterisks denote only a title's 'wide sale or influence' and many vital first edition dates go unmentioned.

Here lies the weakness of *History for their Masters*. In spite of the interesting analysis of the contents of 'over 150 volumes' for her thesis, Valerie Chancellor's research has not really gone deep enough, for publication, into the complicated bibliographical history of her school-book material; with consequent inaccuracies, both of assumption and fact, now being passed on to the unwary reader. (In addition, the book contains two dozen errors in proof reading or printing.)

When both footnote and bibliography, for instance, give only 1849 as the date for an opinion quoted from Trimmer's *History of England*, it can be very misleading to a reader who does not know that Mrs Trimmer died in 1810 and that children's history books were in-variably reprinted with amendments, by different hands, often 'to the present time'. Valerie Chancellor fails to quote even once from the best-selling history in print from 1798 to 1927, by Richmal Mangnall, which she merely lists incorrectly as 'Magnalls [*sic*] *Historical and Miscellaneous Questions* (1800)'. She never compares the texts of different editions or mentions changes in opinions in them, and ignores publishers and the bias they might have brought to bear on textbooks. And she not only omits the name of 'Edward Baldwin' from her index, although he is the author she most often mentions and quotes from, and fails to reveal his true identity as the philosopher William Godwin, but includes in her index and often quotes as representing a typical clergyman of *circa* 1830, 'the Rev Cooper', apparently in ignorance of the fact that this was a publisher's pseudonymous disguise for the hack writer Richard Johnson (1743–93) whose *History of England*, which she lists as '1830 and 1843', first appeared as long ago as 1775.

These faults apart, the book makes an original and useful contribu-tion to the history of education which should 'encourage and illuminate investigations into books used in schools today' (to quote from the Foreword by the late Sir John Newsom).

Hitchin, Herts   Jill E. Grey

**Silver Jubilee: The Story of Didsbury College of Education,
Manchester 1946–71,** by A. H. Body & B. J. Frangopulo,
E. J. MORTON, Didsbury, Manchester, 1971, 90p.

Colleges of education have made a valuable contribution to the
expansion of higher education during the past twenty-five years, increasing their student numbers in greater proportion than any other
sector. They have coped with the emergency training scheme, the
introduction of the three-year certificate course and, more recently,
the four-year B Ed and one-year postgraduate courses. Published
material on this recent period of college history is hard to come by and
therefore any informed contribution is welcome.

Didsbury College of Education is now twenty-five years old and its
history exactly covers the period under discussion. It has a reputation
second to none and its future would appear to be promising. It is in a
sense one of the success stories of the training college world and a book
on its silver jubilee is doubly welcome. It is regrettable therefore that
this book fails to live up to its expectations. It could have been lifted
from the pages of a Victorian ladies' journal without noticeable altera-
tion and some of its deficiencies are those of the colleges themselves.
Its style is sentimentally reminiscent without being informative, en-
lightening or even amusing. At least a third of the book is concerned
with events quite outside and remote from the twenty-five years of
college history. Its many photographs and illustrations reinforce this
view and seem to have been chosen more for their irrelevance than to
illustrate the book's theme.

Eventually one of the authors gives us a brief glimpse of the post-
war emergency training scheme, and something of the atmosphere of
rationing and general shortages is caught, but the only comments of
value are those taken from the Ministry of Education's booklet *Challenge and Response.* Otherwise the reader is presented with a parade of
visiting dignitaries such as R. A. Butler and W. O. Lester-Smith, a
list later repeated by a second contributor.

Finally on page 47 Mr Body hints at one of the problems that faces teacher training today, namely that in the college's first five years of permanent existence (the first four years were 'temporary') it had to make do with rejects from other colleges. Not until 1955 did it make the breakthrough of being able to select only students whose first choice was the college. This little-mentioned fact of being totally dependent on rejects from elsewhere is one that faces many colleges today and may face all unless there are changes in our higher education system. How did Didsbury achieve this breakthrough? What was the formula? No hint is given of the plans, the organisation and the hard team-work that must surely have been involved. Or did it all happen by accident? Mr Body's account can only give substance to the view that in teacher training nothing was planned by those immediately involved—things just happened and everyone was taken by surprise.

How, for instance, did the college develop the vital liaison with schools which the authors state was at first 'inexplicably slight and uneven'? Almost every interesting situation is left unexplained. The approval for the implementation of a £10 million expansion scheme is conveyed to the reader in biblical language on page 53 and (as with Moses' tablets) the decisions that finally emerged appear as God-given, for no clear explanation is offered, nor is any attempt made to relate this plan to national or local needs. Again, after Lord Robbins's visit in 1962, decisions were made to expand numbers to 1,200 and to train graduates, but no comment of value is made on this or subsequent developments. The impact of the B Ed, the development of full-time subsidiary courses and the college's increasingly international connections are given no discussion.

One conclusion from all this is that principals of training colleges (as they were) were nature's subservients, awaiting orders from above and thanking their benefactors whenever bounty was graciously provided. This role would certainly be in line with the (historically) narrow traditions of many colleges, but it is not expected in a post-war LEA college. If such practices do indeed still hold sway, one might well ask whether colleges are fit to take their place as equals in any future pattern of higher education. This strange tradition of muddling along in the 'spirit of Dunkirk'—always short of equipment, with woefully inadequate administrative resources, grateful for the small mercies granted by parsimonious LEAs with one eye on the rates—is a pitiful one. Dr Goldman's recent principalship seems to have questioned this cosy tradition, yet the book is strangely silent on Dr Goldman's three-year period of office, though giving chapters both to his temporary replacement and eventual successor. Surely the problems he met of running and maintaining one of the largest colleges are of vital interest, since the pattern established by the large colleges is likely to be the significant one for the future.

Altogether this is a most disappointing book which, instead of throwing light on important and urgent educational issues, does a disservice to the work of colleges over the past twenty-five years and gives a poor impression of one of the country's largest colleges of education.

Sheffield City College of Education   D. A. Turner

History of Education
The Journal of the History of Education Society

Education and Politics 1900-1951

A Study of the Labour Party

RODNEY BARKER

This is the first comprehensive account of the educational policy of the Labour Party in the first half of this century. It will be of interest to sociologists and educationalists as well as to historians. It complements the traditional approach to English parties which defines them in terms of broad categories such as 'socialism' and 'liberalism', and illustrates what assumptions were held in one area of policy and what light these assumptions cast on the character of the party as a whole. £3

OXFORD UNIVERSITY PRESS

Studies in Adult Education

Now established internationally as an important and progressive journal in the field, it contains scholarly essays and research reports on current aspects of the subject and its little-known history. The extensive review section covers books and periodicals published all over the world. Edited by Professor Thomas Kelly of Liverpool University.

Volume 4 Number 1   **April 1972**

Contents: **The Image of Adult Education,** Bryan Luckham; **Vocational Training in the United Kingdom and France—A Comparative Study,** Colin Titmus; **The Early History of Scottish Popular Science,** John A Cable; **A Museum and its Visitors,** James H Stewart; **The Variation of Memory with Time for Information Appearing During a Lecture,** E J Thomas. Book Reviews. Reviews of other Journals. 104 pages.

Annual subscription £1.75, single copies 90p

DAVID & CHARLES . NEWTON ABBOT . DEVON

Aubrey on Education

A hitherto unpublished manuscript by the author of 'Brief Lives'

Edited by J. E. STEPHENS
University of Hull

John Aubrey worked fifteen years on a treatise on education, but left it, at his death, in a disorderly condition of which he was well aware. The editor, with humility and a clear account of his procedures, has rearranged the material in a readable form which follows Aubrey's own chapter divisions but groups them anew into related parts. £2.75

English Primary Education and the Progressives

R. J. W. SELLECK
University of Melbourne

This study of progressive education is concerned with the primary school in England at a period of vital change in primary school educational thought and attitudes. The 'pioneers' and the 'romantics' are dealt with in detail, and the outlook and achievements of the various schools of thought are carefully and wittily analysed. This stimulating work bears on contemporary issues and will provoke wide discussion.
Students Library of Education £2.00

ROUTLEDGE
London and Boston

JAMES TURNER

The Visual Realism of Comenius

THE *Orbis Pictus* of Comenius is one of the most celebrated school-books. Since the first edition (Nuremberg, 1658) at least 248 editions have appeared in eighteen languages.[1] It is a small encyclopaedia and language tutor for young children; each double page contains a picture followed by a simple explanation in parallel columns in Latin and the vernacular. Each item is numbered in the text, and in the illustration. The preliterate child enjoys the pictures and learns to seek pleasure in books; later he reads his mother tongue in close association with these images, and later still he moves on to Latin. Gradually he is introduced to an appreciation of the order of creation. The 150 chapters deal first with God, the cosmos, and the elements, minerals, the plant and animal kingdoms, and then with human anatomy, economic life, knowledge, morals, politics, recreation, warfare and religion. This article is concerned with the illustrations and their skilful but un-obtrusive contribution to this harmonious order. The unknown artist has created a unique style, exactly suited to the didactic needs of Comenius himself. This will be clarified by comparison with analo-gous books by earlier authors, and with Comenius's other projects and recommendations.

Origins of the Orbis Pictus
Many features of the book were borrowed from already well-established forms. As Robert Alt has shown, most of the material was already illustrated in the German printed bestiaries, herbals, technological treatises, fencing manuals and 'trade-books'.[2] More important than this, illustrated encyclopaedias and language tutors had already been adapted for the purpose of the instruction of children. The Czech Brethren were particularly active in this respect; they are known to have contributed to the broad and comprehensive views of Comenius,

and may well have exerted a specific influence on the *Orbis Pictus*.
The closest predecessors of his book, in format and style, are found in
this catechistic and didactic literature. Learning to read and learning
the rudiments of science, social behaviour and religion were closely
associated in the Protestant catechisms.[3] Comenius organises his book
according to a large-scale division of the universe, beginning and end-
ing with divinity and proceeding through the various stratified classes
of nature and man; this was standard procedure for encyclopaedists,
and for the purpose of instructing the young had already been simplified into a master-pupil dialogue, the *Meister Lucidarius*. This went
into many German and Czech editions, and was an important influence on Comenius's book (see below). The simple 'colloquium'
form, with which *Orbis Pictus* begins, dates back to the early middle
ages and probably earlier,[4] and is essential to the catechism. There are
several polyglot catechisms, some of which use exactly the same typo-
graphical arrangement as *Orbis Pictus*.[5] Several catechisms are illustrated with woodcuts. Early printed devotional books, biblical abstracts,
and emblem-books use the same format—each double-page spread
forms a self-contained chapter, with a woodcut on the top left, a title
in bold type, and the text arranged below and to the right. This is
often in several languages, distinguished by roman, italic, and black-
letter type, as in the *Orbis Pictus*.[6] There is a tendency for the instruc-
tional books, especially in Germany, to use the horizontal rectangular
form of the *Orbis Pictus* woodcuts; while books designed primarily to
illustrate select a vertical or circular frame. The systematic numbering
of phrases in the text and objects in the picture is borrowed from a
reading-book of biblical paraphrases.[7] The phonetic alphabet at the
beginning of *Orbis Pictus*, with its tiny pictures of the animals which
produce the sound of each letter, is found in several ABCs and dates
back to the fifteenth century.[8]

We should remember that the ABC and some form of catechism
were the only reading-matter accessible to most children, and represent a far more widespread means of instruction than the school.
Throughout Europe local and national authorities attached great
importance to these rudimentary texts; Nuremberg in particular

evolved its 'Lesebüchlein'[3] ('little reading-book'), a single volume which would instil, accurately and clearly, the fundamentals of human knowledge, good behaviour, and Christian belief. Knowledge, in these simple but serious books, is never presented as an end in itself; the child is constantly impressed with his *duty*, his proper function in a harmonious church and society, and his place in a larger order. Comenius's great plan for universal education or *pansophia* was dedicated to similar ideals. *Orbis Pictus*, the textbook for earliest childhood, represents the first step to the realisation of this goal. It is useful therefore to think of it as his catechism.

Yet it is more than a means of instruction; it is an act of *exploration*. The child is encouraged to delve into it on his own. The book represents the entire world in portable form, and since the world is 'in order', the child cannot but appreciate its orderliness as he turns the pages. The scope of *Orbis Pictus* is greater than that of any other catechism, and correspondingly its pictures function differently from those of the analogues mentioned above.

In the catechisms the illustrations are exemplificatory and mnemonic. Each Commandment, for example, is headed by a notable biblical example of its transgression. Künstle shows[9] an early carved decalogue where each panel has a hand jutting out in front of it; these hands count from one to ten on their fingers. In early catechisms each sentence of the Apostles' Creed is headed by the apostle from whom it is derived, making a set of twelve, a useful hint to recall the creed itself. This is the standard late medieval use of pictures for teaching; the exemplary, the symbolic and the mnemonic merge together. In later centuries, they separate. The use of sets of pictures to train the memory had a vigorous life of its own. Ratke attacked it as a method of teaching children.[10] Comenius too recognised the problems of this 'forced and tortured' technique, and, although not as uncompromisingly as Ratke, he insists that the development of memory and judgement must not be at odds.[11] The *Orbis Pictus* reflects this insistence. Artificial techniques are excluded as far as possible. Even the allegorical representations of the Virtues tend to show scenes from daily life, where each virtue is in action. We are given neither historical instances, nor any form of synecdoche, but the thing itself; the natural sequence of things, rather than a parallel scheme, reinforces the memory of them.

Other children's picture-books use pictures for narrative. Their main task is to present the material of the bible, followed by instruction in morals, theology and the use of language. In contrast, the *Orbis Pictus* contains no stories,[12] nor does it teach divinity, except in clearly defined instances—the first and last plates, and the chapters on Judaism and Christianity, which are distinguished by a special arrangement of the pictures.

The purpose of *Orbis Pictus* is not simply to train one faculty, nor is it a short cut to the mass learning of a standard adult corpus. The process is more fundamental. The epigraph at the beginning equates the 'Nomenclatura' of the title with Adam's naming of the creatures in Genesis II 19–20. Seeing and naming, for Adam, were inseparable; and so they should be for the child. On the title-page of the Nuremberg *Orbis Pictus*, Comenius proudly claims to show the world of 'all the fundamental things in the world'. Such comprehensive realism has not been side-tracked by accidentals and curiosities; nor have the short-term goals of narrative interest, the instilment of piety, or the reinforcement of memory tempted him from his pansophic intentions.

Comenius's thoughts on pictorial representation

This realism rests on an extensive theory, found at every stage of Comenius's work. It is concisely expressed in the preface to *Orbis Pictus*, as given in Hoole's translation of 1659:

> We can neither act nor speak wisely, unless we first rightly understand all the things which are to be done, and whereof we are to speak. Now there is nothing in the understanding which was not before in the sense. And therefore to exercise the senses well about the right perceiving the differences of things, will be to lay the grounds for all wisdom, and all wise discourse, and all discreet actions in ones course of life.

The presentation of objects, in an accurate and distinguishable way, is thus the main work of the teacher of the young. Without a good grounding in 'sensuals'—objects which the sense can perceive—the child will never grow up to 'act or speak wisely'. His mental life also must be initiated by solid reference to the senses; Comenius was always seeking and inventing ways to bring about the *'reductio intelligibilis ad sensuale'*,[13] the logical transformation of concepts into a form available to the physical senses.

Whenever Comenius refers to the use of pictures, it is always as a part of this process, the laying of foundations by the direct use of the senses. He recommends didactic emblems because they reduce concepts to visible form,[14] and he suggests for the teaching of young children symbols which are 'obvious' or 'direct'. Some of these can be seen in *Orbis Pictus* (Hoole's ed, plates 109–17). The physical world also had problems of representation; systematic astronomy, meteorology and anatomy are not immediately visible. The teacher should therefore use his ingenuity to invent visual aids, diagrams and three-dimensional models. These subjects can also be made more 'visual' by vivid language.[15] Individual objects and substances should wherever possible be brought into the classroom and experienced with all five senses; each school should build up a collection of rare things, such as jewels and perfumes. The *res ipsa*, the 'thing itself', is of paramount importance, and a life-size replica or solid model is the next best thing. Naming and perceiving must be simultaneous at this early stage in education; therefore pictures or wall-charts may be substituted for unobtainable things, enabling all words to be presented with a 'sensual'.[16]

Accordingly, Comenius thinks of book-illustration as an ancillary to learning, almost a last resort; conventional emblems, diagrams and drawings of objects may be used if nothing more vivid comes to hand. There is nothing to suggest the coherence and independence of *Orbis Pictus*. Very early in his career, however, he had recommended an idea of Lubinus, that an enterprising publisher should produce a 'Libellus Imaginum', a little book of pictures, to exercise the sight (pre-eminent among the senses).[17] For the very young, this book would be a major educational tool, teaching the rudiments of the 'Arts and Sciences':

> For here could be drawn mountain, valley, tree, bird, fish, horse, ox, sheep, man, in various ages and heights; light and darkness; the sky with the sun,

moon, stars and cloud; the primary colours; even the tools of the household and the workshop, pots, pans, pitchers, hammers, tongs, etc. And pictures of social ranks [Dignitatum], as, the king with crown and sceptre, the soldier with his arms, the countryman with his plough, the coachman with his waggon, the postman running along. And everywhere an inscription over the top, saying what each one is—Horse, Ox, Dog, Tree, etc.

The plan of the *Orbis Pictus* is clearly present in this enthusiastic account; but a coloured book with single objects labelled with single words is very distant from the final result. Furthermore, in later years the project is rarely referred to. The compactness of the small portable textbook is praised, but such a book should only be illustrated 'where necessary'.[18] For some years Comenius and his contemporaries were engaged on an 'Encyclopaedia of sensuals',[19] but this likewise was not referred to as a true picture-book. Not until 1653 did he produce a first draft of the *Orbis Pictus*, and then he criticises its limitations and explains that it is only a 'miniature encyclopaedia' to make the proper one more clear to the reader.[20] There is nothing in Comenius's writing to account fully for the final emergence of *Orbis Pictus*. He never digresses on stylistic matters, nor gives much indication that the small woodcut may have its own special virtues. He has a hunger for 'concreteness and ease of demonstration'[15] and is eager to assimilate visual expression into his intellectual system; but there is no theory of visual realism, of how pictures function or how they are to be constructed. The harmonious achievement of the *Orbis Pictus* is therefore all the more striking. This achievement can be made clearer by an examination of his other illustrated work.

Comenius's Illustrations

We have seen that Comenius's theories led him to value pictures, but to assign them a subsidiary position. Illustration would thus be sporadic, brought in when the topics stray away from what the teacher can demonstrate, and not integral as in *Orbis Pictus*. This is apparent in the 1656 *Janua*, edited in Schaffhausen by Stefan Spleiss. The copper plates, some at least by Conrad Meyer of Zürich, show miscellaneous useful things. They are grouped thematically but do not follow the numeration of the text, and so cannot be bound in directly. They show anatomical figures, models of the cosmos, maps, tools for surveying and weighing—many themes which are also used in the *Orbis Pictus*. But their organisation is quite different; they form no sequence and have no depth. There is no representation of space beyond the minimal requirements of the diagram. Solid objects cast a little shadow, and the anatomical figures stand on a stylised strip of land, a remnant of the 'Vesalian' landscapes from which they originally derive. This is in contrast to the majority of the plates in *Orbis Pictus*, where the sky is filled with clouds, the horizon extends in rolling hills, and human activities take place in solid, box-like buildings. This *Janua*, however, seems to satisfy Comenius's requirements. The pictures bring to the eye of the child what the teacher cannot supply, or provide in portable form, what he could only draw on the board—the shapes of geometry or the circles of the solar system.

In the same year as *Orbis Pictus*, another illustrated book of his came out. This was the Amsterdam *Vestibulum*, edited by Jacob Redinger. The main body of the text, from sentence fifty-three to the end, is matched page for page by copper plates, probably by Crispin de Pas. Each page is made up of tiny pictures arranged into strips which the reader scans with his eye, following the numbers in the text. The eye has less far to travel than in the *Orbis Pictus*, because of the linear arrangement. There is a wide variety of spatial representations, ranging from plain flat drawings to miniature scenes. Three-dimensional objects throw small shadows, either on the plane of the paper or on an assumed floor. Grouped objects are given enough land to stand on, and workers have a strip of the appropriate terrain or atelier. The full scenes show either a collective noun or a social institution. The scale can vary. Human anatomy is celebrated by large figures occupying half a page, while in the smaller scenes workers are often dwarfed by their tools. The artist has used a flexible and efficient means of representation. He can make lists and describe actions, and show details as well as contexts. Tools, clothes, plants, waggons, or insects are depicted with as much visibility as the small format allows; for example, manual action like sawing is provided with a disembodied hand.

This realism is close to Comenius's declared aim, the presentation of objects '*ad vivam autopsian*' ('for the reader to judge by his own vivid experience') in their orders and suborders. But it is discontinuous. This method, with all its flexibility, cannot *unite* detail and context. The full scenes—the wood on a page of trees, or the room on a page of costumes—themselves become objects and take their place in the list. The visual is subordinate to the scheme of the vocabulary. The individual page is often conscientiously designed, with intriguing interrelations of the frames; but what does it represent?—a synopsis, a mental construction. We are not encouraged to see that the clothes are empty or the plants uprooted; only that they have a certain number and form and are to be named at a certain appropriate point in the book. These illustrations are more ingenious and less thoughtful, more curious and less clear, than those of the *Orbis Pictus*.

By far the most important predecessor of the printed *Orbis Pictus* is Comenius's own manuscript of 1653. This is now lost, but fortunately we can have some idea of its style and content from the author's references and from a printed fragment which has survived.[21] In 1654, while at the Sárospatak Gymnasium in Hungary, he refers to '180 figures' then being drawn and cut in wood, to appear under the name *Vestibuli et Januae Linguarum Lucidarius*[20]—'a clear guide to the Comenian textbooks, *The Porch of Languages* and *The Gateway of Languages*'. The early printed version is actually called *Vestibuli . . . Lucidarium* (the change in gender does not affect the meaning) and is given the alternative title 'a little encyclopaedia of sensuals'. The name *Orbis Pictus* first appears in 1657,[22] and for some years the different titles were used indiscriminately by the author. This earlier draft (which we will refer to as the *Lucidarium*) may not have been completed; this at any rate is suggested by the bibliographical evidence. (The surviving fragment is made up of the first sixteen pages, and is thus one whole printed sheet; the last page has no catchword at the bottom, which seems to indicate that the sheet is complete in itself from the printer's point of view—perhaps therefore it is merely a 'trailer' of the larger work to follow.) Although the title page has no place or printer's name, and the date 'Anno 1653' thus refers to the author's completion of the manuscript, there is no reason to doubt that it was printed in Sárospatak under Comenius's supervision.[23] Since the more sophisticated Nuremberg edition appeared while he was living in Amsterdam, this early sample represents a stage nearer to his initial conception, perhaps even his own drawings.[24]

The two versions differ in title, in language, and in pictorial style; but, as far as we may compare them, the content and prefatory material are very similar. The earlier *Lucidarium* is entirely in Latin, while the Nuremberg edition is in Latin and German,[25] and all subsequent editions have been in two or more languages. The text of the earlier version is simpler, and the style of the woodcuts is cruder. It is this last difference which it is proposed to examine by a systematic comparison of the versions.

fig 1 'Invitatio', *1653*

(a) The '*Invitatio*' (figs 1 and 2). Both plates show a strong affinity to the title-page woodcuts of the late medieval *Meister Lucidarius* (fig 3—from a Strasburg edition, 1503). This is particularly interesting, since after the Reformation the serious purpose of this cosmological, encyclopaedic and liturgical dialogue for children was abandoned. The editions of the years nearer to Comenius's lifetime were diverting and sensational, and did not use the dignified motifs of master, pupil and landscape on their title pages. The old *Meister Lucidarius* culminated in detailed instructions for the young participant in church ritual; after these were suppressed, the gap was filled by more frivolous material—human freaks, or national costumes. Comenius, perhaps with a Czech source in mind, uses his *Invitatio* woodcut to claim an affinity with the serious purpose of the older *Lucidarius*—but his child is to participate not in Roman

Catholic ritual, but in the crafts and institutions of contemporary society.

The two versions of this plate show a deepening symbolism. In the earlier book, the title itself indicates the genre (*Lucidarium*) and the stage of education for which it is intended (*Vestibuli et Januae*). The woodcut (fig 1) indicates master and pupil, and behind them a city gate (*Janua*) a sunbeam (*Lucidarium*) touched by the master's finger, and trees. These represent Comenius's favourite metaphors for the educative process—the light of the sun, the successive entries to a large building, and the growth of a tree. In the later one (fig 2) the

fig 2 'Invitatio', *1658*

title has been compressed into the picture, and each detail is more significant. The verbal title now proclaims the book to be *Orbis Pictus*, which combines the meaning 'the world in pictures' with 'the bright and pretty world'. Now the 'light' metaphor is more striking, since the sunbeam runs directly through the centre of master's and pupil's brains. The city in the background is more complicated, and the teacher's staff draws a line across it; this has the effect of separating off a panel, framed by the staff and the robe. Within these lines a road is seen, leading to a porch with a central gateway, which in turn leads to several spacious buildings on the other side of the demarcation-line. This is a visual pun and refers to an acrostic which Comenius often uses;[26] the successive textbooks—'Porch', 'Gate' and 'Court-yard' together make up the *Way of Learning* (in Latin the initial letters of *vestibulum*, *ianua* and *atrium* make up the VIA). The roomy *atrium* lies outside the scope of this book—to the left of the staff. Further left still we see a grove of assorted trees. The meaning of this is not clear because it seems to refer to several things at once. It may be the grove of Academe—higher education—or perhaps the tangled forest of formal wordlists avoided by the Comenian *Way* (another Latin pun, on '*sylva*'[27]). It is most likely to refer to the cycle of human life. With the help of other plates in *Orbis Pictus* we can distinguish the immature shoots (squat pyramids), the full-grown tree (cedar or oak) and the

fig 3   Titlepage from Meister Lucidarius, *1503*

funereal cypress. In between the grove and the city—between the raw material of human life and the City of Learning (*Urbs Latinitatis*[28])— is a single tree with easily visible branches, one of which is bent in a downward curve and touches the ground. This is a common emblem for education,[29] and rightly stands between the organic and the architectural. The whole plate is thus full of education-symbols.

(b) *Deus* (God) in 1653 is represented by three concentric bursts of light. In 1658 the image becomes more theological, with a trinitarian symbol in the centre. (Hoole in his translation substituted a different symbol more familiar to English readers.[30])

(c) *Mundus* (the World) becomes more rational in the later version; earth, air and sky each take up a third of the unbroken circular frame. Earlier the horizon came half-way up and the top of the circle was broken by a tetragram. The creatures are closer to their natural scales and the human figures are shown in different postures, identical to those in fig 7 below. This seems to suggest that in the final revision, the preparation of drawings for Paul Creutzberger to cut in wood[25] was not done by Comenius but by an artist who, despite his limited skill, took pride in the twisting, balanced nudes and the dramatic landscape of this composition.

(d) *Coelum* (the Heaven) was intended from the first as a *volvella*— a revolving cut-out model of the sort first used in a printed book by Peter Apian in 1540.[31] The inner circle (the world—a tiny landscape) and the outer (the heavens) were printed separately and assembled on a page blank except for the title. The 1653 version, being no more than a sample, prints the image straight on to the page, and gives us only the outer circle.

(e) *Ignis* (Fire) is the last plate of the 1653 sample. The changes once again reveal a strong pictorial sense. In the earlier plate (fig 4) we see

fig 4   Ignis, *1653*

a collection of 'instances of fire'; the presentation is as economical as possible, and the picture is little more than a diagram. A candle burns in broad daylight, a bonfire blazes peacefully in a thunderstorm, smoke is blown in three directions at once, and a spark is struck by disembodied hands; clearly we are not meant to view the picture as a scene. As in the 'ancillary' illustrations for the *Janua* and *Vestibulum*, the realism is piecemeal.

fig 5   Ignis, *1658*

The revised version (fig 5) is very different. The fire is in an indoor grate, one candle, unlit, sits on a table with a flint and tinder, coals and brands are arranged on the hearth; the burning town is framed in the window. A strong perspective scheme dominates the picture, and smaller objects are firmly relegated to scale. The individual items are harder to recognise in this orderly 'room' than in the old diagrammatic plate, but the overall impression of the new version is much more lucid. The place is no longer just a collection of data under one heading—it is a scene, consistent within itself. Detail and context are united.

The new style is obviously much more orderly—and so suited to the aims of the author. In its consistency of scale and event it is more realistic, for Comenius is seeking to express a system of visual realism, rather than a haphazard assembly of items. Even so, fig 5 is not completely realistic: the perspective is incorrect, and the window is purely schematic. It is not a still-life. What sort of realism, then, does the *Orbis Pictus* use?

The *1658* Orbis Pictus
('H' references are to Hoole's English translation)
The formal features of the plates may be summarised as follows. The *frames* are normally the size and shape of fig 5. God and cosmology, however, are depicted in circular frames. The oblong is subdivided only four times; twice into two halves, depicting closely-related activi-

ties (H 69 and 128) and twice into six panels—a special arrangement borrowed from Evenius's depiction of the Old and New Testaments.[7] The *background* is very conventional; open countryside is represented by rolling hills in three planes, the nearest in shadow, the middle one forming an emphatic ridge, and the final one completing the horizon in steeper mountains. Sometimes there are outcrops of rock on right or left, a simplified version of contemporary landscape painting. The sky has large rolling clouds. These features often, but not always, appear through the windows in interiors. The *height of the horizon* varies; it is seldom arbitrary but depends on the population of land or sky, and the necessity to separate items. Thus H 123 *Interiora Urbis* uses a purely medieval system; the town is tipped right up into the air, elevations of the buildings are stuck on like postage stamps, and the surrounding hills seem to huddle under the town. But the preceding plate, *Urbs*, shows a side-view of the city with its towers and roofs naturally jumbled together. The subject of the plate has dictated the perspective. *Vertical divisions* are sometimes used to contrast interior and exterior, and the relative proportions often correspond to the relative extent of the activity indoors and out. The *linear perspective* is very prominent and erratic. In some cases it is nearly correct, in other cases drawn freehand, and once or twice it is drawn 'correctly' on wrong principles—that is, lines which should converge have been drawn accurately parallel. Generally it depicts strong tunnel- and box-like convergences, which fix the eye on the people caught inside them, and uses extraordinarily high vanishing-points. It is localised; sometimes there are two systems in one picture. A building always forms a self-contained box sitting awkwardly on the surrounding terrain and sometimes seeming to tower up from it. *Buildings* are treated very summarily. Their surfaces are plain and often cut away to reveal the contents. Sometimes they are no more than a pattern of lines—a representational habit which dies hard when the subject is a house being built (H 63–4), or falling down (H 6). In contrast *people* are shown active and complete; they rarely cross the frame or overlap one another. This habit is carried out almost superstitiously. But people do not dominate the pictures. As far as possible the *scale* is kept constant and the human figures keep in sober proportion to their surroundings. Occasional towering figures have a reason to do so, like the giant of H 44 or the allegorical figures of H 110–17. Subsidiary parts of the topic are often placed further away. Occasionally the sense of scale is distorted, as in *Sutor* (H 63), where the cobbler is dwarfed by the boots he has made. This is very similar to the handicraft-plates of the *Vestibulum*, and a common source in Comenius's own drawings is a likely explanation. This in turn suggests that many of these formal features were imposed on the author's original material.

Factual consistency is mostly strong. There are some diagrammatic additions—windhead and thunderbolt in the meteorology section, letters and dotted lines in the weights and measures. There are a few fictitious birds; the crane holding a stone, the eagle looking at the sun, and Mahomet's pigeon were firm beliefs, and the footless bird of paradise had the authority of Gesner.[32] There are a few symbolic chimaeras. The first and the last two plates refer the reader out into the mysteries of God, and so are appropriately emblematic. The miracles of the Bible are isolated in tiny frames. In the allegories of virtue only three frames actually violate reality, H 110, 114 and 117, and the effect is slightly masked in the latter by scale.

There are a few exceptions to these rules. The central heart and symmetrical organs shown in fig 6 are probably just a careless medieval-ism. In *Liberalitas* (H 117) the humble recipient of charity is drawn on a smaller scale than the giver—perhaps the only survival of 'symbolic scale'. In the map of Europe (H 108) Bohemia appears as a circle in the middle of Germany. This may also seem careless, but, in *Clamores Eliae*, Comenius wrote 'Europe is the "nucleus" of the lands of the earth, Germany is the heart of Europe, and Bohemia is the heart of Germany . . .'[33] Thus there is a reason, albeit obscure, for this oddity; and we are also reminded of the continuing influence of Comenius's own hand.

The apparent departures from the 'background rule' can also be related to a very careful design. H 39–43 and H 119 are the only oblong frames to have no perspective background. H 119—*Arbor Con-sanguinitatis*—is an odd hybrid. It has heraldic leaves against a white

background and roots visible through the strip of 'hill' which serves
as ground. A very similar representation of a symbolic tree occurs in
an autograph manuscript of Comenius's *Centrum securitatis*. The very
oddity of this plate provides its own isolation; we are reminded of how
few of these commonplace symbolic devices are used.

The other group is more interesting. The anatomical diagrams (H
40 and 41), of which one is reproduced as fig 6, originally derived
from Vesalius. They have
no background at all, and
are thus in marked con-
trast both with their Vesalian model and with the
associated picture of two
figures shown as fig 7 (cf
H 38), where the back-
ground is developed into
a rich composition. In the
anatomical diagram, from
which fig 6 derives, the
human body is set into,
but towers above, a land-
scape (fig 8).

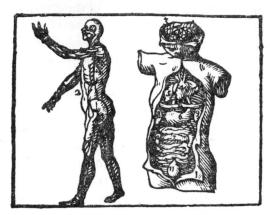

fig 6   Anatomical diagrams from Orbis Pictus

A rudiment of this is
found in Meyer's plates
for the *Janua*. But the
artist in *Orbis Pictus* has
chosen to enlarge the
landscape for the repre-
sentation of complete
human figures, and to
eliminate it entirely from
cut or stripped ones. H
39, 42 and 43 show details
of head and hands, the
five senses and the soul.

fig 7   'The Outward Parts of Man' from Orbis
Pictus

fig 8   Anatomical diagram from Vesalius, De Humani Corporis Fabrica, *1543 (reduced)*

These are represented artificially by separated parts of the body and by a dotted outline of a man. Once again the background is special; these details are drawn on to a suspended cloth like a vernicle, behind which is darkness. Finally, H 37, *Septem Aetates Hominis*, shows representatives of the ages mounting and descending a symbolic block,[34] against plain white. The original Nuremberg edition, however, has taken pains to fill this in with a textured wall, at the expense of the clarity of the composition. This seems to confirm that a definite symbolic plan is being carried out. The differences in background enforce an epistemological difference between the diagrams of incomplete bodies and the full representations of human figures. Such a distinction is quite alien to the *Vestibulum*.

For Comenius the 'visible world' could not be limited to the material. The 'Orb' included activities, institutions, concepts and the ultimate 'realities' of divinity, which merged all the previous realities into a single pattern. The formal cohesion of the *Orbis Pictus* is an attempt, groping and guided, to find a plastic equivalent to this vision. Active and social man is the core of the book. There are no superfluous figures, gazing over parapets or rowing aimlessly, just as there are no sleeping cats, delft plates, or pictures. The usual stock-in-trade of northern European artists, suggestive of pleasant activity, atmosphere and well-being, are absent. The tiny rower in H 137, *Regnum & Regio*, indicates a navigable river on which the king levies a toll. Activity is not suggested but shown directly, and well-being is shown in the orderliness of interior and exterior. Formal devices, in both cases, contribute to the meaning.

The activity of men is presented to the eye by the extreme simplicity of the architectural settings and the compositional devices. 'Set' and 'Scene' in the theatrical sense are useful concepts here. The architecture of the *Orbis Pictus*, unless it forms a subject in its own right (like *Domus* H 66, *Ludus Pilae* H 133, or *Religio* H 144)[35] is highly formal. The high vanishing-points and plain flat walls suggest the 'scene' of a crude theatre rather than a 'scene' in a Dutch realist painting. It is cut away to form edges which often become mere abstract dividing lines—*Partes Domus* H 71 is a good example, where the bottom 'room' on the left is in fact a picture of the back yard. A 'set' presents characters, but it does not advertise, exaggerate or praise; it helps to establish a realistic scale by artificial means. Oddly enough, the informative and entertaining books from which most of the material for *Orbis Pictus* was taken, like Amman's famous woodcuts of trades and estates, do not follow the same rigid compositional rules. They are ingenious and artistic; each plate solves its formal problem in a slightly different way, by overlapping of the planes, domestic detail, superfluous but characterful people, and variations in the angle of view. In *Orbis Pictus*, by contrast, the composition is opened out, pushed back and standardised. There has been a conscious effort at order. All features under discussion tend towards orderliness.

Order for human use is shown in the plates dealing with materials; for example *Lapides* (H 12). The crudest form is furthest off; the nearer to the eye, the nearer to human usefulness and the most worked. A strongly drawn threshold cuts the picture in half. Within it, on a table, lie the most finished and useful stones—jewels, a magnet and a whet-stone. The same distance-symbolism is used in *Faber Lignarius* (H 63). In the rocks are the caves of our ancestors; in the middle-distance, huts and tents; and on the level ground in front, carpenters are building a new house. A 50-50 proportionism contrasting 'domestic' and 'wild' is also used in *Flores* (H 15) and in *Oscines* ('singing birds', H 21) where the house contains birds which can imitate the human voice (three of them); all the others crowd into the left-hand side. The birds are further sub-divided, in the text and in the picture, by their exact place of singing (air, tree or ground). The artist has gone out of his way to enforce the formal symbolism as a means of identifying the place of his subjects according to the criterion of human use. The recessions of perspective give momentum to an intellectual process of categorisation. Human life is the culmination of this movement. By these means the different parts of *Orbis Pictus*, physical, technological and social, are made to share the same reality. Materials, flowers, birds and animals are divided according to human use and shown arranged by human labour. The labourers themselves appear next, set into the appropriate space, surrounded by their essential tools; and the same technique and the same formal symbolism is used to portray social institutions. *Societas Heridilis* (H 121) is divided exactly in half by a wall separating indoors and out; this corresponds to the divided authority of the master over the male yard-servants and the mistress over female domestics.

The representation of these 'societies', conjugal or parental, draws on the didactic emblems of the time. Many of these[36] concern them-selves with domestic and social duties, and so are descendents of the *Zuchtbüchlein* or *Ratbüchlein*, variants of the catechism which instruc-ted children in social behaviour and mentality. They portray the model institution at exemplary moments—at table or diligently working in the parlour. The instructive message is spelled out by the text, by the

orderly composition of the scene itself, and by an extensive but un-
obtrusive symbolism; household tools and decorations, in their natural
appearances and positions,[37] are used to symbolise the human qualities
which decide on their use. This is made quite explicit in the texts.

Comenius uses a similar
technique. The text of
Societas Parentalis (fig 9) at
one point runs (in Hoole's
translation, H 120) 'As the
child beginneth to grow
older, it is accustomed to
Piety 12 and Labour 13
and is chastised 14 if it be
not dutifull. Children owe
to Parents Reverence, and
Service. The Father main-
taineth his Children by
taking Pains 15.' These

fig 9   'An Ideal Family', from Orbis Pictus

numbers refer in the picture to a boy with praying hands, to a
book and a child at a writing-desk, to a birch rod on the table, and
to the palette held by the father who paints at a large easel. These
objects are extremely common in the didactic emblem where they
help to represent the institution of a pious and hard-working family
by symbolic interpretation of its outward appearance. This symbolism is very different from that of the heiroglyphic and esoteric
emblem. The gap between symbol and real thing is as small as possible, and the *'reductio intelligibilis ad sensuale'* is a straightforward
process—'discipline' is shown by a birch rod on the table—whereas
in the 'mysterious' emblem the composition is surreal and the meaning has to be grasped 'at two removes'.[38] In the pictorial realism
used by Comenius the objects are provided by accurate visual
observation, but the form is determined by an intellectual theory of
their place in a larger system. Significance lies beyond the immediate
appearance of the object, but does not contradict it. Such a realism
has an affinity with the didactic emblem, where symbolic and real are

barely distinguishable. In Comenius's picture (fig 9) the birch and the book are glossed symbolically, but the most obvious borrowings from that tradition, the easel and the palette, are simply labelled *laborans* (working). Easel-painting is hardly typical 'work' for the average paterfamilias; the motif has obviously been introduced because of its symbolic meaning,[39] but it is then reinterpreted literally.

What is the origin of Comenius's pictorial realism? The objects derive from popularised versions of the encyclopaedias, herbals, anatomies, trade-books and technological treatises of the northern European Renaissance; some motifs can be traced back to single prints; the social scenes derive from exemplary treatises, emblems and *specula*, while the ethical allegories come partly from this source and partly from Italian iconography. The formal structure, however, does not show such variety; it derives almost entirely from the exoteric emblems of Germany—Taurellus, Mannich and Saubert.[40]

The Originality of Comenius

Orbis Pictus, however, is clearly not an emblem-book. Its first purpose is to show directly the things and actions which make up the universe. It is a revival of Lubinus's idea, a naming-book whose pictures and words run parallel, both of primary importance. As described in the *Great Didactic*, this would have been very elementary, with one thing and one word per picture; social functions would be represented by single figures each with their gesture or attribute.[17] *Orbis Pictus* shows classes of creatures, sets of tools and groups of men, all in their proper place and scale, and their numbers are limited not by a simplistic formal frame but by the actual requirements of the subject. Nothing is superfluous, but nothing seems to have been omitted. This is the encyclopaedic material that must be fitted into a 'little picture book'. Comenius does not discuss how this can be done; most of his recommendations of pictorial methods are very general, and refer to quite a different question—the store of explanatory pictures used in the school when the object itself, or a three-dimensional model, is not available. Pictures are always discussed in terms of general didactics and Comenius nowhere develops a separate theory of how they function. But the problems of actually creating the 'libellum imaginum' must have occupied his mind considerably.

We can see some of his answers in his illustrated work, the fragment of the *Lucidarium* and the 1658 *Vestibulum*, both published under the author's eye, and both likely to reflect his intentions and perhaps his own drawings. These use a flexible mixture of the scenic and the diagrammatic, varying according to the immediate needs of the subject, useful in the schoolroom and in private study. But the Nuremberg edition rejects the diagrammatic and the inconsistent, establishes a standard scale and distance for its objects, and encloses them in a formal structure so stringent that one can talk of 'rules' rather than just 'habits'. Comenius referred to his earlier version as 'something of fresh invention';[41] the claim is fully justified in the later one.

Having left behind the easier techniques of explanatory illustration, does it depend more on the purely pictorial? Robert Alt has shown most of its sections can be traced back to the information-books of the German bourgeoisie; but Comenius's work is a poor specimen by these standards. The composition is archaic, there are no costumes or customs and the rigorous scale-constancy and group-portrayal make it impossible to browse on curiosities and minutiae. But *Orbis Pictus* is not intended to be a trade-book or a herbal; its purpose is to give the young an image of the *orbis sensualium*. This will entertain and inform, but these effects are not pursued for themselves; they are an introduction to a larger system which the child will later have to manage—'in pictures the ignorant can see what they have to do'.[42] The impulse is not empirical—it is enough for the objects to be accurate miniatures of currently accepted representations. The creativity of the artist is limited by his commission, to create a small unit in the large system of panbiblia, itself a contributory part of the pansophic system. The devotion to fact is dictated not by a hunger for realism but by an intellectual policy.

Comenius believed that all human knowledge was founded on sense-data, implying that the early years of human life should be devoted to the direct perception of empirical facts. Whenever he discussed primary education, the stage of the *Vestibulum* and *Janua*, he showed how each exercise of the senses was the starting-point of the corresponding mental discipline of later years.[43] Each fact carries its epistemological label. This systematic attitude to the factual is reflected in *Orbis Pictus*. We are always aware of the organising intellect; it appears in the classification of objects and the order of their succession. The special formal features also impose orderliness, and we have seen how they have a symbolic function. But the symbolism is at the service not of the arcane but of didacticism, of the intellectual policy of pansophism. The proper placing of objects in the systematic universe, and the central position of man, are built in to these pictures. This gives *Orbis Pictus* its strong unity. Everything is dedicated to the purpose of teaching.

In the same way its sources are found not in the mainstream of adult art and writing, but in the particular forms evolved for education —the catechism, the *Elucidarius*, the *Lesebüchlein*, the exoteric emblem, and children's posters. All these contribute to the *Orbis Pictus* but the final product remains entirely original. In its clarity, comprehensiveness and systematisation, it is distinctively Comenian and it employs a distinctive realism, combining the factual and the symbolic in a consistent way. The model was found satisfactory throughout Europe for more than a century.

Pembroke College, Oxford

References

1　The most detailed bibliography is K. Pilz, *Die Ausgaben des Orbis Sensualium Pictus* (Nuremberg, 1967). I refer always to the wood-cuts of the original edition of *Orbis Pictus* (hereinafter referred to as *OP*); but the edition most available in English facsimiles is Charles Hoole's hastily-engraved London edition of 1659, which differs slightly in numbering. To avoid confusion, all chapter-references will be to Hoole, referred to in the text by the letter H.

2　*Herkunft und Bedeutung des Orbis Pictus* (Berlin, 1970).

3　Cp I. Dyhrenfurth, *Geschichte des deutschen Jugendbuches* (Zürich and Freiburg-i-B, 1967) ch 1; and the *Bibliographie der Nürnberger Kinder und Jugendbücher, 1522–1914* (Bamberg, 1961) under *Teutsche Kinder Tafel*, Luther's *Kleine Katechismus*, and J. Saubert's *Lesebuechlein*.

4 Cp W. H. Stevenson, *Early Scholastic Colloquies* (1929) and G. N. Garmonsway ed, *Aelfric's Colloquy* (1939).

5 One striking example, which divides the printed line after each significant phrase, like *OP*, is Thomas Ingmethorpe's Hebrew-English *Short Catechisme* (1633); Comenius may have seen it.

6 Cp David Bland, *A History of Book Illustration* (2nd ed, 1969), esp under Beham. His references to *OP* are only useful as a summary of *idées reçues* (154–5). Mathäus Merian the Elder also produced popular biblical illustrations; Comenius knew and recommended them, and they form the immediate source for five out of the six panels of H 147, and probably also the oval light-bursts in H 36.

7 Sigismund Evenius, *Gottselige Bilder Schule* . . . (Nuremberg, 1637). The title goes on to link this picture-book with the more orthodox catechism.

8 Klaus Schaller, *Die Pädagogik des* . . . *Comenius* . . . (2nd ed, Heidelberg, 1967), illustrates this fully.

9 K. Künstle, *Ikonographie der Christlichen Kunst* (Freiburg, 1928), fig 49.

10 Schaller,[8] 326–32.

11 The basic text for Comenius's work is his *Opera Didactica Omnia* (Amsterdam, 1657; Prague, 1957), hereafter referred to as *ODO*. His *Consultatio Catholica* was edited from the MS in 1966 (Prague). Part of his work has been translated into English, notably V. Jelinek, *The Analytical Didactic of Comenius* (Chicago, 1953) and M. W. Keatinge, *The Great Didactic of John Amos Comenius* (1910). This note refers to *ODO* II 120 (Jel 139).

12 With the exception of the eponymous Fall story in H 36—'Man'. The top left-hand corner of Hoole's plate 98 seems to be narrative; the scholar reads quietly while the town burns. This is not in the original—the London engraver has failed to recognise a torch-bearer.

13 *ODO* II 126 (Jel 148).

14 *Cons Cath* II 187 and 544. Cp note 13.

15 Cp *ODO* I 116–17 (Keat ii 187) praising Fludd's description of meteorology.

16 *ODO* I 370, II 149 (Jel 190), 166, 256, III 27, 38, 835; *OP* (Hoole fA5v–6); *Korrespondence* (ed A. Patera, Prague, 1892), 130. For wall-pictures, cp *ODO* I 80 (Keat ii 131)—but these should be 'historical monuments etc'—and 108 (Keat ii 173). The latter reference throws some light on the *condensation* of *OP* . . . the wall-charts should be an 'epitome' of the textbooks used—'*tum Textus* (*nervosa brevitate tum Imaginum and Emblematum picturis*'.

17 *ODO* I 171–2 (Keat ii 264–5) and II 80 (an uninformative repeat of the idea).

18 *ODO* III 27.

19 Cp G. H. Turnbull, 'Plans of Comenius for his Stay in England', *Acta Comeniana XVII* (Prague, 1958), 19, and C. Webster, *Samuel Hartlib* . . . (1970), 20. Mr Webster informs me that the discussions took place around 1635, and that the main proponent of the Encyclopaedia was William Brooke.

20 *ODO* III 835 and note 21, *encyclopaediola*.

21 This *editio praecox* was first brought to light in G. H. Turnbull, 'An Incomplete Orbis Pictus of Comenius, Printed in 1653' in *Acta Comeniana XVI* (Prague, 1957), 35–58 and is also reproduced in *OP* (facsimile, Osnabrück, 1964). The unique complete sheet is housed in Sheffield University Library (Hartlib Papers, VII 106), and is the property of Lord Delaware; all reference to it is made with their kind permission and co-operation. Part of another (corrected) has been recovered from binders' waste in Hungary by Dr J. Bakos of Sárospatak. Its complete title, including a MS addition probably by Comenius, runs *Vestibuli et*

Januae Linguarum Lucidarium (*sen encyclopaediola sensualium*) *Hoc est Nomenclatura Rerum ad autopsian deducta.*

22 In *ODO* III 802—an even briefer sample with a footnote promising a prope Nuremberg edition.

23 There is no substance whatever in H. Rosenfeld's suggestion that the *Lucidarium* was printed in Nuremberg in 1657 without Comenius being able to see it. (*Archiv für Geschichte des Buchwesens*, vol 6, Frankfurt, 1965, pp 878–98). Bibliographical evidence backs up commonsense in suggesting Sárospatak as the place of printing and 1653–4 as the date.

24 The classic statement of the opposite point of view is W. Toischer, 'Die Entstehung des OP', *Zeitschr. für Gesch der Erziehung und des Unterrichts III* (Berlin, 1913, vol 4, 170ff); this was written before the discovery of the *Lucidarium*.

25 H. Kunstmann ('Die sichtbare Welt Comenii', *Der Welt der Slaven II*, Wiesbaden, 1957, 377–93) shows that the German translation is probably the work of S von Birken, and that the blocks were cut by Paul Creutzberger. An examination of Creutzberger's known work (The Bible, ed Dilherr, Nuremberg, 1670) does not reveal an original personality.

26 *ODO* II 163 (Jel 60) and III 119.

27 *ODO* I 319.

28 *ODO* I 321. Both these references are to a panegyric by David Vechner, who pursues Comenius's metaphors to the brink of absurdity.

29 Cp L. van Puyvelde, *Jordaens* (Paris and Brussels, 1953), 162, and Conrad. Meyer, *Nützliche Zeitbetrachtung* (Zürich, 1675, but in circulation earlier), plate 1.

30 Cp Georg Stuhlfauth, *Das Dreieck* . . . (Stuttgart, 1937).

31 *Astronomicum Caesarum* (Ingolstadt, 1540) and cp Schaller,[8] 335.

32 Conrad Gesner, *De Avium natura* (Zürich, 1555), 611.

33 M. Blekastad, *Comenius* . . . (Oslo and Prague, 1969), 720.

34 The rising and falling steps leading from cradle to coffin seem to have been first used in a woodcut by Jörg Breu (the Younger) in 1530. A later imitation by C. Bertelli reduces the structure from an archway to a block with niches, as in *OP*. See V. R. S. van Marle, *Iconographie de l'Art Profane* . . . (The Hague, 1931), figs 189 and 190, and F. J. Dubiez, *Cornelis Anthoniszoon van Amsterdam* . . . (Amsterdam, 1969), fig 25.

35 In these cases the perspective is nearly correct, and the surfaces are realistically textured.

36 Eg Johann Saubert (the Elder), *Duodekas Sacrorum Emblematum*, part 4 (Nuremberg, 1630), plates 10 and 11; Conrad Meyer, *Nützliche Zeitbetrachtung*[29] and loose sheets, eg *Tischzucht* (1645). Meyer's prints originated as *Neujahrsblätter* (see Dyhrenfurth[3]) didactic posters given to the children of Zürich by the city library. The first ones were created by Meyer after Jacob Cats' *Kinderspel*. The latter is completely different in form, however, and clearly belongs to Dutch realism (see J. Cats, *Houwelyck*, Amsterdam, 1644, fA5).

37 Meyer shows, as well as allegorical pictures, the tools of sewing, spinning and dusting, a lamp, knives and a sharpener, books, a palette, and the husband painting (plate 3). Saubert[36] (plate 10) shows a birch, books, a palette and brushes, and a canvas mounted on an easel. The painter also appears, among other education-symbols, in the titlepage of *ODO*.

38 George Herbert 'Jordan (I)' l 10. The distinction between the esoteric and the exoteric tradition is discussed by Edgar Wind, *Pagan Mysteries in the Renaissance* (2nd ed, 1968). Comenius only uses esoterica in the section on Ethics, and then

only sparingly; 'opportunity' in H 110 is a heiroglyph (cp Wind, fig 53) but most of the objects or scenes in these plates are either elementary similes, like the scraping man in H 117, or illustrative scenes, like the drunkards in H 112. (The foreshortened vomiter comes from later eds of Holbein's death-dance.) The weird figures are further isolated by the text ('Justice is painted . . .') and by formal symbolism—they stand on the foreground while scenes and similes are further off on the next ridge. The whole section is prefixed by the 'Choice of Hercules', a definitely exoteric fable where 'the terms of the argument are literal and fixed' (Wind, 205).

39   I suggest that the 'painter' symbol combines the proverb *nulla dies sine linea* (not a day without a line, ie on the canvas) which refers to industriousness and derives from Pliny's account of Apelles, and the widespread image of the child's mind as *tabula rasa*, originating in Aristotle.

40   Cp N. Taurellus (Oechslein), *Emblemata physico-ethica* (Nuremberg, 1595; also later eds), especially the plates from fF8 to fG8; J. Mannich, *Sacra emblemata . . .* (Nuremberg, 1624); and Saubert.[36]

41   *ODO* III 1046.

42   St Gregory quoted in the introduction to Evenius;[7] cp Schaller,[8] 334.

43   *ODO* I 167–9 (Keat ii 259–62) and 171–2 (Keat ii 264–5).

DIANA HARDING

Mathematics and Science Education in Eighteenth-century Northamptonshire

NORTHAMPTONSHIRE, reasonably stable and prosperous during the eighteenth century, was one of the most populous counties in England at that time. Six main rivers formed important connections with the nine surrounding counties, and six main roads linked London and the north of England. These brought trade and social contacts which were vital to the development of Northamptonshire. Another influential feature was the existence of a large number of sizeable estates and a numerous body of gentry. Farming was the main source of wealth for most of the gentry, for the London markets relied on Northampton-shire sheep, cattle, horses, dairy produce and grain. As the rate of enclosure increased, people drifted to the neighbouring market towns where the leather and textile industries were heavily dependent on the agricultural life of the county.

The close relationships between the agricultural and urban areas had been intensified by the growing importance of market towns during the seventeenth century.[1] Throughout the eighteenth century Northamp-ton, the largest of the fourteen county market centres, was a focal point in community life for it was the meeting place, not only of farmers and traders, but also of the gentry, who were important in county politics and administration. Such activities produced a notable rise in the numbers of professionals, including schoolmasters, scriveners, lawyers and medical men. An important result of this growth was the emer-gence of Northampton, during the eighteenth century, as the intellec-tual centre of the county.

It is against this background that the educational accomplishments of Northamptonshire must be judged. Dr Nicholas Hans has claimed that the eighteenth century was, perhaps, the most interesting period of English education: it was not only a period with schemes and philosophical works as brilliant as those of the seventeenth century, it was also a period which saw the realisation of many modern educational ideas.[2] Much of the interest in new subjects and new methods has been focused on the growth of science and mathematics, a trend which originated in the seventeenth century and gained momentum during the Agricultural and Industrial Revolutions. In Northamptonshire, the most interesting developments were to be seen in the dissenting and private academies and schools, in the activities of learned scientific societies, and in the work of individual teachers and writers who influenced thought and learning far beyond the boundaries of the county itself.

Mathematics and Science in academies and schools

It was in the industrial areas of Northamptonshire, dominated by the middle classes and Nonconformist churches, that the private schools and academies which departed most strikingly from the traditional patterns of education were to be found. In the eighteenth century, the term 'academy' referred to a school which offered training in a range of subjects beyond the level of simple, elementary skills. Some were multilateral, offering languages, humanities, mathematics and science. Then there were the technical academies, sometimes referred to as commercial schools, which were very important in that they met the needs of the ambitious, urban, middle-class society by education 'for trades'.

The subject matter of mathematics teaching often varied according to the skill of the master and the size of the school, but it could be described as a complex range of specialisms, including algebra, geometry, surveying, navigation, mechanics and astronomy. The most comprehensive courses offered in Northamptonshire were to be found in the technical academies run by John Noble, Benjamin Shelton and William Grey. The first commercial school advertisement in the *Northampton Mercury* referred to 'arithmetic vulgar and decimal, practice, square and cube root, superfices and solid measure, navigation and surveying'.[3] John Noble and William Butlin, who were joint proprietors of an academy in Bearward Street, Northampton, in 1747, offered 'arithmetic vulgar and decimal, extraction of roots, book keeping, geometry, trignometry, mensuration, decimals, scale and dividers and sliding rule, practice and theory of gauging, surveying, astronomy and navigation.'[4] At Daventry, Benjamin Shelton, and later his widow, provided courses in 'arithmetic, surveying, measuring timber etc., navigation, astronomy and algebra.'[5] In 1744, John Hill of Welford taught 'Geometry, Trignometry, Merchant Accounts, Mensuration of Superfices and Solids, Surveying and Gauging.'[6] An almost identical course was offered by a contemporary, William Gray of Whittlebury.[7] Other proprietors were less explicit. Thomas Cross of Northampton advertised 'more complex mathematical sciences', in 1762,[8] and T. and J. Cornfield of Guilsborough referred in 1794 to 'the less abstruse parts of the mathematics'.[9]

A number of men describing themselves as writing masters also taught some elementary arithmetic and accounting. The simple training which they offered was usually designed for the lower middle-class students who could afford only modest fees. The general picture which emerges in Northamptonshire towns is of a number of small establishments where the proprietors often supplemented their incomes by teaching privately outside their own schools, and by taking up part-time appointments in local endowed schools. But the *Northampton Mercury* provides direct evidence of a steady succession of writing masters in Northampton, who built up quite successful schools. John Lee, who described himself as a writing master, ran a large establishment in Gold Street in the 1730s. He boarded some pupils and taught, in addition to writing, 'arithmetic, foreign exchanges, merchant accounts and book keeping'. In 1735 he claimed that, in the previous five years, three hundred students had been successfully prepared by him 'for trades'.[10] Other successful writing schools in Northampton were opened by Henry Woolley and John Smith. Henry Woolley who ran a school in Gold Street for 'youths qualifying for business'[11] was also secretary to the Infirmary, a friend of Philip Doddridge and a business partner of Richardson Wood, the grammar school master. John Smith started a day and evening school in Bridge Street which was later continued by other masters in St Giles Street.[12] Throughout the recorded history of these schools, arithmetic and merchant accounts always featured in the curricula.

A number of mathematics teachers mentioned in advertisements[13] cannot be traced through normal reference materials and it is likely that they had themselves received little formal education and became interested in mathematics and science through their own reading, experiments and observations. Many of these men combined teaching with professional work, surveying being the most usual. In contrast, we know that a few of the prominent mathematicians living in the county were also part-time teachers and some interesting publications were produced by Northamptonshire men, notably *An Easy Introduction to Mechanics* (1768) by John Ryland of Northampton; *Synopsis of Logarithmetical Arithmetic* (1783) by Thomas Sargeant also of Northampton; *Mathematical Essays on Several Subjects* (1785) by John Hellins of Green's Norton; *Navigation made easy to the most common capacity* (1790) by John Malham; and *A Treatise on Land Surveying* (1799) by Thomas Dix of Oundle.

Some prominent writers and teachers were associated with the famous dissenting academy brought by Philip Doddridge to Northampton from Market Harborough in 1729. Doddridge's Academy was at first accommodated in a house in Marefair, and later in a substantial house in Sheep Street, which belonged to Doddridge's friend and patron, the Earl of Halifax. After Doddridge's death in 1752, the Academy moved to Daventry and was placed under the supervision of Caleb Ashworth and later under Thomas Robins and Thomas Belsham. When the latter resigned in 1789 the Coward Trustees arranged for the Academy to return to Northampton, but in 1798 the trustees felt obliged to close it because its liberal views had become a matter of concern to those who feared the spread of revolutionary ideas from France. During the lifetime of the Academy the teachers and students contributed much to the widening of the curriculum and, despite the fact that the dissenting academies' most important function was the teaching of religion, mathematics and science were always available to the students. Doddridge, however, had some reservations about the amount of time required for mathematics and science, and, although he taught algebra according to his own scheme, he deplored 'pursuing too long some abstruse mathematical enquiries'.[14] In 1732 the Coward Trustees made a grant towards apparatus for lectures in experimental philosophy, but in 1745 Doddridge told his friend Samuel Clarke that the course 'takes up a good deal of time and pains, though we do little more than make the experiments with a short account of the purposes they are intended to explain'.[15] However, science remained on the curriculum and in 1771 the Coward Trustees provided for an observatory.[16] It is also relevant to record that Joseph Priestley was a student at Daventry; that Stephen Addington, who entered the Academy in 1746, later taught in Market Harborough and produced school text-books, including an *Arithmetic* in 1765; and that Caleb Ashworth, student in Northampton and principal tutor in Daventry, produced *A Treatise on Plane Trigonometry*.

In more precise terms, the work of Doddridge's Academy, between 1729 and 1751 included geometry and algebra for first-year students, with trigonometry, conic sections, celestial mechanics and natural and experimental philosophy in the second year.[17] When the Academy removed to Daventry, Ashworth himself was largely concerned with teaching mathematics, but other tutors of this subject included Noah Hill, Thomas Belsham, Timothy Kenrick and William Broadbent.

One of the most interesting examples of mathematics and science teaching in eighteenth-century Northamptonshire was that of John Ryland, the Baptist minister who removed his academy from Warwick to College Street, Northampton, in 1759.[18] His printed curriculum for 1781 may still be seen on a faded and torn exercise book in College Street Chapel, and his *Plan of a Truly Liberal Education* included science and mathematics. The latter was described as 'especially Practice or a Method of Computation with Certainty and Expedition' and included the 'Principles of Geometry', the 'Mensuration of Land in Heights and Distances', 'County Book Keeping' and 'Merchant Accounts'. Ryland was assisted in mathematics and science teaching by a Mr Wells.

Ryland's methods of teaching were interesting. He was keen to provide practical work from the boys' environment and experiences, and one account tells of an exercise in migration in which he called his students early one morning to observe the birds gathering on the academy roof.[19] Other practical work included walks in search of plants for the school herbarium; the keeping of pets, such as the hermaphrodite pigeon which lived in the school garden; and the collection of specimens. Evidence of such work may be seen in an exercise book which belonged to his son.[20] It was intended as a record of the 'Natural History of Butterflies and Moths' and, on the outside, he listed three reference works: *Fundamental Entomologiae or an Introduction to the Knowledge of Insects*, translated from Linnaeus by W. Curtis, apothecary, and sold by Peach of Cheapside in 1772; *Instructions for Collecting and Preserving Insects, particularly Moths and Butterflies* by the same author; and *Outlines of the Natural History of Great Britain and Ireland* in three volumes, by John Berkenhout, MD. In the exercise book Ryland's son drew and described each insect that he observed, stating where he had seen it and what he knew about it.

Practical methods of teaching mathematics were described by Ryland in his *Address to the Ingenuous Youth of Great Britain*. Here he stated that: 'Arithmetic can never be enough taught' and mentioned two masters who had done much to promote it—Dr Stephen Addington of Market Harborough, an ex-student of Doddridge's Academy, and Mr Daniel Fenning of Leicestershire.[21] Of his own students he wrote that they 'work every question in single proportion in four different statings, in order to strengthen their minds and their reasoning powers'.[22] According to Ryland, geometry was the best subject for youth after divinity and history. He claimed that schoolboys should be able to master six books of Euclid 'in a way of play . . . by working the theorems in the sand',[23] and clear practical instructions were given to any young man who wanted to attempt the scheme. The master was required to arm himself with Le Clerc's *Practical Geometry*, a large pair of compasses and a ruler. He could then take twenty to thirty boys into the playground and teach them so that they understood the first principles of geometry very rapidly. Practical experiments with simple equipment were described to help boys understand cohesion, water in capillary tubes, pumpwork, optics, spheres and the orrery. To show simple mechanics, especially levers, the master was encouraged to find a fire shovel, tongs and a poker. A spinning-wheel could be used to illustrate the power of a wheel and axle, marbles would explain the nature of percussion and the laws of motion, the falling ball could explain gravity and spinning tops the motions of the earth. Some experiments must have been entertaining: 'The twisting of a chambermaid's mop will show the nature of the centrifugal force of the planets'.[24]

There was great interest in Ryland's use of cards to teach school subjects. His geography cards were later published by Bowles of St Paul's Churchyard, and his optics cards, improved and augmented by James Ferguson, were printed in London in 1820. Similar cards were used to teach geometry, anatomy and astronomy. In the latter subject, Ryland devised a 'living orrery' for seventeen boys. The biggest stood in the middle of the playground, representing the sun. The others, standing at proper distances, were sixteen planets. Each boy had a card, giving his distance, magnitude, period and hourly motion and, when asked to orbit, each one repeated these details. One pupil referred to such methods as 'eccentricities'. (This is probably a pun, since one of the parameters defining the orbit of a planet is called its eccentricity.)

As Ryland had devised such useful methods, he was keen to publish them, and his works included: *Elements of Geography*, which was introductory to *Longer Treatises on the Use of Globes* and *An Easy Introduction to Mechanics, Geometry, Plane Trigonometry, Measuring heights and distances, Optics, Astronomy*.[25] These publications were, however, only a small part of Ryland's work and it would be misleading to over-emphasise his influence on mathematics and science teaching. At a time when most Baptists disliked the new learning, feared unorthodox opinions and distrusted university education, Ryland was an original. But his *Plan of Education* (1792) showed that 'the substance and spirit of the Christian religion'[26] was the real material of his 'truly liberal education', and, as his main aim was to win pupils for Christ, he obviously found it necessary to compete with other local academies by offering twelve to twenty-year-old students a means of livelihood as well as a disciplined, religious environment. It is likely, therefore, that his materials and methods in mathematics and science teaching were similar to those used in other local academies, and particularly Doddridge's Academy.

In time, such institutions as Doddridge's and Ryland's Academies came to be regarded as precursors of modern universities. In eighteenth-century Northamptonshire they influenced, and were influenced by, the work of other local schools, and their closure in the last decade of the century marked the end of an important period in the educational history of the county.

Societies, Lectures and Exhibitions
Since Northampton was the intellectual centre of the county, it is not surprising to find that the real interest in mathematics and science education was most apparent in that town. During the 1740s, which was the period when Doddridge's Academy and several other smaller academies were growing in popularity, a Philosophical Society was established in the borough. There had previously been Gentlemen's Societies in Spalding, Peterborough and Stamford which were concerned with aspects of scientific work and which attracted a number of local gentlemen, but the Northampton society seems to have been more influential. It started as a meeting of five members: S. Paxton, G. Paxton, — Poole, B. Goodman and H. Woolley, writing master and first secretary to the Infirmary.[27] They were later joined by Sir Thomas Samwell of Upton, MP for Coventry, Joseph Jekys, Lord of the Manor of Dallington and Infirmary treasurer, Dr Philip Doddridge, the Academy proprietor, and his usher, Samuel Clarke, and a James Ferguson, possibly the lecturer referred to later.[28] The society attracted a number of gentlemen from town and country, including several medical men connected with the Infirmary, which had itself been founded in 1743. Little is known about the members of the society, but there is evidence of their interest in science, and the philosophical lectures which were held in Northampton during this period grew from their work. The society kept barometer readings and a rainfall chart; in 1743 Mr Poole gave a lecture on comets, and in 1744 Philip

Doddridge delivered two papers to the society entitled 'The Doctrine of Pendulums' and 'The Laws of Communication of Motion, as well in elastic as in non-elastic bodies'. At about this time some of Doddridge's students at the Academy were deeply engaged in a course of experimental philosophy so they too would have been interested in the meetings of the society.[29] Also, it is likely that a number of the highly-educated, local friends of Doddridge were connected with the society, notably James Stonehouse[30] and Mark Akenside of the Infirmary;[31] James Harvey, the devotional writer from Weston Favell;[32] and Richard Grey, vicar and schoolmaster of Hinton and author of *Memoria Technica*.[33]

Another interesting figure, of humbler and more obscure origin, was William Shipley, drawing master in Northampton until 1750, when he went to London to establish his own academy.[34] It was Shipley who germinated the idea of a 'Society for the Promotion of the Arts' to encourage arts, useful inventions and discoveries by offering rewards and honours, and to do the work not already covered by the Royal Society. A practical experiment of the type encouraged by Shipley was being tried out in Northampton during the period when the Philosophical Society was growing. This was the venture in cotton-spinning, financed by Edward Cave, who was a patron of the Infirmary and founder-editor of the *Gentleman's Magazine*.[35] The carding and roller-spinning machinery used by Cave was an invention of Lewis Paul. Though the Northampton venture failed, Arkwright patented an identical principle in 1769.

The growing interest in science was partly practical, in response to the changing needs of industry and agriculture, and partly a fashionable hobby. Anyone interested in improving his basic skills, or in studying mathematics and science to assist his career in commerce could attend one of the evening classes organised in the main towns by specialist private teachers. But the more general demand for scientific knowledge was met by a class of itinerant lectures, and their courses in natural philosophy were very popular with middle-class audiences, including many ladies.

The *Northampton Mercury* provides detailed evidence of local lectures designed to attract sizeable audiences. Visitors to the town included two of the most important lecturers in experimental philosophy in England, John Warltire and James Ferguson. Warltire, who published details of his course of lectures in experimental philosophy,[36] spent much of his time working in the Midlands. He made his reputation as a chemist and spent many years working with Darwin on experiments with air, and with Priestley on experiments with water.[37] He also gave private chemical lectures to Robert Darwin and the sons of Josiah Wedgwood.[38] Warltire's lecture tours in Northamptonshire, which included visits to Northampton, Daventry and Towcester in 1763, and Northampton, Kettering and Wellingborough in 1799, seem to have occurred before and after his period of residence in the west Midlands.[39] It is likely that he had not established a reputation when he first visited Northampton, for he charged only moderate fees and, although he did produce some experiments to show the properties of air, his main concern was with astronomy, which was a particularly popular subject at this time. The *Northampton Mercury* advertisement for his visit in 1763 describes a course similar to the one detailed in his published *Analysis*.[40]

One year after Warltire's first visit, James Ferguson hired 'a very large room' at the 'Red Lion', Northampton, for his course in experimental philosophy. Ferguson, who was self-educated, came to England from Banffshire in 1740, and won distinction as an instrument-maker and teacher. His lectures were both popular and profitable and he received gifts from many distinguished people, including George III, whom he visited often.[41] His advertisement for a course of lectures which appeared in the *Northampton Mercury* in 1764, is reproduced on page 149.

The other lecturers who worked in Northamptonshire were less prominent than Warltire and Ferguson.[42] Adam Walker, another autodidact, who came from Yorkshire, made two visits. After teaching at Ledsham and Macclesfield Schools, Walker set up his own establishment in Manchester, where he met Priestley, who encouraged him to go to London in 1778. He took a house in Hanover Square, but travelled to many towns in Great Britain and was engaged to lecture

EXPERIMENTAL PHILOSOPHY.

On Monday *the* 3*d of* September, *at Four o'Clock in the Afternoon, in a very large Room at the* Red-Lyon *in* NORTHAMPTON,

MR. FERGUSON, F.R.S. will begin a Course of twelve PHILOSOPHICAL LECTURES; in which the following useful and interesting Subjects will be explained, and experimentally demonstrated by a great Variety of simple Machines and compound Engines, *viz.* The Mechanical Powers, the most advantageous Construction of Pyrometers, Cranes, Wheel-Carriages, Water-Mills, Wind-Mills, and Pile-driving Engines. The Laws of Fluids, the Construction of various Kinds of Pumps and other Hydraulic Machines. The Method of finding the specific Gravities of Bodies, and detecting counterfeit Metals. The Structure of the Air-Pump, and its Use in shewing a great Variety of capital Experiments relating to the Pressure, Spring, and other Properties of the Air. The Use of the GLOBES, and the Art of Dialling. The apparent Motions of the Heavens by a curious Armillary Sphere. The Laws by which the Planets move, and are retained in their Orbits, the annual and diurnal Motions of the Earth, and the Doctrine of the Tides, demonstrated by Means of a Machine called the *Whirling-Table.* The diurnal and annual Motions of the Planets, the different Seasons, the Motions and Phases of the Moon, the Harvest-Moon, the Causes, Times and Phænomena of Eclipses shewn by the ORRERY, and the Motion of the Comets by the *Cometarium.*

In this Course every Thing will be explained and demonstrated in such a plain, easy and familiar Manner, as may be understood by those who have neither seen or read any Thing of the like Nature before, if the Subscribers will but look and be attentive.

The Subscription is One Guinea, to be paid at the first Lecture; and the Subscribers are then to appoint the most convenient Hours for their daily Attendance afterwards.

Advertisement for James Ferguson's Philosophical Lectures, 1764

See Harding, 'Mathematics and Science Education', pp 139–59

PHILOSOPHY.

MR. PITT, LECTURER on NATURAL and EXPERIMENTAL PHILOSOPHY, most respectfully begs Leave to inform the Lovers and Encouragers of Science, That he purposes to begin his COURSE of LECTURES, on Monday, October the 29th, at Half past Six o'Clock in the Evening, at the BLACK BOY INN, NORTHAMPTON.

The Course consists of all the most Curious and useful new and entertaining Parts of PHILOSOPHY, which will be delivered in eight or twelve Lectures, on the following Subjects; viz. ELECTRICITY, MECHANICS, ASTRONOMY, HYDRASTICS, HYDRAULICS, MAGNETISM, OPTICS, PNEUMATICS, AEROLOGY, and CHEMISTRY. These Lectures are illustrated by an extensive Apparatus which has been greatly improved since his last Visit in 1785.

The Design of this Course is to show how the natural Strength may be assisted by Art, and how to construct Machines for that Purpose; to explain the wonderful Properties of Matter in Earth, Air, Fire, and Water; and to investigate those Laws, by which the ALMIGHTY regulates, governs, and continues all the Celestial Motions; to account for the general Appearances resulting therefrom, and, in short, to make Mankind wiser and better. And as the Knowledge of Nature tends to enlarge the human Mind, and give us more noble and exalted Ideas of the God of Nature, it is presumed this Course will meet with Encouragement.

⁎ Subscribers to pay 10s. 6d. for a Course of Eight Lectures, or 15s. for Twelve Lectures, as they follow in the Syllabus, which may be had (gratis,) at the Lecture Room.

A single Lecture, Two Shillings.

Mr Pitt's advertisement, 1792

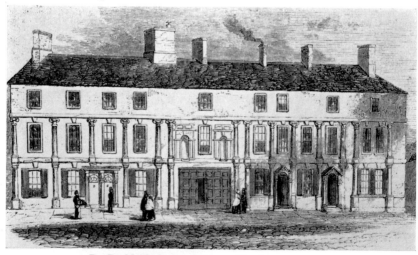

Dr Doddridge's Academy at Northampton, 1751

See Harding, 'Mathematics and Science Education', pp 139–59

This Day, *and the following Days of the Week*, *at Three o'Clock in the Afternoon, will be shewn, at the Vicarage-House in Gold-ftreet*, North-ampton, *at Half a Crown a-piece*,

By the ORRERY,

THE Motions of the Planets in general; their Srations and Retrogradations; the Annual and Diurnal Motion of the Earth; and the Increafe and Decreafe of Days and Nights; the Phafes of the Moon, and her Motion in her Orbit; and the Eclipfes of the Sun and Moon.

Experiments relating to Electrical Attraction and Repulfion; particularly, the Face and Hands of a Boy, fufpended horizontally by Cords, attracting and repelling light Bodies, and Sparks of Fire darting out of every Part of his Face and Hands with a fnapping Noife, by only rubbing a Glafs Tube at his Feet.

Advertisement for a demonstration of the Orrery, 1736

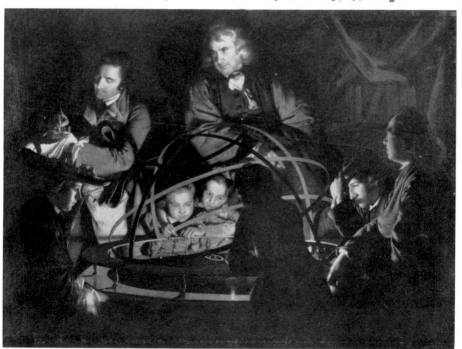

A philosopher giving a lecture on the Orrery, c 1763 (from a painting by J. Wright in Derby Art Gallery, by courtesy of the Courtauld Institute of Art)

See Harding, 'Mathematics and Science Education', pp 139–59

Sidney Webb (courtesy of National Portrait Gallery)

Beatrice Webb (courtesy of National Portrait Gallery)

See Brennan, 'Educational Engineering with the Webbs',

at Eton, Winchester and Westminster Schools.[43] In 1783, Walker advertised a course of twelve lectures in Northampton, costing one guinea, and delivered on three weekdays.[44] He claimed to use the finest collection of apparatus in Britain at that time, much of which had been inherited from a Mr Griffith. Perhaps this was the 'Mr Griffis' who lectured at the 'Hind' in Northampton in 1754.[45]

The exact subject matter expounded by the lecturers under the heading of experimental philosophy varied. Not all the advertisements described their work fully, but three are of interest: Archibald Spens on mechanics, hydrostatics, pneumatics and optics;[46] James Ferguson on mechanical powers, the laws of fluids, specific gravity, properties of the air, globes and astronomy;[47] and a Mr Pitt on electricity, mechanics, astronomy, hydrostatics, magnetism, pneumatics, optics and chemistry.[48] Pitt was particularly proud of his extensive apparatus, which he sometimes detailed in advertisements (see page 150). It is not surprising that the elaborate experiments promised by some of the lecturers necessitated the use of large rooms, and that this is why the 'Red Lion' and 'Black Boy', both major urban inns, were commonly used in Northampton.

Most of the lecturers who visited Northampton offered instruction in experimental philosophy, but there were a few exceptions. The first two courses mentioned in the *Northampton Mercury* were concerned with anatomy, and are likely to have been of professional rather than general interest. In 1722 Martin Warren, a native of Northamptonshire and Fellow of Emmanuel College, lectured with G. Warren, a Cambridge surgeon, and, three years later, John Murray conducted a course in humane and comparative anatomy.[49] In contrast, a number of more spectacular lectures were designed to attract large audiences, such as the one which featured the horizontal suspension of a boy to illustrate electrical attraction and repulsion. Then, there was the lecture by Mr George Alexander described as 'A Lecture on Heads'; and the astonishing performances of Dr Graham, in 1790.[50] The latter's subject was 'Health, Long Life and Happiness', and was described as a short oration on 'The Influence of Female Beauty and Virtue over the Hearts and Fortunes of Men'. James Graham, who was a famous quack doctor, invited people with diseases that had baffled medical skill to apply to him. The newspaper reported that 'the Doctor's eccentricities are very numerous and singular' and, indeed, his visit to Northampton occurred at a time when many people were beginning to consider him insane.[51] No doubt he attracted huge audiences.

The real value of the lecture system, which Dr Kelly has described as 'the remote ancestry of University Extension teaching',[52] was that it enabled scientific knowledge to become more widespread. The same can be said of public exhibitions which were of great interest in Northampton. In 1773 a Grand Philosophical and Mathematical Exhibition was held in the Great Room of the 'Saracen's Head' and 'met with such universal applause' that the organisers were encouraged to plan different performances each night for a week.[53] A few exhibitions were brought from London,[54] but it is rather difficult to judge their quality as advertisements suggest that some were designed for popular entertainment rather than education.

Mathematicians

A more reliable indication of the growth of scientific inquiry in the eighteenth century was the work of individual mathematicians. During this period a number of Northamptonshire contributors began to make a significant impact in the *Ladies Diary*, a publication described in the *Gentleman's Magazine* as 'that small but valuable publication in which almost every English mathematician who has arrived at any degree of eminence for the last half century has contended for fame at one time of his life or other'.[55] The two most prominent Northamptonshire contributors were Thomas Cowper of Wellingborough and John Landen of Peakirk near Peterborough.

Cowper was regarded by Benjamin Martin as among the first practical astronomers of his time, but he had to direct his energies to many different aspects of science in order to make a living. He was a member of a fairly affluent Quaker family, but, as Thomas would not apply his energies to his father's business of serge-maker and wool-comber, and persisted in reading when he should have been working, the father left his property to a brother. To support himself, Cowper became a teacher of arithmetic, navigation, surveying, dialling, gauging, algebra and fluxions; but he later gave up tutoring to become a land surveyor. His scientific achievements were considerable. In astronomy, optics and mathematics he was eminent. He corresponded with several important people and, in 1760, Benjamin Martin wrote to offer Cowper the opportunity 'to go to Bencoolin to observe the transit of Venus. . . . Such an undertaking will render your name memorable to all posterity. Your being a good mathematician induced me to think of you as a very proper person.' Cowper did not accept the invitation though it was sponsored by the Royal Society, but he wrote regularly to Green, the astronomer who did go to the South Seas to observe Venus.

In addition to Green, the astronomer, and Martin, the mathematician, Cowper included among his friends Captain Heath of Upnor Castle, a celebrated astronomical calculator, and Thomas White of Corby. Much of Cowper's time was taken up as a land surveyor in Oxfordshire and Huntingdonshire and in connection with the Wellingborough enclosure. Nevertheless, he managed to make regular contributions to the *Ladies Diary* between 1743 and 1753, and to produce astronomical calculations for a periodical known as *The Palladium* in 1773. From a local point of view, one of his most interesting exercises was a question he set, which required the calculation of distances from a cottage in Wellingborough to the visible steeples of Irchester, Rushden and Higham Ferrers.[56]

During the period when Thomas Simpson was editor of the *Ladies Diary*, his friend John Landen of Peterborough was regarded as 'a very respectable contributor' and 'undoubtedly one of the greatest Mathematicians that this or any other kingdom has produced'.[57] Landen, like Cowper, worked as a surveyor, making mathematical calculations in his leisure time: 'Had it been otherwise, it seems highly probable he would have extended his researches in Mathematics to which he was most enthusiastically devoted, much further than any other person has done'.[58] Fifteen important pieces of work by Landen were published during the second half of the century, including *The*

Residual Analysis, Mathematical Memoirs and several contributions to
Philosophical Transactions.[59] Although Landen was highly respected
for his work, he lived a retiring life, earning his living as land agent
to Earl Fitzwilliam from 1762 to 1788, and spending his spare time in
study and in attending the Gentlemen's Societies.[60] Possibly he did
some teaching, for another contributor to the *Ladies Diary* was Peter
Walton, described as 'Descip. Landenii'. In addition to his work for
the *Diary*, Landen communicated his findings on calculus to the Royal
Society. From 1754 the results (given in *Residual Analysis*, 1764) were
presented by Thomas Simpson; then, in 1766, Landen was elected as
a Fellow. He then proceeded to produce a theorem, known by his
name, for expressing a hyperbolic arc in terms of two elliptic arcs.
Also of particular interest were his explanations of Newton's errors
in calculating the effects of precession, and Stewart's in computing the
sun's distance from the earth. His results for experiments in rotary
motion (a subject which proved too difficult and laborious for most
mathematicians), were different to those of Euler and D'Alembert; and
he was still trying to explain them during his final illness.

John Hellins, another of the contributors to the *Ladies Diary*, was
not a native of Northamptonshire (as Cowper and Landen were) but
he did some interesting mathematical work while in the county. The
son of a Devonshire labourer, he was apprenticed as a cooper until he
was nearly twenty, but taught himself mathematics and became a
schoolmaster at Bishop's Tawton in Devon: 'he was one of those
extraordinary men, who, deprived of early advantages, have elevated
themselves by force of genious and of industry to a level above most
persons blessed with a regular education'.[61] At Bishop's Tawton,
Hellins became friendly with the notable mathematician Malachy
Hitchins, who encouraged him to take an appointment at the Royal
Observatory. Whilst so employed, he qualified for Holy Orders, and
in 1783, owing to the patronage of Henry, Earl of Bathurst, he was
appointed curate of Green's Norton in Northamptonshire and vicar
of Potterspury in 1790. Although Hellins was a devoted parish priest,
his most distinguished work was in science and mathematics. In 1796
he became a Fellow of the Royal Society, and by that time had made

many contributions to periodical publications and issued several books of his own.[62] His mathematical ability was so widely known that, when Wyndham was preparing his new military system in 1806, Hellins finished all the calculations.

None of the other contributors to the *Ladies Diary*[63] appear to have enjoyed the status of Cowper, Landen and Hellins, but their presence in the county, together with that of many lesser mathematicians, was obviously an important feature in the life of the local community.

Conclusion

The existence of interesting scientific and mathematical work in eighteenth-century Northamptonshire appears to have resulted from three important factors. Firstly, it is clear that these subjects were becoming more accessible and relevant to a larger number of people; secondly, it would appear that the greatest impetus came from the towns, particularly Northampton; and, thirdly, there were the contributions of scholars and teachers either made privately or through academies, societies and public lectures. These interrelated factors indicate that Northamptonshire offered a favourable environment for the growth of modern scientific and mathematical ideas. This was in turn probably due to the size, stability and comparative prosperity of the county, to its easy contacts with London and to the considerable influence of the Dissenters.

Technical High School for Girls, Longport, Canterbury

References

1　A. Everitt, *Changes in the Provinces in the Seventeenth Century* (Leicester, 1969), 24.
2　N. Hans, *New Trends in Education in the Eighteenth Century* (1951), 6.
3　*Northampton Mercury*, 11 September 1721.
4　Ibid, 2 March 1747.　　　　　5　Ibid, 9 November 1772.
6　Ibid, 21 February 1774.　　　7　Ibid, 27 May 1776.
8　Ibid, 22 March 1762.　　　　9　Ibid, 5 July 1794.
10　Ibid, 28 January 1736.　　　11　Ibid, 13 October 1755.
12　Ibid, 1 Feb 1762; 22 Mar 1762; 7 Feb 1780; 29 Apl 1786 and Poll Book, 1774.
13　Mathematics teachers: Caleb Ashworth, Thomas Belsham, William Broadbent, Timothy Kenrick, Benjamin Shelton, Titus Wadsworth (Daventry); Thomas

Cornfield (Guilsborough); William Butlin, Thomas Cross, Philip Doddridge, Thomas Hague, Thomas Harris, John Lacy, John Noble, John Collett Ryland (Northampton); Thomas Dix (Oundle); John Landen (Peterborough); John Hellins (Potterspury); Edward Laurence (Stamford Baron); John Hill (Welford); Thomas Cowper (Wellingborough); William Gray (Whittlebury); John Malham (residence unknown).

14   J. Orton, *Memoirs of Philip Doddridge DD* (1824), 165. The Coward Trustees had a copy of Doddridge's algebra manuscript.
15   J. D. Humphreys, *The Correspondence and Diary of Philip Doddridge* (1829), III 109.
16   H. McLachlan, *English Education under the Test Acts* (Manchester, 1931), 173.
17   Ibid, 147.   18   *DNB*, L, 56.
19   J. Culross, *The Three Rylands* (1897), 40.
20   At College Street Chapel, Northampton.
21   J. Ryland, *An Address to the Ingenuous Youth of Great Britain* (1792), 124.
22   J. Culross, *The Three Rylands* (1897), 124.
23   Ibid, 125.   24   Ibid, 126–7.
25   *An Easy Introduction to Mechanics, Geometry, Plane Trigonometry, measuring heights and distances, optics, astronomy; to which is prefixed, an Essay on the advancement of learning by various modes of revelation* (1768).
26   J. Ryland, *Address* (1792), 108.
27   S. Paxton—possibly Samuel (Deed in NRO 1768, YZ 4718);—Poole—possibly Edward who was at Peterborough 1725, or Robert, medical and theological writer (*DNB*). G. Paxton and B. Goodman not traced.
28   W. Whellan, *History, Gazeteer and Directory of Northamptonshire* (1849).
29   J. D. Humphreys, *The Correspondence and Diary of Philip Doddridge* (1829), 404, 516.
30   *DNB*, LIV, 417.   31   *DNB*, I, 208.   32   *DNB*, XXVI, 282.
33   *DNB* XXIII, 200 and J. Nichols, *Anecdotes of the Eighteenth Century* (1812), I, 425.
34   *DNB*, LII, 112.
35   *Victoria County History* II, 334.
36   J. Warltire, *Analysis of a Course of Lectures in Experimental Philosophy* (1769).
37   In his paper on experiments on mechanical expansion of air, 1788, Darwin described experiments made with the help of Warltire. Priestley and Warltire worked on experiments which, in Cavendish's hands, led to discovery of the composition of water (see R. Schofield, *The Lunar Society of Birmingham*, Oxford, 1962, 185–8).
38   Ibid.
39   *Birmingham Life* I, 246. R. Schofield, 185–7, 199, 268.
40   *Northampton Mercury*, 10 October 1763.
41   *DNB*, XVIII, 343.
42   Courses in experimental philosophy were given by Archibald Spens 1736; Mr Griffis 1754; John Warltire 1763 and 1799; James Ferguson 1764; Mr Pitt 1778, 1785 (and sons), 1792; Mr Walker 1783 and 1796.
43   *DNB*, LIX, 42.
44   *Northampton Mercury*, 13 October 1783.
45   Ibid, 6 January 1754.   46   Ibid, 4 October 1736.
47   Ibid, 7 September 1764.   48   Ibid, 17 April 1778.
49   Ibid, 1 October 1722 and 8 November 1725.
50   *Northampton Mercury*, 4 November 1765, 2 December 1771, 30 October 1790, 6 November 1790.

51 *DNB*, XXII, 323.
52 T. Kelly, *A History of Adult Education in Great Britain* (Liverpool, 1962), 101.
53 *Northampton Mercury*, 19 August 1773.   54 Ibid, 17 June 1795.
55 *Gentleman's Magazine*, March 1790.
56 J. Cole, *The History and Antiquities of Wellingborough* (Wellingborough, 1837), 268–70.
57 *Gentleman's Magazine*, March 1790.   58 Ibid.
59 Publications of John Landen:
    1754 *Philosophical Transactions*, vol 48, 'An Investigation of some theorems, which suggest several very remarkable properties of the circle'.
    1755 *Mathematical Lubrications*.
    1758 *A Discourse on the Residual Analysis.*
    1760 *Philosophical Transactions*, vol 51, 'A new method of computing the sums of a greater number of infinite series'.
    1764 *The Residual Analysis.*
    1768 *Philosophical Transactions*, vol 58, 'Specimen of a new method of comparing curvilineal areas'.
    1770 *Philosophical Transactions*, vol 60, 'Some new theorems for computing the whole areas of curve lines'.
    1771 *Philosophical Transactions*, vol 61, 'Theorems for computing fluents'.
    1775 *Philosophical Transactions*, vol 65, 'Theorems for finding the length of any arc of a conic hyperbola'.
    1777 *Philosophical Transactions*, vol 67, 'A new theory of the motion of bodies revolving about an axis in free space'.
    1780 *Mathematical Memoirs*, vol I.
    1781–3 *Tracts on the summation of converging series.*
    1785 *Philosophical Transactions*, vol 75, 'Solution to experiments on rotary motion'.
    1790 *Mathematical Memoirs*, vol II.
60 *DNB*, XXXII, 48.
61 G. Baker, *History of Northamptonshire*, II, 222.
62 Publications of John Hellins:
    1787 *The Young Algebraist's Companion.*
    1788 *Mathematical Essays on Several Subjects.*
    1776–95 Contribution to the *Ladies Diary.*
    1795–1814 Contributions to the *British Critic.*
    1780 onwards, nine papers in *Philosophical Transactions.*
    1791 Two tracts in Masere's *Scriptores Logarithmetici.*
63 Contributors to the *Ladies Diary*:
    1743–53 Thomas Cowper of Wellingborough.
    1748–67 John Landen of Peterborough.
    1750–73 Stephen Hodges of Wellingborough and Althorpe.
    1758–9 Peter Walton.
    1761–2 Thomas Harris of Bugbrooke.
    1776–95 John Hellins of Greens Norton and Potterspury.
    1792–3 Newton Bosworth of Peterborough.
    1798–1800 John Hawkes of Finedon.
    1800 and after, Thomas Kirkton of Peterborough.

For plates, provided by the author, see pp 149–51

ANTHONY BISHOP and
WILFRED JONES

The Act that never was: the Conservative Education Bill of 1868

A CYNICAL and frivolous piece of political window-dressing or a serious and important attempt at educational reform? Marlborough's 'saccharine scheme'[1] or a great opportunity missed? What should be the historian's verdict on the education bill prepared by the Third Derby Administration and presented to parliament in March 1868?[2] To offer an answer to this question it is necessary to ask several others: What was the measure designed to achieve? Why was it introduced? How much work went into its preparation? Why did it fail?

During the 1860s among the principal issues of an educational nature that attracted parliamentary attention were the problem of ministerial responsibility for educational policy; the fragmentation of the various central authorities for education; the provision of rate aid for education and the closely allied matter of local education authorities; and the providing for the needs of the 'neglected districts'—those 11,000 or more parishes which derived no assistance, in the form of education grants, from the Exchequer.

Attempts to deal with each of these questions were made—mostly by private members—with depressing frequency throughout the fifties and sixties, but without any tangible, or at least satisfactory, result. Then, quite suddenly, the Derby cabinet in 1867 decided to introduce legislation that, in the context of the times, was little short of revolutionary. The main, though by no means the only, purpose of the proposed measure was to unify the central authority for English education, to enhance its status and to assign to it a more constructive role. In choosing this aspect of educational reform as its priority for treatment, the Tory government showed realism as well as prudence. A good case could be made for claiming that just then the central administration of education was in more urgent need of improvement than was the local; and such a proposition certainly appeared to present fewer difficulties so far as its passage through parliament was concerned.

The defects of the central authority for education at that time were many and varied. In the first place no single unified authority existed; instead there were no fewer than three major and four minor authorities. On the one hand there was the Education Department, which administered the elementary code; the Science and Art Department, which provided grants for technical instruction; and the Charity Commission, which with the Court of Chancery exercised some jurisdiction—deficient though it was—over the endowed schools. On the other hand, there were the War Office, the Admiralty, the Home Office and the Poor Law Board which were responsible respectively for the army and navy schools, the reformatories, and the pauper schools.

In the second place the political control of publicly-provided education was divided, inadequate and otherwise unsatisfactory. As the result of a decision made in 1839 whereby the superintendence of the education grant had been placed with a Committee of the Privy Council, the Lord President (as chairman of all such committees) found himself the *de jure* minister of education, although he was not so entitled; as the result of a statute passed in 1856, a Vice-President of that same committee was created with the object of enabling the government to provide the Commons—to the supposed mutual benefit of both parties—with an educational representative. As a result of both actions there arose the greatest confusion and ambiguity over ministerial responsibility. But the incongruities did not end there, for since the Charity Commission was an extra-parliamentary and virtually autonomous body, it lacked adequate representation in, and was subject to no effective control by, either House. Worse still, it was the custom of successive administrations to place the supervision of any new public service in the hands of either the Privy Council or the Home Office, with the consequence that the Lord President found that his duties ranged over a very wide area—from keeping a watching brief over the affairs of the Channel Islands to the issuing of charters to companies and corporations, while the Vice-President was compelled to devote much of his attention to such extraneous matters as dealing with outbreaks of cholera and with the payment of cattle inspectors. Most disturbing of all, the Education Department's policy-making power, not merely its day-to-day administration, had come to reside more and more in the person of the permanent secretary, a trend which by the mid-1860s had occasioned alarm among members of both Houses and both parties. By that time the dangers that might arise from placing public education in the hands of politicians were felt by many to be less serious than those that had already arisen as a result of leaving it in the hands of irresponsible officials. Furthermore, the office of Lord President was such that it could safely be disposed of to inoffensive and ineffectual noblemen who might be relied on not to show too much interest in (far less enthusiasm for) educational matters, and the office of Vice-President was such that few politicians with imagination, talent or even ambition were prepared to accept it.

In the third place, the direct, as distinct from the derived, powers of these ministers were limited in the extreme. Largely in order to make the proposal to establish a central authority for education less unpalatable, Lansdowne, the then Lord President, had insisted that the functions of the Committee of Council should be confined to the superintendence of the application of parliamentary grants for the education of the poor. This meant that the minister had no *statutory* powers of initiation. He could, and did, introduce new grant regulations, but he was not under any legal obligation—nor even empowered —to *promote* the education of the people.

Thus there was considerable room for improvement so far as the executive element in the educational service was concerned, and over the years politicians of varying stature and differing persuasions had come to recognise the fact; some, indeed, argued that the improvement of the country's educational system was dependent upon it. By 1867 Earl Russell felt so strongly about the lack of unity and control at the centre that, in December of that year, he called on the Lords to support a resolution on the subject. He moved 'That the appointment of a Minister of Education by the Crown, with a seat in the Cabinet, would in the opinion of the House, be conducive to the public benefit'. In commending this motion to his fellow peers, Russell thought that it would be admitted that:

> there should be in this, as in other countries, a Minister of Education, who would be capable of taking into consideration all affairs relating to education, and whose whole attention should be devoted to the furtherance and improvement of our educational system.[3]

Replying for the government, the Duke of Marlborough, the Lord President, opposed Russell's resolution on two main grounds. He had, he said, very great objections to the appointment of a Minister of Education both because the universities would in some measure be accountable to such a politician, and because, if past experience were anything to go by, a development on these lines would create more problems than it solved.[4] This was a reference to the unsuccessful attempt, made after the 1856 measure, to promote greater unity in educational administration through the agency of HM Inspectorate.

Marlborough's audience could not have known that at the very moment he was inviting them to reject Russell's proposals he was preparing legislation designed to carry them into effect. The reason for this inconsistency (to put no finer point on it) is not altogether clear, though there is more than a suspicion that it may have formed part of the Tories' predilection for 'dishing the Whigs' by stealing their policies.

Whatever the explanation, Marlborough and his colleague, Lord Robert Montagu, the then Vice-President, had, by the date the debate took place (2 December 1867), already sought the advice of their senior civil servants on possible changes in educational administration, and Montagu had even submitted to the Lord President detailed plans for reorganising the central authority.

The most interesting of the official documents was that written by Henry Cole, the influential secretary of the Science and Art Department. Asked to supply the Vice-President with a 'few notes on Public Education' he summarised the general principles upon which its administration should, in his view, be based:

I consider that elementary education, secondary or technical instruction, the management of public libraries, galleries and museums and all the votes for education, science and art, should be concentrated in the administration of them, so far as the expenditure of public funds is concerned, under the sole authority of the same minister of the crown.

This Minister of Public Instruction ought not, I think, to be the Lord President of the Council. The work is ample enough to engage the sole attention of a minister who, I venture to say, ought to rank as a Secretary of State. He would sit in either House, according to the circumstances of the Cabinet. There should be an under-secretary also in Parliament.

In my opinion, the present work at the Privy Council office, with all the calls for charters, health, cattle plague, quarantine, &c. made upon the attention of the Lord President, makes it impossible for that high functionary to devote sufficient time to numerous questions involved in public instruction, viewed comprehensively.

To enlarge elementary education, making it truly national, to reform educational charities, to increase technical instruction throughout the United Kingdom, to reorganise the British Museum, the National Gallery, the National Portrait Gallery &c., so as to make them work efficiently and harmoniously together, are functions which ought not, I conceive, to be treated as of secondary importance to any others.[5]

Equally condemnatory of the existing system and equally radical in his proposals for improving it was Montagu himself. In a memorandum on the constitution of the Education Department, dated 28 November 1867, he concentrated his criticisms on the three features that he, in company with others, found most disturbing. The Committee of Council, he pointed out, possessed no control over the administration of educational endowments, and this control, as the Newcastle Commission had been at pains to emphasise, was 'the first object for consideration in any practical and comprehensive educational scheme'. Secondly, the Committee was ill-fitted to discharge even its current responsibilities; far less was it capable of supplying those deficiencies in educational provision that were generally acknowledged to exist. Finally, he drew attention to the unsatisfactory nature of the political control exercised over the Education Department. From the draft Report of the Select Committee on Education which had appeared the previous year, he quoted the remark that 'the agency of the Committee in the ordinary business of the Education Department, whether administrative or legislative, is anomalous and unnecessary'. He felt that the time had come to replace it by a different kind of executive authority.

Montagu then proposed the establishment of 'a permanent Board or Council of Education to act under and subject to the complete control of the Lord President', and he supplied an extensive list of arguments in support of such a scheme. He contended that it is 'manifestly for the benefit of the general public that all charity business should be conducted in and by one Department'; that, given the existing state of endowment legislation, it seemed hardly possible to effect any beneficial change in the law as it applied to public education until the statutory powers of the Charity Commissioners had been extended and redefined; that the proposed change would render the council the central and only department for all educational purposes and that it could be utilised to give the Council of Education increased responsibility in the opinion of the public; that it presented the only means by which to afford the Lord President the assistance and co-operation of a strong working board for all ordinary business; that it would provide a remedy for the present evils of divided responsibility; and that it would lend additional weight to a department of state over which it had been stated a cabinet minister should preside.

There followed a detailed set of recommendations designed to give substance to the main proposal. The plan was to convert the Charity Commission into a Department of the Privy Council and to reconstitute the Committee of Council on Education as a Committee of Council on Education and Charities. For the purpose of carrying into effect the necessary legislation, a council or board would be established composed of five administrative officers responsible to the Lord President. In the first instance the membership would consist of the three serving Charity Commissioners, Ralph Lingen, the secretary of the Education Department, and Henry Cole, who would 'take the Science and Art Department and Technical Education'. The Vice-President of the Committee of Council would also become a member of such a board or council, and enjoy the power to vote.[6]

Montagu concluded his memorandum by observing that such proposals would 'tend to render a comprehensive Government Bill complete, and perhaps popular'; and he warned that they were not capable of being treated separately. 'Any Bill short of being comprehensive will only appear to be an effort to "prop" up a bad system. There is no use in increasing either the number of schools, teachers or school children, while the central authority is known to be unable to control them.'[7]

Advised then as to the principal defects of the English educational system—the lack of a unified and dynamic central authority; the failure to supply the needs of the neglected districts; the inadequacy of the provision made for the efficient administration and wise application of educational endowments—and briefed as to the most suitable means of rectifying them, the Duke of Marlborough, as Lord President, prepared the necessary legislation. In this he was aided by Lord Derby, the Prime Minister, who as early as 1856 had been converted to the desirability of appointing a single responsible minister of education.

The Conservative plan was hammered out in cabinet and some idea of the discussions which arose can be gained from the letters which passed between Derby, Disraeli (then Chancellor of the Exchequer), Lord Stanley (Foreign Secretary) and the Queen.[8] Disraeli informed Stanley in January 1868 that Marlborough had unfolded his scheme to him. The Chancellor thought it large, almost complete, yet moderate and prudent. It would, he conjectured, require frequent cabinets and minute discussion. He told Derby that any forced decisions at that moment on such controversial issues as conscience clauses, rating and boards of management might break up the cabinet; the latter had, however, decided unanimously that legislation was necessary, that it should be preliminary yet not insignificant, and that an education minister was needed whose duties should be very large and no longer confined to the revised code. Such a minister should deal with elementary and pauper education, endowments, the Science and Art Department, and Irish education. If the bill were to include less than this it would not 'satisfy the present temper of Parliament and the country'. On 4 February Disraeli wrote to the Queen (who had evidently shown some interest in the matter) repeating that the cabinet were unanimous regarding the education bill. Two days later, in a letter to the Prime Minister, he expressed the view that the bill might be regarded as a strictly preparatory measure, the government keeping the 'great question' for the next parliament. It would need to be introduced into the Lords ('we want education discussed by Dukes and Bishops') and it would, in any event, 'have a beneficial effect on all'.

Marlborough presented his measure in the Upper House on 24 March 1868. Its full title was 'An Act to regulate the Distribution of Sums granted by Parliament for Elementary Education in England and Wales; and for other purposes'. In his speech on the first reading he outlined the Conservative thinking which had led up to the bill.[9] The government, he said, hoped that the hatchet of discord over elementary education would be buried, and that it wanted to frame a plan which should be the foundation of a national system of education.

As a solution to the problem of the neglected districts and of the shortage of elementary school places generally, Marlborough offered the Tory alternative to rate aid, for some years regarded by many as the panacea to some of the country's educational ills. The Conservatives had consistently opposed rate support on the ground that to finance schools in this way would be to place the control of education in the hands of ratepayers who, it was feared, would weaken Anglican influence. There was apprehension, too, that 'democratic' control would upset the social pattern which Conservatives were anxious to maintain. The Derby administration's proposal was, in the first instance, simply to expand state aid. All bodies, religious or secular, which applied for grants to build new schools, or to enlarge existing ones and to maintain them, would be accommodated, subject only to safeguards designed to ensure efficiency and to maintain standards. Special assistance would be extended to small, poor schools. The act would also have removed all interference by the state in religious matters and, of equal significance, would have included a conscience clause for application in single-school areas.[10]

Doubtless the government believed that, once it had freed exchequer aid from religious strings, non-sectarian bodies interested in education would join the national system, claim the grants and build many new schools. The one stipulation was that these must not be run for private gain.[11] More optimistic Conservatives hoped that the act would produce enough elementary schools to supply current needs —working on the assumption that the pupils remained at school for six years. However, if it did not, the responsible minister would be empowered to order an educational census of any area thought to be deficient in elementary education for the poor, and to indicate what measures were required to provide for any well-defined want.[12] Marlborough himself suggested that one such measure might be the application of endowments to the benefit of elementary education.

The necessity of legislating anew upon the problem of educational trusts was emphasised elsewhere in Marlborough's speech. 'We find', he remarked, 'that a most voluminous Report of the Middle Class Endowed Schools Commission has lately been laid upon the table . . . It would be impossible for any Department of the State to take up the matter unless it were specially organised for the purpose, and unless there were persons appointed by the Crown to take this great subject under their cognizance, and to initiate measures on their own responsibility.' This was, in fact, one of the many reasons which had led the government to decide that there was enough work and a sufficiently large field of enterprise to engage the attention of a special department of the state. It was, furthermore, the government's intention to seek approval for the appointment of a sixth Secretary of State who would have 'the whole range of educational matters under his consideration and control'. Such a minister would not only administer the Privy Council grants but also, on his own responsibility, 'look into the various subjects connected with the education of the country and propose to Parliament such schemes as he may think are calculated to promote the cause of national education'. And, because the government felt the great defect of the existing system of education to be that it was not 'initiative', but merely followed in the wake of voluntary efforts, it proposed to create a department which should have the responsibility of originating measures that might be for the benefit of the country and 'to put into the hands of the new minister all those powers which will be necessary to enable him to perform those functions'.[13]

When the bill came up for its second reading on 24 April,[14] Marlborough elaborated on the wide-ranging responsibilities of the additional Secretary of State, since the need for such an office-holder was questioned by several peers. It seemed to be assumed, he explained, that the proposal to create such a minister had reference simply to those duties which were now connected with parliamentary grants and with the administration of education as it was then conducted by the committee of Council. If this were so then he agreed that an appointment of this kind would not be expedient. But when members considered how various and important all the functions of the new Education Department were, he thought that the appointment of a responsible Minister of Education, 'capable of dealing with the subject in a comprehensive spirit, and of framing measures with the view of consolidating and uniting the different branches of primary and secondary education into one great whole, would be likely to be productive of the greatest possible advantage'.[15]

These were bold and imaginative proposals, designed to rectify the principal shortcomings of the nation's educational system virtually at a stroke. But the grand design came to nothing, and the reforms it purposed to achieve were instead introduced piecemeal at intervals over the ensuing hundred years. The central authorities for elementary, technical and secondary education were not combined until 1899; primary and secondary education were not articulated into an integrated system until 1944,[16] and until that date, too, the Minister of Education was not placed in 'control' of education nor given the statutory power and duty to 'promote' it; and he was not accorded the rank and dignity of a Secretary of State, together with what may be assumed to be an accepted right to cabinet membership, until as recently as 1964.

The fate of Marlborough's bill is soon told. On 18 May it was withdrawn,[17] since, owing to a change in the political fortunes of the government, it had no prospect of becoming law that session. In the autumn of 1868 Disraeli, the new Prime Minister, went to the country clearly expecting that the newly-enfranchised urban working class would show their gratitude by returning the Conservatives to office. Instead, the working class showed their independence and brought back the Liberals. But a change of government need not, of itself, have doomed the measure. What really proved fatal to it was not so much the change of administration as the changes in the leadership of the two great parties. At the close of 1867 Russell, now seventy-five, resigned as leader of the Liberals in favour of Gladstone; in the following February Derby, suffering increasingly from ill-health, relinquished the premiership to be succeeded by Disraeli. As a result, the two most influential statesmen who strongly advocated a fundamental reform in the machinery of government so far as education was concerned, and whose support was crucial to its realisation, were replaced by two others whose enthusiasm was never more than lukewarm. Disraeli, in this as in other areas of public policy, was governed as much by expediency as by principle. He quickly saw, or imagined he saw, the political advantage to be gained by advancing such a measure, but once that advantage had been lost he just as swiftly abandoned it. Thus in 1874 when, restored to office, he was in a position to transfer—as envisaged in Marlborough's bill—the administration of educational endowments to the central authority for education, he declined to do so, returning the rehabilitation and reform of the endowed schools instead to that extra-parliamentary body, the Charity Commission. And in the same year he rejected a motion calling for a select committee to consider the question of ministerial responsibility for public education, observing that he personally would be 'sorry to see what is called a Minister of Education established in the country with an entire or with a considerable control over all educational establishments from the primary schools to the august universities'.[18] He had not expressed such sentiments six years before. Gladstone, too, disapproved of a general-purpose education department headed by a cabinet minister, but for different reasons. He objected on principle to the proliferation of government departments and especially to any that proved powerful enough to secure cabinet representation, fearing the adverse effects of such developments upon the efficiency of that body.

Another, though doubtless secondary, factor that sealed the fate of the bill was the publication in December 1867 of the Report of the Schools Inquiry Commission. In considering what might be the most suitable form of central authority for supervising the reform of the endowed schools, it recommended that, in the absence of a Minister of Education, the most appropriate agency would be an autonomous body virtually independent of parliament and beyond direct ministerial control. One of the members of that commission was W. E. Forster, and when he came to legislate for the endowed schools it is not perhaps surprising that he chose the kind of central authority that he had himself advocated, rather than the one which the Conservatives, following the advice of the Newcastle Commission, had favoured. Eventually, the Tory alternative was adopted, but not for another thirty years; and by then it was too late easily to reverse some of the more unfortunate consequences of the earlier decision.

A further possible reason for the abandonment of Marlborough's far-reaching bill was the need to give full attention to the more immediate Public Schools Bill. In 1868 the Conservatives became increasingly alarmed by vigorous assertions in the Commons that public schools' endowments were no different from other educational endowments and should not be dealt with separately to the sole benefit of the upper classes. For this reason the opposition urged that the Public Schools Bill be left to the reformed parliament. The Conservatives did not choose to drop this bill. Anxious to hive off rich endowments to upper-class education, they hurried through the necessary legislation in the short period of office left to them. Marlborough himself declared that delay must be avoided at all costs.[19]

To return to Marlborough's bill, it is in fact possible to argue that it was superior in many ways to both pieces of educational legislation that his effective successor enacted. The creation of a Secretary for Education would not merely have raised the status of the department at a particularly crucial period in the development of the service, it would also have brought order and cohesion to its central control. Elementary, secondary and technical education and probably teacher-training would have been developed side-by-side in accordance with an overall educational policy subject to full parliamentary control. Much of the administrative confusion that until the close of the century bedevilled the system at both the local and national levels would have been avoided; and much of the political inferiority from which the central authority for education continued to suffer for so long could well have ended there and then.

Indeed, so radical, far-sighted and progressive in many respects was the Tory bill that historians may be forgiven for doubting—as many of them do—that it was meant as a genuine attempt at legislation at all. However, Disraeli had endorsed the idea of an education minister as long ago as 1855. The problem of educational expansion was necessarily shelved whilst the ministry grappled with reform but became the government's main social concern in the first post-reform session. Disraeli's initial attitude to Marlborough's plan seems to have been to think in terms of political tactics—'what parliament will take and what will secure the government' (Hardy), but he seems later to have been completely won over by Derby.[20]

If the Conservatives *were* guilty of a frivolous pretence, then they disguised their true intentions remarkably well. The elaborate preparations, the detailed planning, the frequent (and apparently often heated) cabinet discussions, the personal correspondence between ministers and with the Queen, the debates in parliament, all these provide evidence of serious intent. The Liberal (Bruce's) bill was also abandoned so that it would seem that both parties came to realise that an election would have to take place before a popular education measure could be enacted.

In the end, the realisation of the Conservative plan was prevented by ill health, old age and a fickle electorate. This combination consigned the 1868 Education bill to the limbo of forgotten but noble failures. But for this the name of Marlborough might have been associated with achievements other than those arising from mere military prowess.

Philippa Fawcett College, London
C. F. Mott College, Liverpool

References

1 A. J. Marcham, 'The Myth of Benthamism, the Second Reform Act, and the extension of popular education', *Journal of Educational Administration and History*, vol II, no 2, June 1970, 25.

2 Marlborough's Bill—'An Act to Regulate the Distribution of Sums granted by Parliament for Elementary Education in England and Wales, and for other purposes'. Short title—Education Act 1868. H of L 1868, iv, 227.

3 Hansard, 3rd Series, CXC, col 478.

4 Hansard, 3rd Series, CXC, cols 493–506.

5 H. Cole, *Fifty Years of Public Work*, vol 1, 350.

6 In a subsequent discussion on the memorandum it was pointed out that, although there were to be five permanent members, 'the determination of the Lord President shall be final . . . It is not intended to make the whole Board perform the work of each person. Each member is to do the duty of his separate department. Omit the term "Board" if it objected to: but simply say that so many persons are to perform the duties subject to a general power of consultation.' (Disraeli Papers BIX/B/1. Unsigned printed paper on the constitution of the education office.) The Board of Education was, in fact, designed to operate along similar lines to the existing Board of Admiralty. Marlborough's bill made provision for a Secretary of State, five Principal Secretaries and five Under Secretaries for Education. (Sections 5 and 7, Part 1.)

7 Public Record Office Ed 24/54. Memorandum by the Vice-President on the Privy Council of Education.

8 Monypenny and Buckle, *Life of Disraeli* (1916), vol 4.
Disraeli to Lord Stanley, 17 January 1868, 577.
Disraeli to Derby, 30 January 1868, 579.
Disraeli to Queen Victoria, 4 February 1868, 580.
Disraeli to Derby, 6 February 1868, 581.

9 Hansard, 3rd Series, vol CXCI, cols 105–29.

10 For agreement on the Conscience Clause see Canterbury to Marlborough, 31 December 1867 and 18 January 1868, Marlborough Papers, vol 11, nos 160 and 174.

11 Part 1, Section 19, clause 1 of the bill.

12 Part 11 of the bill.

13 Hansard, 3rd Series, vol CXCI, cols 119–29.

14 Hansard, 3rd Series, vol CXCI, cols 1305–31.

15 Hansard, 3rd Series, vol CXCI, col 1326. The use of the word 'primary' as opposed to the traditional term 'elementary' appears to have been deliberate.

16 One might add that only in 1971 was the education of severely mentally handicapped children transferred from the Ministry of Health to that of Education, and that approved and reformatory schools are still the responsibility of the Home Office.

17 Hansard, 3rd Series, vol CXCII, cols 405–11.

18 Hansard, 3rd Series, vol CCXIX, col 1618.

19 Hansard, 3rd Series, CCXIII, cols 1701–9.

20 P. Smith, *Disraeli, Conservatism and Social Reform* (1967), 80–112, and W. D. Jones, *Lord Derby, and Victorian Conservatism* (Oxford, 1956), 333, for discussion of Tory education policy.

EDWARD J. T. BRENNAN

Educational Engineering with the Webbs

THE name of Sidney Webb is associated inevitably with the early
years of the Fabian Society. Though not, in 1884, a founder member,
Sidney had quickly established himself as one of its leading lights
and, along with Bernard Shaw, Graham Wallas and Sydney Olivier,
made up the redoubtable 'Fabian Quartet'. The part played by
the Fabians in planning the fabric of the welfare state has, of course,
been immense; the extent of their involvement in shaping many
of today's educational institutions has become known only in recent
years.

It is in the context of educational change that the policies of Webb
and the Fabians are to be identified the most completely. This is not to
underrate the contribution of eminent members of the society in the
day-to-day administration of bodies such as the London School Board.
The names of Annie Besant, Graham Wallas and Stewart Headlam immediately come to mind. But, of course, the school boards' days were
numbered. Within the society their spokesmen, Wallas and Headlam,
were powerless to prevent Webb's 'sweet reasonableness' carrying the
majority along on the crest of a centralising wave. Long before the
1902 legislation was introduced into parliament, Sidney's recommendations had been adopted as official Fabian policy.

If we look at those Fabian tracts which are concerned with the subject of education, we see that nearly all were written by Webb. And
even in those cases where authorship is not acknowledged we have it
on the authority of E. R. Pease, secretary to the society for twenty-five
years, that the same hand was responsible. There are two exceptions
only. J. W. Martin, an ex-school board teacher, wrote two highly informative tracts[1] but as a result of meeting a female member of the
society in the United States, decided not to return to England. Hubert
Bland, one of the society's earliest members, waited until as late as

1905 before writing a tract, but this was restricted to the subject of free meals for schoolchildren.[2]

The Fabian Society was one of the flowerings of the movement in the 1880s towards the collectivist solution of Britain's social and economic ills. Socialism was emerging as a force to be reckoned with. Whether it spoke through the Marxist voice of H. M. Hyndman's Social Democratic Federation, or through the medieval Utopian outlook of William Morris's Socialist League, or through the Guild of St Matthew, whose main tenet was that socialism was Christianity translated into politics, the choice facing those who so fervently believed in social amelioration seemed so often to be a stark one: revolution or utopianism. That Britain chose neither of these alternatives was the peculiar contribution of the Fabian Society, that extraordinary body of middle-class intellectuals, who were to wield an influence out of all proportion to their numbers.

Fabians, almost by definition, have never been revolutionaries. Their linchpin, at any rate in the early years, was 'the inevitability of gradualness', social change being effected through the existing political parties. To do this it was of course necessary to permeate those parties with socialist doctrine. In this way the Fabian belief in 'the national minimum' could be translated into reality. To this was added the *cri de coeur* of 'national efficiency' and—curiously for a socialist pressure group—'imperial efficiency' whose educational implications were the training of an imperial race.

Belief in 'the national minimum' went right across the board of Fabian planning: factory legislation, sanitation, housing, local government, the Poor Law, public education in all its aspects. For what Sidney saw, quite unequivocally, was that public education is a facet of socialism in action. In a significant little book, *Socialism in England*, published in 1890, he writes, a little too complacently perhaps, considering his later activities: 'this branch of industry has been virtually nationalised, without loss of stimulus or failure of enthusiasm'. Socialism, in other words, was beginning to work.

The essence of Fabian method is quite simple to comprehend— at least in retrospect. Give people the facts and figures and they are bound to become socialistic in outlook. Margaret Cole has admirably caught the flavour of moral superiority that pervaded their outlook and lent vigour to their programmes of political education:

> The Fabian Society had come to believe that out of the mouths of the other side, out of their own papers, their own records, and their own statistics, Socialists could convict capitalism of inefficiency as well as immorality and leave it without a leg to stand on.[3]

The society gave the public the facts and figures in the shape of the *Fabian Tracts*, twenty-five out of the first sixty written by Webb himself. And although the techniques of mass communication were comparatively unsophisticated at the time, those that did exist were exploited to the full. A torrent of memoranda and circulars cascaded forth and the press was captured whenever occasion demanded. It should perhaps be said that an unfortunate by-product of the policy of permeation is the distaste of those who come to realise that they too have been manipulated. There were as a consequence periods in the career of the Webbs, not least in the aftermath of the education legislation of 1902–3, when their unpopularity, especially in left-wing circles, was extreme.

Although by chance, as it were, I have used the plural form of the surname, Beatrice has not as yet been specifically referred to. This is an omission which may seem inexcusable. My concern so far, however, has been with the Fabians and Sidney's role therein. It was not until after her marriage to Sidney in 1892 that Beatrice joined the society for, according to Bernard Shaw, she regarded its members in the first place with mixed feelings.[4]

As for 'the partnership' itself, what should be made clear is that it is impossible to unravel with any degree of certainty the individual contribution made by either Sidney or Beatrice in any of their joint enterprises. This is a difficulty which all who have written on the Webbs have had to acknowledge. Even in those areas where each seemed to be carrying out a clearly differentiated role, as for instance in Sidney's chairmanship of the London Technical Education Board, or Beatrice's work as a member of the Royal Commission on the Poor Law, the impact of each upon the thinking and decisions of the other must have been considerable. Their natures were complementary and in all their undertakings there was inevitably a process of mutual permeation.

Few married people have ever shared their lives more completely. It is doubtful whether after their marriage either ever acted independently of the other. This being so, then the naïveté of attempting to identify their individual contributions to educational change is at once apparent. It is for this reason that I have chosen to write of the Webbs in the plural, even though in terms of decision taking and extent of literary output Sidney's contributions may appear to be the weightier.

It has been said that when Sidney entered public life in 1892 he was guided in his activities by 'a grand design' for educational improvement and that with this considerable advantage he was able to direct his political flair and remarkable industry to the promotion of the ends he had formulated. Scrutiny of the early *Fabian Tracts* would suggest that this is an assertion of dubious validity. That he regarded education as a necessary item in any programme of social reform is evident in tracts such as *Facts for Londoners* (1889), *Questions for Parliamentary Candidates* (1891), and *Questions for School Board Candidates* (1891). Education also receives some attention in that most seminal of all left-wing publications, *Fabian Essays in Socialism*.[5] But in these writings he is obviously quite satisfied with the existing administrative framework, for it would appear that Sidney, along with most socialists of the day, regarded the school boards as the instruments in whose hands educational advance could continue to be entrusted.

There is even on occasion a seeming disregard of the importance of education as part of a left-wing political programme. Certainly there is no mention of the subject in either *Questions for London County Councillors*[6] or the important *London Programme*,[7] both written with the 1892 local elections in mind. If 'a grand design' was taking place, Sidney was singularly cautious in enlarging upon its structure either to fellow Fabians or to Beatrice Potter.

In the case of so assiduous a diarist as Beatrice, it might be expected that any similar aspirations on her part would have been faithfully recorded. The answer is simple to determine. Neither in *My Appren-ticeship* nor in the manuscript diaries is there any evidence to support the assumption that an educational 'grand design' was in fact beginning to emerge before 1892. In fact when the subject is mentioned at all there is a vehement rejection of state intervention in education—'the most dangerous of all social poisons', as she described it in 1884.

The truth was that theirs was what A. V. Judges has described as 'a functional theory of education'.[8] There was in the beginning no 'grand design'. It was their active engagement in all manner of educa-tional undertakings that enabled the theory to emerge. Increasingly alarmed by experiences of obscurantism and obstructionism on the part of politicians and officials, dismayed by what they considered to be the fumbling incompetence of those responsible for Empire in the very heyday of imperialism, the Webbs more and more became the advocates of national and imperial efficiency, and they came to see education as the instrument to that end. Each paid lip service to the notion that education can bring about individual fulfilment but one is never convinced that they believed such an aim to be important, unless, that is, it could be developed within a matrix of social dues and obliga-tions.[9]

Sidney's concern with educational engineering was not realised in the House of Commons, which in fact he did not enter until 1922, but in the context of local government. His election as one of the members for Deptford on the London County Council was in part an outcome of the Fabian belief that 'municipal socialism' had to take place before the real collectivisation of English society at the national level could succeed. Whether the 'municipal socialism' of the Fabians was radically different from the earlier 'gas and water socialism' of the Radicals in the large cities of the provinces is rather doubtful. What is less doubtful is that, quite apart from the broad lines of strategy mapped out in ad-vance by the society, Sidney especially was deeply committed to the reform of the public services of London, a city which he believed was lagging behind every other city in Britain in putting its house in order.

It should not be forgotten that Sidney was a native of London and to his dying day loved the place with a passion of surprising intensity that was in no whit diminished by an awareness of the squalor and degradation that existed within yards of his birthplace near Leicester Square. 'Hell is a city much like London',[10] was a line of poetry he was forever quoting. It is probable that this predilection for Shelley was more the result of its value as a political imperative than for its aesthetic qualities, for Sidney's lack of sympathy towards the arts was so notorious as to give rise to a crop of unfavourable anecdotes, often recounted, let it be said, by critics anxious to undervalue the achievements of the Webbs by drawing attention to their more egregious qualities.[11] If poetry, and indeed the arts as a whole, had any function at all for Sidney it was as a spur to action, certainly not for reflection which, particularly on the banks of Cam and Isis, he disapproved of completely.

That London did not necessarily have to remain in its sorry state is evident in this excerpt from *The London Programme*:

> By himself the typical Londoner is a frail and sickly unit, cradled in the gutter, housed in a slum, slaving in a sweater's den and dying in the workhouse infirmary. Collectively he is a member of the greatest and most magnificent city the world has known, commanding all the latest resources of civilisation and disposing of almost boundless wealth.

The amelioration of the lot of his fellow Londoners was therefore the task to which Sidney now bent his energies, but his interest in improving the capital's educational provision as part of the collectivist programme seems to have emerged but a few weeks before his election to the London County Council in February 1892. Only a remarkable political flair and the trust that men of all persuasions were ready to place in him during these early years can explain the fact that within a few weeks he had emerged as chairman of the council's first Technical Instruction Committee, later to be called the Technical Education Board.

Before the inadequacies of technical education could be put right, they had to be chartered by the sort of expert indispensable to Fabian policy making. The appointment of Llewellyn Smith, secretary of the National Association for the Promotion of Technical Education, and fellow worker with Charles Booth in his classic *Inquiry into the Life and Labour of the People of London*, to survey the possible scope of technical education in the metropolis, was a crucial one, for the *Report* that emerged some months later was so comprehensive that it was to serve as a blueprint for the next decade.[12]

The board, very much the brainchild of Sidney, could now go ahead, not just as another committee of the LCC, but one which enjoyed a remarkable degree of independence from its parent. As well as twenty members of the council, it included fifteen representatives of groups as diverse as the London School Board, the Headmasters' Association, the City Livery Companies and the London Trades Council. The plan to have mixed representation was very much Sidney's own. The advantages were obvious; for through this device potential opposition could be disarmed and suspicions allayed. In order to guarantee success, however, he virtually nominated every other member, including, incidentally, three other Fabians.

Sidney was chairman of the board for nearly the whole of its existence.[13] Through it he was able to advance the cause of municipal socialism both directly through the expansion of the LCC's educational empire and indirectly in helping to persuade the government of the day that the future local control of education should be based upon the county council pattern and not upon the school boards, whose *ad hoc* virtues were becoming increasingly distasteful to Fabian planners.

Webb was able to exploit three parliamentary measures to sanction the policies he began to implement. There was the Technical Instruction Act itself, passed in 1889 and permitting the raising of a penny rate. There was secondly the Local Taxation Act of the following year which provided a remarkable windfall through the celebrated 'whiskey money'. The story of its passing is by now so well known that there is little purpose in recounting it once again.[14] What was rather strange was that before Webb's election to the council, the LCC had taken no action whatsoever to place itself in front of this cornucopia; an omission which seems remarkable when one considers that its bounty was such that, despite considerable expenditure over the next ten years, the council never was forced into the position of raising the rate permitted under the Technical Instruction Act.

The third parliamentary measure was an enabling act which allowed the county councils to provide scholarships. The Technical Education Board now had all the statutory authority it needed to go ahead in providing what Sidney, doubtless with his own educational background very much in mind, considered to be absolutely necessary: two educational 'ladders', one for climbing by day, the other in the evening. They were badly needed. Before 1892 there were, for a school roll of 680,000, only one thousand scholarships. The odds against an elementary school boy winning one were 150 to 1; for a girl the odds at 500 to 1 were even more heavily weighted. By 1903 Sidney could claim that there was in London a better scholarship provision than in any German, French or American city.[15]

But more important perhaps than the development of the 'capacity catching machine', an indispensable means of bringing about the meritocratic state so dear to Fabian hearts, was that the public money given to scholarship winners from the elementary schools began to revive many of London's endowed secondary schools from their hitherto depressed condition. And not only did the grammar schools benefit but the polytechnics, art schools and all manner of technical institutes also received generous grants from the TEB coffers.

With assistance there came inspection. Both elements provided an adhesive which to an ever-increasing extent bound together the diverse parts of London's educational provision, despite its administrative ambiguities, into something which could be regarded as a system. Webb, who made this claim, was of course an interested party and we should perhaps regard his assertion with a degree of scepticism. However, it was certainly the opinion of the Bryce Commission in 1895 that 'London was the only place for organised secondary education'.[16] But here again it should be said that there is some evidence to show that the commission had undergone a degree of Fabian permeation, though not perhaps to the extent that Beatrice so fondly believed.[17]

It was never Sidney's policy to start new schools as such, even though the Board was empowered to do so. The creation of new schools would mean delay and was quite likely to cause unnecessary friction—with the London School Board on the one hand, and the endowed secondary schools on the other. Far better to give a shot in the arm whenever this was possible. Besides, to set up its own schools would have meant the loss of a splendid opportunity to lock together the disparate elements of London's educational provision. Radical critics might, on principle, bemoan the giving of public money to non-public institutions. To Webb, with 'his gift for making ideas viable', it was a political necessity.

But it was higher education, one always feels, which really engaged the Webbs the most deeply. To Sidney, the polytechnics were particularly significant in that the instruction they provided was in many cases up to university standard and their *clientèle* was drawn from what was referred to in contemporary circles as a *nouvelle couche sociale*, marks of approbation which bear a remarkable resemblance to recent official pronouncements.[18] Fortified by this double affirmation of their virtue, Sidney was able to persuade an at times reluctant TEB to give large sums of money to the polytechnics, so that during his tenure of office they grew in number from five to twelve. They also grew in scope and status, so much so that by 1900 many of their classes had been included in the new London teaching university, itself the creation of Sidney and his friend, R. B. Haldane. The university's readiness to embrace the polytechnics, not to mention the London School of Economics, to its bosom was partly the consequence of the bait that Sidney so adroitly and persistently dangled in front of it—the prospect of financial assistance from the LCC.

What we have seen in recent years—the growth of the original polytechnics into chartered and independent universities—is, it might appear, but a logical extension of the capacity for growth that is inherent in all educational institutions. In turn the London polytechnics are in the process of being replaced by a whole new generation of polytechnics, situated not just in London but in all the major industrial areas of the country.

At the heart of the Webbs' interest in higher education was their

ardent belief in national efficiency and their dismay at the way in
which Britain's industrial supremacy, already past its peak, was being
increasingly eroded at the end of Victoria's reign. Not that they were
narrowly chauvinistic. Sidney for instance, writing about London
University in the new century, saw its role as combining 'a sane and
patriotic imperialism with the largest minded internationalism'.[19] But
without question they were sick and tired of a fumbling and in-
competent amateurism and, like many of their generation, they saw
in the example of Germany not so much a threat as an ideal.[20] The
Technical Instruction Act itself had been one response to the challenge
of foreign competition; now, by virtue of his responsibility for the
provision of technical education in the capital of Empire, Sidney set
up various fact-finding committees whose duty it was to inquire into
such objects as the teaching of chemistry and 'the application of
science to industry', fields in which continental powers such as Germany were by all accounts forging ahead.

'National efficiency' and 'imperial efficiency' more and more became
Fabian articles of faith and the answer was seen, perceptively or otherwise, in terms of educational change. The close association of Webb
and Haldane which resulted in the setting up of Imperial College in
1903 has to be seen in this context. The case for 'the Charlottenburg
Scheme', as it was usually referred to by the joint partners in the
enterprise, was in fact largely based on the evidence to be found in
Llewellyn Smith's Report to the LCC—evidence which painted a
stark picture of the loss to Germany of the techniques pioneered by
Britain in fields such as electro-chemistry and the coal-tar industry.
This was the evidence used by Webb when he wrote Lord Rosebery's
appeal to the chairman of the LCC for an annual grant; it also provided
the ammunition for Haldane in the course of his endowment-raising
visits to financial and industrial magnates like Lord Rothschild, Sir
Julius Wernher and Alfred Beit.

There was an obvious extension of the principle of national efficiency
in the field of teacher training. It is true that the initiative for the
start of the London Day Training College, now the London University Institute of Education, had come from the London School

Board in July 1899. But it was Webb who master-minded the operation, a process which was not made easier by the antagonism of Ramsay
MacDonald and 'the working men' on the LCC who, for reasons
which are not surprising when the psychological consequences of
permeation are taken into account, felt that the venture was but the
latest unfortunate flowering of Fabian behind-the-scenes activities. In
fact, so sensitive had the antennae of suspicion become that they were
unwilling to comprehend that the request had come from their own
school board.

The 'favourite child of the Webbs',[21] however, was without question,
the London School of Economics, brought struggling and kicking into
the world in 1895 by a doctor and midwife who for years were in a
state of chronic anxiety about the survival prospects of their offspring.
A good deal has been written in recent years on the subject of the
LSE, mostly in an attempt to understand the root causes of its turbu-
lence during the late 1960s. A brief recapitulation of those events may
nevertheless be of interest, as the story does provide a remarkable
insight into the Webbs' 'disinterested Machiavellianism', as it pleased
Beatrice, somewhat euphemistically, to refer to it.

One recent Director of the School has conceded that the circumstances surrounding its birth well deserve the adjective 'picturesque':[22]
the extraordinary windfall of £10,000 entrusted to Webb under the
will of Henry Hunt Hutchinson, the obscure Derby solicitor, to
promote 'the propaganda and other purposes of the Fabian Society
and its Socialism, and towards advancing its objects in any way that
may seem advisable'; the fund-raising opportunism of Beatrice in
snaring Charlotte Payne-Townshend; the good fortune and pre-
science of the Webbs in sensing the quality of W. A. S. Hewins[23]
during a chance encounter in the Bodleian; the calibre of the early
teachers working in conditions which would have daunted lesser
spirits.

Beatrice's immediate reactions to the news of Hutchinson's bequest,
confided to the intimacy of her diary, are interesting, in that they show
that the creation of a higher educational establishment devoted to
research and teaching in the social sciences was much more appealing

than the prospect of spending the money on political propaganda.[24] Some years previously, Sidney had enthused over the quality of the teaching of economics in the Massachusetts Institute of Technology, but the spur to action—that is, experience in the field of educational administration—still lay in the future. Matters were very different in 1894 when the 'Gresham University' Committee stressed the need for London to have the sort of studies pursued in Paris in the *Ecole Libre des Sciences Politiques*, one of the *grandes écoles*. Now, as chairman of the TEB, Sidney was very much concerned with remedying what he saw to be the deficiencies in London's higher education. Not surprisingly, the news of the Hutchinson bequest came as manna from the heavens.

Beatrice was jubilant that the prospect of training the experts so badly needed in the pursuit of national efficiency, could now begin in all seriousness:

> It looks as if the great bulk of the working men will be collectivists before the end of the century. But Reform will not be brought about by shouting. What is needed is *hard thinking*. And the same objection applies to sending nondescript socialists into Parliament. The radical members are quite sufficiently compliant in their views: what is lacking in them is the leaven of knowledge. So Sidney has been planning to persuade the other trustees to devote the greater part of the money to encouraging *Research* and Economic study. His vision is to found, slowly and quietly, a '*London School of Economics and Political Science*' a centre not only of lectures on special subjects but an association of students who would be directed and supported in doing original work. Last evening we sat by the fire and jotted down a whole list of subjects which want elucidating—issues of fact which need clearing up. Above all, we want the ordinary citizen to feel that reforming society is no light matter and must be undertaken by experts specially trained for the purpose.[25]

The most pressing problem that the Webbs had to face was whether spending the money in this way could be sustained, if their decision were ever to be challenged in the courts. Hutchinson's attitude towards his wife and daughter had been niggardly, to say the least. There was always the risk that they might challenge the will on the grounds of his diminished responsibility. One obvious response was to increase the annuity left to the widow. Even so, had not the dead man's daughter, Miss Constance Hutchinson, agreed with the Webbs that there could be no better way of spending the money than starting a higher educational establishment devoted to research and teaching, the plan might well have misfired.

The 'old gang' of the Fabian Society was less tractable. Much more attractive to them was the idea of devoting the whole of the money to the purposes of left-wing propaganda, or alternatively creating 'a big political splash' by subsidising members of the Fabian Executive, not to mention the Independent Labour Party, to stand for parliament. Neither course of action held much appeal for the Webbs. That Sidney was uneasy, however, is evident if we trace his tactics during the twelve months that elapsed between the news of Hutchinson's death and the start of the LSE in the autumn of 1895. Matters came to a head when the names of the lecturers were published and the identity of those outside bodies which had agreed to give support was made known. It was all very well to enlist the financial help of such strongholds of capitalism as the London Chamber of Commerce, but in the process assurances had had to be given that nothing of a socialistic character would be introduced into the curriculum. Even Bernard Shaw stood aghast at Sidney's byzantine manoeuvrings. Voicing the dismay of the Fabian 'old gang' at what appeared to be a diverting of socialist resources from their rightful purpose, he indulged in a splendid display of Shavian fireworks in a letter to Beatrice:

> You see we must be in a position at any moment to show that faith has been kept with Hutchinson. If Webb is ever publicly convicted of having served up the County Council and the Chamber of Commerce on toast to the ghost of Hutchinson, everyone will laugh and think it an uncommonly smart thing. But if he is even suspected of having tampered with a trust of ten thousand pounds from a private benefactor, then we shall lose our character for being straight in money matters; and none of us can afford to do that. And it is so very simple to avoid anything of the sort. All that is necessary is to avoid shocking the common sense of the public and the ILP or Fabian critic by talking about academic abstraction and impartiality. Even if such a thing were possible, its foundation out of Hutchinson's money would be as flagrant a breach of trust as handing it over to the Liberty and Property Defence League, since it was expressly left to endow Socialism. Further, the Fabian executive must not be told that it has nothing to do with it. It was by an act of special providence that Bland was absent on that disastrous occasion. He would certainly have moved then and there that the subject

be dropped and that the Fabian executive, having no control of the Hutchin-son bequest, declines to make itself responsible for its administration by discussing it in any way. To me the attitude of Martin, who is quite friendly to us, is very alarming. He is willing to admit good-naturedly that nothing else could be done; but it is quite evident that he also feels that if the money had been left to him, he would have managed very differently. Much more terrifying is the temporary (let us hope) suspension of Webb's wits. The moment I read that prospectus in the *Chronicle*, I saw that it would have to be carefully explained to the Fabians. My dismay when Webb did not even understand why the subject had been put on the agenda paper was acute. Please shew him this letter and allow it to rankle.[26]

Sidney, however, had already sought the advice of counsel in the person of R. B. Haldane—'that steadfast fellow conspirator for the public good', as Beatrice was to describe him in later years. Not only did Haldane confirm the right of the Hutchinson Trustees, of whom Webb was chairman, to act without consulting the Fabian Society, but he was able to confirm that the study of economics and other branches of social and political science could be regarded as a perfectly legitimate way of promoting Fabian socialism. Secure in his apparently impregnable legal fortress, Sidney was able to face his fellow Fabians in his favourite posture of 'sweet reasonableness'.

One notable Fabian who had criticised Webb for appropriating socialist funds for his own educational ends was Ramsay MacDonald. Despite the fact that he was offered and accepted one of the Hutchin-son lectureships in the provinces—for part of the legacy was in fact devoted to the purposes of political education—he neither forgot nor forgave the Webbs for their seeming addiction to higher education. Beatrice for her part was inclined to interpret MacDonald's hostility, not so much to his avowed beliefs that educational priorities lay in the area of elementary education, but as the result of pique and jealousy, following his failure to be appointed to the staff of the LSE.[27]

The passing of the years seems to have intensified this mutual dis-like. As a result of one of Sidney's favourite strategems MacDonald was given a place on the TEB. But to no avail: his antipathy was in no way lessened and the Webbs' educational policies were consequently more and more difficult to implement. For example, in 1903, in a correspondence which was malicious but entirely logical, MacDonald wrote to the Principal of London University, alleging that the university had embraced to its bosom an institution that was politically 'committed'. The consternation of Sir Arthur Rucker and Archibald Robertson, the Vice-Chancellor, was at once apparent[28] and the implications for the LSE extremely serious.

Despite his anxiety, Sidney was quite secure. The ground had been well prepared. He could show that the Hutchinson money had never formed part of the school's actual endowment and that both its financial backers and its teachers represented all shades of political opinion. Ramsay MacDonald must doubtless have been puzzled by Sidney's lack of consistency over the years, but Shaw's admiration for the political expertise of his friend presumably grew as he saw the real motive for the inclusion of right-wing academics amongst its lecturers.

All in all the period was a critical one in the life of the LSE, and Sidney was on tenterhooks wondering from what direction MacDonald would strike next. In the previous summer, for example, he had launched an attack on both Sidney and the School on the grounds that LCC money was being used to propagate socialism and that there were too many Fabians on the governing body! Sidney was extremely apprehensive, as is evident from reading his letters to Beatrice who at the time had taken Bertrand Russell's first wife, Alys, away on holiday to Switzerland, in an effort to create some distraction from the latter's growing marital difficulties. But although what we learn of the marriage breakdown from the first volume of Russell's *Autobiography* may make us a trifle sceptical of the author's claim that human conduct should be 'based upon love and guided by reason', the episode had one beneficial effect—if only from the point of view of the student of the period—for Sidney and Beatrice wrote to each other nearly every day and this was a crucial period, not only in the life of the London School of Economics, but also in the wider parliamentary arena.

The infancy of the LSE had been a precarious one. The perpetual and nagging problem was the raising of more money, and the manner by which the Webbs tracked down their prey makes a fascinating study in fund-raising opportunism. This was perhaps epitomised in their treatment of the newly discovered Irish millionairess, Charlotte Payne-Townshend. Before they met her they had already learned of her socialistic predilections and once the acquaintance was made Beatrice earmarked her as the future soulmate of Graham Wallas who, however, apparently bored her 'with his morality and learning'. Despite this setback they did persuade her to give £1,000 to the School, endow a women's scholarship and rent the top half of the premises in Adelphi Terrace which the School was using at that time. 'It was on account of her generosity to our projects and "for the good of the cause" that I first made friends with her', said Beatrice, with a candour that was almost disarming.[29]

Fortunately for Charlotte, she got value for her money, since Beatrice then suggested that she should join them, in the summer of 1896, on one of their working holidays, and it was at the rectory of Stratford St Andrew, near Saxmundham, that she met her fellow countryman, Bernard Shaw, for the first time. After they were married, the Shaws lived above the school in a state of apparent domestic felicity. Over the years Charlotte continued to be a tower of financial strength in the various Webb undertakings, although there seems to have been little love lost between the two women.[30]

Regularity of income for the new institution was naturally easier to ensure by virtue of the fact that its creator happened to be the chairman of the LCC's Technical Education Board. The way in which Sidney was able to persuade reluctant working men on the board to agree to public money being given year after year to the LSE is a remarkable illustration of his political skill, although once again it should be said that by the turn of the century his credit was fast being exhausted. Matters came to a head with the passing of the Education Acts of 1902 and 1903. As a result of their activities, the Webbs became so isolated that Beatrice was forced time and time again to hit back, although what she had to say had mostly, out of respect for the laws of libel, to be reserved to the privacy of her diary. What seems to have irked her particularly was the fact that 'the working men' within the dominant Progressive Party of the LCC were now refusing to be moulded to the approved Webb pattern:

. . . they are not much to be proud of—a good deal of rotten stuff; the rest
upright and reasonable but coarse-grained in intellect and character . . . the
ordinary Progressive member is either a bounder, a narrow-minded fanatic,
or a mere piece of putty upon which any strong mind can make an impression,
to be effaced by the next influence—or rather the texture is more like gutta-
percha, because it bounces back to the old shapeless mass of prejudice
directly you take your will away.[31]

The truth was that neither Beatrice nor Sidney really appreciated, and
certainly had not anticipated, the strength of the working men's feeling
for the school boards, brought into existence by a Liberal government
and possessing all the shining virtues of 'primary democracy', a concept for which the Webbs with their growing attachment to the goal
of 'national efficiency' were coming to acquire a proportionate distaste.

It had been obvious for some time that the Unionist government
which had been returned in 1895 was determined to curtail the powers
of the school boards. That the Church of England should be exerting
pressure was neither illogical nor surprising, but it later came as
something of a shock for radicals and socialists of all complexions to
realise that one important left-wing group, namely the Fabian Society,
was beginning to work towards this end.

The use of the word 'beginning' is quite deliberate, for there is
nothing to show that before he brought the TEB into existence Webb
was hostile to the school boards. Study of one of his earlier tracts,
Facts for Londoners, written in 1889, makes it quite apparent that he
regarded control of elementary schools by the London School Board
as being axiomatic. Indeed in the previous year the Fabian Society
and the Social Democratic Federation had joined forces to defeat the
clerical majority on the London School Board, and one result had
been the election to the board of two prominent Fabians, Annie
Besant and Stewart Headlam. Tracts such as *Questions for Parliamentary Candidates* and *Questions for School Board Candidates*, both
written in 1891 with important elections in mind, assume that any
school receiving public money will automatically come under school
board control. Astonishingly, *Questions for London County Councillors*,
written with the author himself a candidate for office, eschewed any
mention of the subject of education; as did his *London Programme*,

the *vade mecum* of all aspiring municipal socialists. Certainly, if Sidney did believe in these early years in county council involvement in education, he did not chose to reveal his intentions to his fellow Fabians.

It was only in the fullness of time that the Webbs felt it necessary to clip the wings of the school boards, and once again one is struck with the realisation that Fabian intervention was dictated by the demands of administrative efficiency. This point is fully developed in Alan McBriar's penetrating contribution to *The Webbs and Their Work* in which he describes how a growing awareness of unnecessary expense, the unhealthy cleavage between elementary and higher education, and the inevitable confusion which results when authorities overlap in their functions, caused Sidney of necessity to become a centraliser.[32]

According to Beatrice, Sidney had returned from their world tour in January 1899 determined to bring about county council control of public education. The immediate result was the most potent of all Fabian tracts, *The Education Muddle and the Way Out*. The outlines of the tract were discussed by the society later that year, and the reader is immediately struck by the similarity between its contents and the major provisions of the education act that emerged three years later. The failure of Graham Wallas and Stewart Headlam to stem the centralising tide that was apparently obsessing the Fabians is by now well known. The Webbian formula was adopted. The tract, the 106th to be put out by the society, appeared in its final form in January 1901, but before its publication Sir John Gorst had asked for fifty galley pulls to be sent along to Whitehall, there to be perused by civil servants and governmental colleagues.

Strange to relate, there is no evidence to suggest that Sidney was ever identified with Gorst's administrative harassing of the school boards. Although he was chairman of the TEB in 1897 when the Education Code was amended so that, under clause 7, South Kensington grants could be paid to one authority only in each area, he made no move to apply for such recognition. In fact the board took no action until November 1898, a time when Sidney was many thousands of miles from home. The application was made by William Garnett, secretary to the board,[33] through Edward Bond, the new Moderate chairman. The challenging of London School Board expenditure by the two ratepayers representing the Camden School of Art, which was to lead eventually to the Cockerton Judgement, was again engineered by Garnett.[34] Sidney may well have enjoyed a wry satisfaction at the way things were moving. Outwardly, at any rate, there is no doubt at all that from 1899 to 1902 he appears as the advocate of conciliation, seeing his role as that of comforter of outraged school board sensibilities.

And although Tract 106 recommended the giving of rate aid to the voluntary schools and the sweeping into limbo of the great majority of the school boards, there was never any suggestion on Webb's part that the largest and most efficient boards should disappear. This innovation of Morant's came as a complete surprise. For, according to Fabian criteria, size was indispensable to viability, an article of faith which seems today to have won general acceptance in both the economic and administrative spheres. In spite of Sidney's growing dislike of *ad hoc* bodies on principle, he knew that the large school boards were efficient and he never presumed to recommend their dissolution.

As far as the issue of rate aid to the voluntary schools was concerned, the Webbs' stand both puzzled and dismayed their non-conformist and secular friends, who never really understood how two avowed socialists could in all conscience adopt such a position. But, for that matter, neither could the Webbs ever understand the feelings of outrage displayed by non-conformists and secularists. The truth was, of course, that Sidney was so intent on pursuing administrative efficiency that the giving of subsidies to church schools seemed to him to be of minor consequence. Rationalist and sceptic he might be, but if millions of people wanted this sort of education, there seemed to him to be no reason why they should not be given it. His agnosticism was essentially non-militant and this his critics simply could not understand, nor indeed forgive.

Beatrice for her part remained something of a mystic throughout her life, and was even more tolerant about public money being given to the voluntary schools. One of Bertrand Russell's more amusing anecdotes, deriving from his friendship with the Webbs, tells how Beatrice particularly favoured the Church of England on the grounds that, at any rate, it had the merit of being a state institution. Beatrice's apologia is both succint and topical—even in the context of the 1970s:

> I could only shelter myself by the argument that the reform of the Church was not the work I had undertaken to do, or which I was trained to consider. The practical alternatives before us constituted a very simple issue; whether we were to throw our weight against the continuance of the present form of religious teaching and help to establish pure materialism as the national metaphysic; or whether we would accept, provisionally, as part of the teaching in the schools, the dogmas and ritual of the Christian Church of today. For my own children, and for those of other people, I deliberately believed the lie of materialism to be far more pernicious and more utterly false than the untruths which seem to me to constitute the Christian formula of religion. Moreover, we are face to face with the fact that the vast majority of the English people, are, as far as they think at all, convinced Christians. By insisting on secular education, I should not only be helping to spread what seems to me a bad kind of falsehood, but I should be denying to others the right to have their children taught the creed they hold to be positively true. I see no way out of the dilemma, but the largest variety possible of denomina- tional schools, so that there may be the utmost possible choice for parents and children, and, let me add, the widest range of experiment as to the results of particular kinds of teaching on the character of the child and its conduct of life.[35]

Only one school board was excluded from the scope of the 1902 Act and that, ironically enough, was London's. London was altogether too sharp a thorn to be handled with comfort, as Sir John Gorst took care to point out. There were many Conservatives who hated the LCC for its socialistic policies and were now thinking in terms of control by the new-fangled apparatus of the metropolitan boroughs.[36]

Thus it was that next year Sidney was faced with a renewal of the wire-pulling and lobbying which had been a feature of his life during the passing of the 1902 Bill. And this time, he had to do without the help of Morant who, pleading the excuse of 'a rotten staff'[37] and over- work, declined to co-operate.[38] The crux of Webb's campaign was to persuade the Anglican bishops that the LCC would be more generous to the voluntary schools than the boroughs, which would be unduly dominated by the disproportionate presence of elementary school teachers on their councils. Strictly speaking, however, borough control was not the only alternative, for the government had become so disturbed by the growing non-conformist discontent in the country that there was even talk of retaining the *status quo*. With this as a possible outcome, Sidney's second tactical objective was to persuade LCC Progressives, including men of the calibre of John Burns and Ramsay MacDonald, that it would be madness to oppose the extension of county council control. This proved to be a difficult, not to say frustrating, task.

The manoeuvrings with Unionist MPs, wining and dining the Prime Minister, the nocturnal conversations with Anglican bishops and Roman Catholic cardinals, the canvassing of the professional associations, the creation of a favourable public opinion through the leader columns of the press—all reveal Fabian tactics at their peak of efficiency and, perhaps it is only fair to add, at their starkest and most repellent.

The success of the Webbs' campaign can be seen in the London Education Act which emerged on the statute book in the spring of 1903. Sidney had been extremely worried by the various government proposals over the previous weeks: the plan for a vast *ad hoc* authority on the lines of the Water Board, which was replaced in turn by the plan for a smaller board with LCC representatives in a majority—but still in essence contaminated by an allegiance to 'ad hoccery'. After all the doubts and uncertainties the outcome for Sidney was highly satisfactory, for the act ensured that London was to be treated in exactly the same way as the rest of the country: LCC control was to be supreme.

The Fabians, and Sidney particularly, have been seen by some educational historians as adopting an unhelpful and somewhat perverse role in this critical period of English social history. The pre-1902 development of the higher grade schools and the emergence of more 'realistic' curricula have been interpreted as adumbrations of post-1945 educational reform. But after 1902, with the demise of the school boards and new policies at the Board of Education, all this disappeared.

In this view, the Fabian Society played a prominent part in a sorry story. This is certainly the judgement of Brian Simon in his *Education and the Labour Movement*.[39] In this work the author very skilfully disentangles the threads of socialist policies during the period. The Fabian thread appears to be the only one which leads in the wrong direction in the administrative labyrinth.

That the Fabian Society appears in a maverick role during the period cannot be denied. Neither can the feeling of outrage on the part of non-conformists, secularists and the advocates of primary democracy who saw the abolition of the school boards as a completely reprehensible step. The Fabians had played no part in the events leading up to the suppression of the higher grade schools; that they had played an active part in the shaping of the legislation of 1902–3 is indisputable, as also is the knowledge that they were supported by no other left-wing organisation.

The important question that should be posed, however, is how far the critics of the Fabians in the early years of the century were being truly objective in their reactions to the abolition of the school boards. In a book which is encyclopedic in its range and dazzling in its insights, Professor Simon does not, it would appear, think this a very important question. It is the viewpoint of the writer of this article that the justification of the more commonly accepted radical interpretation should be based, at least in part, on an analysis of the composition of the boards over a period of thirty years. Such an analysis has yet to be made.

Were the school board representatives in fact made up of sea-green incorruptibles dedicated to an active role in the emancipation of the working class through a widening of educational opportunity? How many of the 2,500 boards were really like this? We need go no further than Brian Simon's book to realise that lethargy and obscurantism so often prevailed. From 1885 to 1897 'Diggleism', an outlook invariably to be met with when the interests of ratepayers are given free rein, was supreme on the London School Board. No piano, for instance, was installed in any London board school between the years 1891 to 1897. The Manchester School Board, which was one of the better ones, was dominated by clerical interests for the whole of its existence. Even in towns where schools boards were created, it was quite often the case that their function was simply to enforce attendance at the existing voluntary schools.[40] There were, furthermore, pockets of socialists who did not idealise the boards and said so openly. Sometimes, as in the case of the Glasgow socialists, they knew all too well that the cumulative voting system of the boards militated against working-class representation.[41] Can it possibly be that in retrospect the recollection of their purity was somewhat stronger than the reality?

The prevailing fear of the Left was that the new LEAs were likely to be dominated by propertied and moneyed interests. It should be said that there was some justification for their fear in the original bill, which proposed that the co-opted members of the new education committees should be in a majority of one. When that bill was withdrawn, the LCC formula that the representatives of the county councils were to be always in a majority was written into the new legislation. As far as the future was concerned, there was certainly less possibility of clerical dominance on the county and borough councils, even with a large co-opted element, than had been the case with the boards. As for Sidney, it was quite unthinkable that the placing of public services like education under the control of the county councils would lead in any other direction than towards the realisation of the collectivist utopia. Compared with a miscellaneous grouping of *ad hoc* bodies, they were much more strongly placed to achieve this goal.

In the light of Labour Party thinking over the last twenty years, it may be of some interest to consider whether the Webbs had any egalitarian inclinations. The answer is fairly easy to determine: Sidney and Beatrice were essentially believers in excellence and professionalism, buttressed, let it be said, by a notion of 'the national minimum' in all fields. Beatrice especially was inclined to be intolerant of frailty and weakness in her fellow human beings. Their view of the fabric of society was that it was essentially hierarchical and would continue to be so.

In comparing their own social philosophy with that of R. B. Haldane, Beatrice in the hindsight of the 1920s had this to say:

Haldane believed more than we did in the existing governing class: in the great personages of Court, Cabinet and City. We staked our hopes on the organised Working Class, *served and guided*, it is true, by an élite of unassuming experts who would make no claim to superior social status, but would content themselves with exercising the power inherent in superior knowledge and longer administrative experience.[42]

This is an interesting remark, refreshing in its directness and candour, but not, however, untypical of the diaries which she kept for so many years.

An élite based upon birth or wealth was to be replaced in the fullness of time by a meritocracy, whose goal would be the pursuit of 'national' and 'imperial efficiency'. These new mandarins or samurai were to be selected by tests and were to climb by means of 'the scholarship ladder'. The most cursory inspection of *Who's Who* for 1972 will give some indication of the effectiveness of the Fabian dream.

Cambridge Institute of Education

References

1   J. W. Martin, *State Education at Home and Abroad* (Fabian Tract no 52, 1894); also *The Workers' School Board Programme* (Fabian Tract no 55, 1894).
2   H. Bland, *After Bread, Education* (Fabian Tract no 120, 1905). Bland was married to Edith Nesbit, whose writings, especially *The Railway Children*, look like ensuring for her a permanent place in the pantheon of children's authors. According to W. H. G. Armytage, their addiction to the movement was so strong that they named one of their children Fabian. At least one of her children's stories is dedicated to him.
3   M. Cole, *Beatrice Webb* (1945), 49.
4   On one occasion at least as 'a rabble of silly suburban faddists'. K. Muggeridge and R. Adam, *Beatrice Webb* (1967), 130.
5   *Fabian Essays in Socialism*, ed Bernard Shaw (1889).
6   S. Webb, *Questions for London County Councillors* (Fabian Tract no 26, 1891).
7   S. Webb, *The London Programme* (1891).
8   A. V. Judges, 'The Educational Influence of the Webbs', *British Journal of Educational Studies*, vol x, no 1 (November 1961), 37.
9   Their view of education as serving 'extrinsic' rather than 'intrinsic' ends is very much in evidence in *Soviet Communism: A New Civilisation?* (1935).
10 An aphorism which the Fabian, William Clarke, said was rather unfair to hell.
11 The latest biography of Beatrice, the vastly entertaining work by Kitty Muggeridge and Ruth Adam, is not free from a certain ambivalence in this respect.

12 Hubert Llewllyn Smith, *Report to the Special Committee on Technical Education* (1892).
13 Chairman 1892–8, 1901–2; Vice-Chairman 1899–1901.
14 Except for the purpose of recalling that finest mixed metaphor of all time: only a very indignant Irish MP could have accused the government of 'throwing down an apple of discord which has burst into flames and flooded the country'.
15 S. Webb, *London Education* (1904), 26.
16 *Final Report, Royal Commission on Secondary Education* (1895), 37.
17 Bryce, Llewellyn Smith and Michael Sadler were personal friends. Another member, Henry Hobhouse, was Beatrice's brother-in-law.
18 These assumptions now underpin the binary system.
19 S. Webb, 'London University: A Policy and a Forecast', *The Nineteenth Century*, June 1902.
20 See, for example, Beatrice's reactions to Sir John Gorst's ill-fated Education Bill of 1896. 'The discreditable failure of this complicated measure is only another instance of how impossible it is nowadays to succeed in politics without technical knowledge of the great democratic machine. The last Liberal Government went out discredited because their members were mere prigs thrust into office—the present government are going the same way. "In these matters I am a child", says Balfour! We do not want clever school boys at the head of our great departments . . . Who would trust the building of a bridge to a man who started with such an infinitesimal knowledge of engineering as Balfour and Gorst have of national education and its machinery?' B. Webb, *Diary*, Whitsun, 1896.
21 The tag bestowed on it by William Beveridge.
22 Sir Sydney Caine, *The History of the Foundation of the London School of Economics and Political Science* (1963), 4.
23 1865–1931, first Director of the London School of Economics. Resigned in 1903 on his conversion to Tariff Reform, and was for fourteen years secretary to Joseph Chamberlain's Tariff Reform Commission. Under-Secretary of State for the Colonies, 1917–19.
24 B. Webb, *Diary*, 21 September 1894.
25 Ibid.
26 *Webb Papers*, G. B. Shaw to B. Webb, 1 July 1895.
27 'He is not good enough for that sort of work—he has never had the time to do any sound original work or even learn the old stuff well'. B. Webb, *Diary*, 18 April 1896.
28 See, for example, *Webb Papers*, Robertson to S. Webb, 31 December 1902.
29 B. Webb, *Diary*, 16 September 1896.
30 'Charlotte does not really like me any more than I really like her: our continued friendly and mutually respectful relations and quite genuine loyalty and friendliness towards each other are a testimony to good manners in the widest sense—to tolerance and kindliness on both sides'. B. Webb, *Diary*, 1 May 1925.
31 B. Webb, *Diary*, 8 July 1903.
32 Alan M. McBriar, 'Sidney Webb and the LCC' in *The Webbs and Their Work* (1949), 81–2. Also ch VIII of his excellent *Fabian Socialism and English Politics, 1884–1918* (1962).
33 Formerly assistant to Clerk Maxwell at Cambridge, then Principal of the Durham College of Science in Newcastle where his energies had earned him the nickname of 'William the Builder'.

34 W. Garnett, 'A Retrospect: How the County Council became the Local Education Authority for London', *The Educational Record*, April 1929.
35 B. Webb, *Diary*, 5 June 1902.
36 *Webb Papers*, Gorst to S. Webb, 24 June 1902.
37 B. Webb, *Diary*, December 1902.
38 *Webb Papers*, Robert Morant to S. Webb, mid-May 1903. In fairness to Morant, it should be said that at the end of 1902 he had drafted a bill for London which had been killed by Walter Long.
39 Brian Simon, *Education and the Labour Movement 1870–1920* (1965).
40 As in Macclesfield, for example. N. L. Pole, *The Macclesfield School Board* (Advanced Diploma dissertation of the Cambridge Institute of Education, July 1971).
41 Simon, 226, no 1.
42 B. Webb, *Our Partnership* (1947), 97.

Acknowledgement

The author wishes to thank the London School of Economics and Political Science for giving permission to quote from the Passfield Papers.

For plates, provided by the author, see p 152

MARJORIE CRUICKSHANK

The Denominational Schools' Issue in the Twentieth Century

THE issue of denominational schools in this country is one which successive ministers in the post-war period have treated with the utmost respect. Whatever modifications have been made in the details of the 1944 settlement, its basic principles have been maintained, and in the same breath that individual ministers have announced adjustments, they have emphasised their determination to keep intact the balance of the dual system. Clearly, professional advisers have warned their political chiefs of the delicacy of the problem and of the difficulties and dangers involved in any major reconsideration of principles. Ministers have restricted themselves therefore to minor revisions and parliamentary critics have been discouraged from widening the area of debate.

Historically the dual system is rooted in the traditional conflict between Church and Dissent. Formally it was incorporated in the famous compromise solution of 1870, which provided for the continued existence of voluntary elementary schools associated with particular churches alongside public elementary schools to be built and partially maintained by the new local authorities, the school boards. The distinction between the two types of school was clear-cut. In contrast to the board school which was restricted in its religious teaching to undenominational instruction, the voluntary school was free to teach the faith of a particular denomination and to rear its children to become worshipping members within a religious community. Financially, voluntary schools were at a disadvantage compared with board schools since, though both types of schools received state aid, the latter alone were supported by aid from the local rates.

Philosophically the issue concerns the liberty of the individual, the fundamental right of parents to have children educated in schools of

non-conformist "for"

their choice. Expressed in this way as a democratic principle it sounds very simple; but in the circumstances of a mixed community, where the rights of the minority conflict with the wishes of the majority it can be deceptively simple. Certainly in the early years of the twentieth century the powerful body of Nonconformist opinion claimed then, as it had done in preceding decades, that any distinctive teaching, which went beyond the common ground of bible teaching provided by public authorities and available to all, should be regarded as an extra to be paid for by the religious communities who desired it. In a situation where the full acknowledgement of minority rights would have been offensive to the majority, the state endeavoured to preserve a balance, to establish an equilibrium between the freedom of individuals and the freedom of the people as a whole.

As compared with arrangements in other western countries the English compromise has included unusual features. Here church schools have always been part of the national system of education. They have not, as for example, in France and the USA, been divorced from a wholly secular state system, and the vitality of the denominational sector has ensured not merely survival but firm partnership within the national framework. In England, the issue of Church and State has never assumed the form of a conflict between secularists and clericalists, for religion has never been banned from publicly-provided schools. Indeed, the strongest opponents of clericalism, the Nonconformists, have consistently pressed for the universal teaching of undenominational religion.

A unique feature of the dual system has been the distinction between the financing of the two types of school. The relationship of denominational schools to the wholly public sector has been rationalised in terms of financial penalty, in Gladstone's words, 'a void' which the denominations must fill from their own resources. After 1902 when responsibility for maintenance of church schools passed to the new Local Education Authorities, the financial void corresponded to the cost of buildings and repairs. In 1944 the principle was retained by the requirement that managers should pay the total cost of new school buildings (except for school places for 'displaced' pupils) and 50 per cent towards repairs.[1] Today, though the proportionate contribution has been reduced, the principle remains. In the words of Sir Edward Boyle (now Lord Boyle), Opposition spokesman at the time of the latest revision, 'If certain people want a voluntary school with the education reflecting a particular religious atmosphere, it is right that they should pay something for it.'[2]

In the various negotiations over the last thirty years, the proportion of costs to be contributed by the denomination has been determined by the practicalities of the situation, both by the needs of denominationalists in an inflationary world and by the consideration of other interests. Essentially, arrangements have been designed to enable the denominations to make provision comparable with that of county schools. The request for a 75 per cent grant towards all building costs, which in 1944 was judged to be unrealistic, was very largely met by the 1959 Act. Some seven years later, when Roman Catholics were pressing for 85 per cent grant in order to enable them to participate in programmes of comprehensive reorganisation, a figure of 80 per cent, available for the first time without reservation for new schools, was finally agreed upon. In the words of the then Secretary of State, Anthony Crosland, '85 per cent would have been considered by many to be inconsistent with a voluntary school system, it would have brought the principle of the dual system into question, and perhaps even placed it in jeopardy'.[3] Clearly much backstage calculation and bartering goes on before the announcement of a final figure which is acceptable all-round.

Not surprisingly the dual system of schools has been criticised on grounds of expensive duplication and administrative untidiness. Today, as in the post-Hadow era, the whole programme of school reorganisation is complicated by dual control. Even on routine matters of administration, local officials often find the degree of independence of the voluntary school sector irksome and are apt to refer slightingly to the amateurishness of voluntary school managers. Teachers, too, are far from insensitive to the problems of clerical managership and on professional grounds their unions have long opposed such practices as clerical 'right of entry'. For a variety of reasons many teachers who were themselves students at denominational colleges, prefer not to seek appointment in denominational schools.

Compulsory provision of religious observance and religious instruction in all state-aided schools was an integral part of the 1944 settlement with the churches. Contemporary opinion today, particularly among young teachers and student teachers, is critical of the desultory teaching which often occupies that part of the timetable designated Religious Education in county and controlled schools. Demand for compulsory, as distinct from the previous optional provision, was a product of wartime pressure, a reaction against Fascist ideology with its emphasis on the State at the expense of individual and family. Members of a generation which had seen children wrenched from their parents and brought up in 'the spirit of the community' to become 'New Germans', were stirred to demand more positive teaching of western values in the form of religion. The first public reference to the need for educational reform came in 1941 in the form of a joint request by Anglicans and Nonconformists for provision of sound religious teaching in the schools.[4] Acceptance of the so-called Archbishops' Five Points was incorporated in the general agreement, so that religious instruction according to Agreed Syllabuses should be given in all county schools and those voluntary schools which became controlled schools.[5]

At a time when fresh legislation was under discussion in 1968, the then Secretary of State, Michael Stewart, declared himself in favour of retaining the compulsory provision. He declared the requirement to be 'non negotiable', but he asked for 'articulate support of parents throughout Britain to withstand the tremendous pressure for abolition'. The response was hardly encouraging. In general the adult population tolerates religion for its children. Possibly parents associate it with moral teaching or in some vague way consider it to be an influence for good.

Politically the success of Butler's war-time bill was rooted in extensive all-party negotiations. It is a lesson which post-war ministers have taken to heart and successive adjustments have been introduced as agreed measures. The old political feuds, long associated with

church schools, are now revived only in reminiscences. Memories of
Nonconformist resistance following the 1902 Act were evoked more
than sixty years later in parliamentary debates by the member for
Bedfordshire, Brian Parkyn, who recollected that his grandfather 'went
to prison on a number of occasions fighting against Church schools
and even the very gold chain which I am wearing went to court several
times and was brought back'.[6]

The intensity of the 1902 controversy left an indelible memory on
contemporaries. Even in World War II, Churchill had regarded any
revision of the Balfour Act as political dynamite. In 1942 the terms
of his reprimand to Butler would have discouraged a lesser man. 'We
cannot have any Party politics in wartime', he had written. 'The religious issue would raise these in the most acute and dangerous form.'[7]
For their part, Roman Catholic veterans had been terrified lest new
negotiations would resuscitate the old Liberal 'contracting out' proposals, and they had made clear their determination to remain within
the national system. On the Nonconformist front, too, some of the
negotiators had found it hard to forget the past, though fortunately
Dr Scott Lidgett, the great Free Church statesman of the time, had
been so repelled by former acrimony that he had come out in support
of a compromise solution.[8]

In the event it had become clear that a major resettlement came
within Butler's definition of 'the art of the possible'. Within a period
of forty years the whole milieu had so changed that the issue left the
general public unmoved. In our own secular society indifference is
even more marked; the emotional protests of the past, the mass meetings, passionate oratory and press publicity echo the high feeling and
crude intolerance of an age that has gone. In particular, time has
eroded former public antipathy towards Roman Catholicism as a
religion alien in association and allegiance. In the localities Catholics
no longer have cause to fear the sort of discrimination which operated
against them in earlier years. Evidence of Roman Catholic trust and
reliance in the impartiality of the central authority at a time when they
had cause to fear local prejudice accounts for the large number of
Catholic schools on the direct grant list today. As the Donnison Report

of 1970 pointed out, almost one-third of direct grant schools are Catholic schools including twenty-seven in the Liverpool archdiocese alone.[9]

The divisiveness in Liverpool was brought into sharp focus as late as the thirties, when the Local Education Authority refused to implement the terms of the 1936 Act (a once-and-for-all measure which provided for up to 75 per cent assistance towards the cost of reorganisation of denominational schools on Hadow lines), and had to be brought to heel by the Board of Education. Today such a confrontation between Protestants and Catholics would be inconceivable in a city where the religious communities are no longer socially isolated and where the ecumenical movement has helped to dissolve old friction and hostility.

In the twentieth century, Nonconformity has probably suffered most from the general decline in religious affiliation. Even before World War I the power of political Nonconformity had disappeared, and during the inter-war years it continued to lose ground as a social force. Yet throughout the long years of decline, its leaders refused to contemplate any revision of the 1902 Act which entailed expenditure of additional public money on denominational schools. Instead, they nourished the vain hope that by a process of attrition such schools would disappear altogether. Even during World War II survivors among the old militants warned Butler of the 'sunken rocks' which he was liable to encounter in raising the issue. In contrast to their general attitude of reluctant acquiescence in the 1944 settlement, a younger generation of Nonconformity gave its blessing to the latest financial revision which was brought forward as an agreed measure in 1966.[10]

Today opposition to further financial aid to denominational schools comes not from Nonconformity but from a vocal group of humanists, in particular from the British Humanist Association, a body of professional people who present their case with crisp cogency. Indeed, in the latest parliamentary debates the humanists tabled the only adverse amendment to increased subsidies. On grounds of the principle, they express objection to 'closed schools' and to 'closed headships', rungs on the promotion ladder, which, they claim, are barred to general

applicants. Like the Nonconformists of old they have attacked particularly the existence of denominational schools in single-school
areas.[11] Unlike the Nonconformists, however, they have consistently
opposed the teaching of religion in county schools. Their claim to have
public support would seem dubious, since popular polls have produced very different results. A comparison of the different poll
questions reveals how apparently innocent distinctions in wording can
produce conflicting response.[12]

In the general evolution of attitudes during the twentieth century,
Anglicans have often appeared inconsistent and vacillating. As representatives of an Established Church they have had to look beyond
their 'domestic' role as the owners of schools, to a 'general' role of
responsibility for the teaching of religion in all public schools. However, their counsels have been so fraught with dissension that they
have pursued no firm policy. Each diocese has been left to decide for
itself.[13]

For Anglicans the great age of school building had already passed
by 1900. Even the generous terms of the 1936 Act had failed to elicit
from them viable schemes for the new post-primary (special agreement) schools. It was for their schools that Butler had devised in 1942
'controlled' status whereby the Church retained the school building,
the right to give two periods a week of denominational instruction and
the right to minority representation in the management of a school.
To all other intents and purposes, however, the school was to become
a county school. In effect, however, local managers frequently clung
on to their all-age schools, which survived as aided schools into the
fifties and sixties. Their poverty produced some strange expedients,
as in the case of one urban school in 1948, where the nineteenth-
century galleries were repaired rather than replaced on grounds of
economy.[14]

Today the controlled schools of the Church of England outnumber
the aided schools. Compared with 20 per cent of the school population
in Anglican schools in 1938, 5 per cent now attend Church aided
schools. Significantly, only 2 per cent out of the entire secondary
school population are in these schools. The strength of the Anglican

aided commitment therefore lies in the primary sector, particularly in rural areas such as East Anglia and in towns of the North West, traditionally Anglican strongholds. The majority of the buildings of aided primary schools, however, are survivals of the all-age era, and the current policy of replacement of Victorian primary schools, launched by the present Secretary of State, Mrs Thatcher, will reduce the Church's stake in this sector. Already many of the small village schools have been compulsorily closed. On average Anglican aided schools are diminishing at the rate of forty a year and controlled schools at twice that rate. In the post-war period money for new aided schools had come from the sale of school sites, a source which has dried up in more recent years. All evidence seems to suggest a considerable contraction in the numbers of Anglican aided schools in the future.

In 1970, the Durham Report on Religious Education, *The Fourth R*, stressed the need for the Church to retain a share over the whole range of the public system so that its representatives could speak with authority on every sector.[15] By deliberate policy the stake in teacher education has been increased. Support for colleges rather than schools is, of course, less burdensome economically, and under a system of direct state grants, Church colleges enjoy a wide measure of autonomy. Amid the financial stringency of the thirties, the Church had been compelled to close colleges. In the post-war years, however, and particularly since the publication of the Robbins Report in 1963, provision has been energetically expanded—between 1963 and 1970, students in Church of England colleges have increased from 9,000 to 18,000— and the entire image of the colleges has been transformed. With great vision new colleges—the first to be built by the Church in the twentieth century—have been established in the university centres of Canterbury and Lancaster, bringing the total number of Anglican colleges to twenty-seven.

Churchmen clearly see the expansion of their provision for future teachers, both graduates and non-graduates, in relation to fulfilment of their dual 'general' and 'domestic' role in education. Their expenditure in teacher education is grounded in the belief that the context of ethos and values within which education takes place is of vital importance. It is clear, however, that today, in contrast to past practice, there is less overt emphasis on distinctive attitudes and values. Indeed, among Churchmen themselves there is disagreement in their conception of the fundamental purposes of Church colleges.[16] It would perhaps be illuminating to take some soundings of the opinion of past and present students on their experiences, and to ascertain how the actuality has corresponded with expectations. After all, students *choose* to go to Church colleges, though it would appear that their religious ardour, measured in terms of attendance at chapel and course work, is not conspicuous. Anglican decision to give prominence to teacher education can be judged only over a long term.

Today it is no longer the Established Church but the Roman Catholic community which has the largest number of fully denominational schools. With well over 700,000 children in its aided and special agreement schools it now caters for 9 per cent of the school population. From the time of Manning, Roman Catholics had drawn strength from the consistency of their objective, a place in a Catholic school for every Catholic child. Their purpose had been clear, to save children from 'the dangers of perversion' which they risked both in the proselytising schools attached to Protestant churches and in the board schools with, in Manning's words, their 'featureless, phantom common Christianity'. Their own schools stood for Catholicism, not only as a faith to be taught, but as a life to be lived. In the numerous Irish communities the school was part of the denominational enclave, associated with religious solidarity and social exclusiveness.

The Hadow Report of 1926 was the first threat to the traditional self-contained parish, since the proposed post-primary schools would of necessity be interparochial. In fact, despite the Roman Catholic response to the 1936 Act, their post-primary schools did not materialise until after the war; and at the time of the 1944 Act, the typical Roman Catholic elementary school was still all-age in organisation, shabby and sub-standard in its buildings.

During the fifties and sixties, Roman Catholic education was transformed by a massive building programme. Provisions for 'displaced pupils' under the 1944 Act and later concessions under the 1959 Act were exploited to the full. Subtleties of distinction sometimes proved difficult. In the words of Edward Boyle in 1966, 'the metaphysics of when a place is a new place and when it is a transferred or substituted place had become pretty fantastic'.[17] In effect it was the movement of population which necessitated the extension of building grants to all new schools. The 1967 Act, associated with comprehensive reorganisation, provided for just such an extension.

Roman Catholic post-war educational effort has been impressive. In the school sector overall expansion has doubled the provision of places, in the field of teacher education seven new colleges have been added to the existing nine and between 1963 and 1970 the college population has risen from 4,500 to 11,000. Soaring costs had brought the sum expended on school buildings alone to £40 millions by 1967, compared with an estimated £9 million in 1944. Over the country as a whole, some two-thirds of Catholic children are in Catholic schools. However, proportions vary between areas, and in growth regions in the South almost half of the Catholic child population attend county schools.[18]

Faced with comprehensive reorganisation Roman Catholic authorities have responded by a policy of rationalisation. Resources are therefore in process of being diverted from the private to the public sector with its wider intake, a change of status for individual schools from independent to voluntary aided. Similarly, many of the direct grant schools, formerly selective in their entry, are being adapted to fit into local patterns of reorganisation as 'upper' schools. Though Roman Catholic authorities value highly the financial arrangement associated with direct grant status, they find no difficulty in merging their direct grant schools (which have more than 90 per cent of their pupils financed by Local Education Authorities) into comprehensive programmes.[19]

In post-war years the climate of negotiations between Church and State has altered dramatically, a change which has been reflected in the character and outlook of Roman Catholic leaders themselves. In the past, even as late as the early forties, the aggressive and high-handed tactics associated with prelates like Archbishop Downey of Liverpool stirred up inevitable reaction. Butler himself had found it most difficult to make contact with the veteran leaders, whose apparent indifference to all points of view save their own, he had found distinctly unhelpful. In contrast, the statesmanship and realism of Roman Catholic negotiators in recent years has contributed to the smoothness of discussions and to successive alleviations of the financial burden. It is not without interest that at the second Vatican Council, reference was made to the fairness of the English settlement by Cardinal Heenan.

Comprehensive reorganisation has brought a new challenge to the denominations. In principle both Anglicans and Roman Catholics are keen to co-operate with local schemes. Anglicans seem reconciled to a reduction in their 'domestic' role, though as a function of their 'general' role they wish to retain provision for religious education in all county schools. (Their attachment to 'controlled' status would appear to be minimal.) Already Catholics have built comprehensive schools in new housing areas; elsewhere they are in process of adapting existing schools to new patterns. However, there is no longer unity within the Roman Catholic Church on the principle of segregated schools. Critics do not hesitate to question the relevance in contemporary society of perpetuating an educational exclusiveness associated with penal days, and to urge exploration of other methods of inculcating the Faith.[20] The current ferment must bring reappraisal of policy. Some parents who are keen to retain Catholic primary schools express their preference for inter-denominational secondary schools. It may well be, therefore, that experiments with interdenominational schools in exceptional areas will lead to the development of a network of joint Christian schools. Similarly a broadening of the foundations of denominational colleges of education on ecumenical lines may correspond to future needs.

The English solution to the denominational issue has been empirical. Its illogicality is in contrast to the rational solutions adopted by the USA and by Scotland, the one excluding denominational schools both from the public system and from public aid, the other integrating them without financial discrimination into the state system. Both systems, however, have been under pressure in recent years. In the USA, though temporary devices such as dual enrolment have been adopted to ease the financial difficulties of the parochial schools, the problem of inequality of school provision remains. In Scotland, the rigid segregation of children into Catholic and Protestant schools, particularly in the city of Glasgow, has nourished bigotry and intolerance to a degree unknown in England for many decades. Indeed, many of the English Catholics, who have applauded the so-called Scottish solution, would find it little to their liking at close quarters. In the long run the great merit of the less logical English system is its capacity to respond to changing needs and circumstances.

Today, there are many in England who find segregated schools anomalous at a time when by conscious endeavour the attempt is being made to break down between children barriers of class, race and colour. Events in Northern Ireland would seem to substantiate their view. Among denominationalists, a number of Roman Catholics are for the first time uncertain where they stand. For their community the increasing mobility of the population poses new financial problems. Quite a different problem is presented by the difficulty of staffing their schools with practising members of their own community, teachers who are able and willing to give religious teaching.

It was the legislation of the mid-twentieth century which brought the extension of the dual system, hitherto confined to the elementary sector, into secondary education. In the intervening quarter of a century the proportion of children educated in fully denominational (aided) schools has shrunk to less than half. Ahead lies the great bulge in secondary education. Official estimates forecast a rise in school population from the present 8 million to 10 million in 1980 and 11 million in 1990. There seems little possibility that the denominational sector can keep pace with the rising school population. The likelihood is rather that future negotiations will seek to restrict the main denominational contribution to the lower age-range in primary and middle schools. At that point the state may well be able to offer generous terms to the voluntary sector. As the area of education under

THE STRENGTH OF THE VOLUNTARY SCHOOL SECTOR IN THE TWENTIETH CENTURY

Council (County, after 1944) and Voluntary Schools, 1903, 1938 and 1969

Year	COUNCIL		CHURCH OF ENGLAND		ROMAN CATHOLIC		OTHERS	
	Schools	Pupils	Schools	Pupils	Schools	Pupils	Schools	Pupils
1903	6,003	2,870,213	11,687	2,338,602	1,058	337,295	1,494	421,160
1938	10,363	3,540,512	8,979	1,125,497	1,266	377,073	308	44,403
1969	*County*		*Aided and Special Agreement*		*Aided and Special Agreement*		*Aided and Special Agreement*	
Primary	14,581	3,462,210	2,637	365,145	1,941	489,495	43	7,517
Secondary	4,481	2,513,386	144	59,960	532	235,399	87	45,674
Total	19,062	5,975,596	2,781	425,105	2,473	724,894	130	53,191
			Controlled		*Controlled*		*Controlled*	
Primary			3,737	448,178	1	27	116	16,525
Secondary			70	29,122	—		153	80,354
Total			3,807	477,300	1	27	269	96,879

direct denominational control contracts, churchmen—Anglicans and Roman Catholic alike—may well look afresh at their role over the entire field of education and they may seek to extend, to further education, facilities which they already offer in higher education. In the last resort, the extent and range of denominational and interdenominational effort will depend not only on direction from above but on conscious decision and co-operation of members of the religious communities, of parents, teachers and of students themselves.

University of Keele

References

1 Education Act, 1944, clauses 102, 103 and 104.
2 Hansard, 6th Series, vol 735, col 905.
3 Ibid, 840.   4 *The Times*, 13 February 1941.
5 Education Act, 1944, clause 25.   6 Hansard, op cit, col 884.
7 R. A. Butler, *The Art of the Possible*, 1971, 94.
8 Marjorie Cruickshank, *Church and State in English Education, 1870 to the Present Day*, 1963. Chapter 7 gives a detailed account of the negotiations.
9 *Public Schools Commission*, Second Report, vol 1, 1970, para 112.
10 Lord Boyle pays tribute to influence of Michael Stewart, *The Times*, 12 Feb 1971.
11 Eg, *Religion in Schools*, British Humanist Association, 1967, paras 30–3.
12 On religious education very different answers were recorded by the following: 1965 New Society Survey by National Opinion Polls, 1969 British Humanist Association Survey by National Opinion Polls and 1966 Schools Council Survey by the Government Social Survey.
13 Inefficiency and division of control within the diocese has been criticised in a commission under the chairmanship of the Bishop of Carlisle, *Partners in Education, the Role of the Diocese*, 1971.
14 Managers' Minutes, School of St George & St Giles, Newcastle-under-Lyme, 1 September 1947. Repair qualified for grant under the heading of 'fair wear and tear'. Removal, constituting improvement to building, would not qualify for grant. The galleries were not removed until 1958.
15 Report of the Commission on Religious Education in Schools, 1970, para 549.
16 R. A. Adcock and J. Elliott, 'The Significance of the Durham Report for the Church Colleges of Education', *Education for Teaching*, 84, Spring 1971, 28–43.
17 Hansard, op cit, 904.   18 *The Tablet*, 24 April 1971.
19 The Manchester LEA, for example, has distinguished between non-denominational direct grant schools, where it will cease to take up places after 1971, and denominational (RC) direct grant schools where it will continue to take up places pending the outcome of discussion on their role in the comprehensive system. *Education*, 2 July 1971.
20 Eg, criticism expressed by the Catholic Renewal Movement in A. E. C. W. Spencer, *The Future of Catholic Education in England and Wales*, 1971.

Book Reviews

Education Since 1800, by Ivor Morrish, ALLEN & UNWIN, 1970, pp 244, £2.25 cloth, £1.40 paperback.
Society and Education in England since 1800, by P. W. Musgrave, METHUEN, 1968, pp 152, £1.25 cloth, 62½p paperback.
English Popular Education, 1780–1970, by David Wardle, CAMBRIDGE UNIVERSITY PRESS, 1971, pp 182, £1.75 cloth, 60p paperback.

Each of these three books attempts to solve a problem common to all who teach the history of English education, since about 1800, in colleges or university departments of education—namely to provide students with a survey of this major topic which is brief, scholarly, accurate, readable, cogent, and thought-provoking. It must be said at once that none of these authors solves the problem, or indeed comes within sight of doing so. The student will do better to stick to Professor Barnard or to the relevant chapters of Professor Armytage. Mr Morrish's book is the least satisfactory of the three. He admits that the book can be 'little more than a *coup d'oeil* of the development of education since 1800': in fact it appears to consist largely of a re-hash of most of the official reports of the period, followed by an odd tailpiece of four chapters on Herbart, Froebel, Froebelianism and Montessori, and Dewey. It contains horribly little directly about schools or children; it says some very naïve things (the Sunday School movement 'established that religious leaning which state education has had in this country ever since'; Robert Lowe was 'anything and everything but an educationist'); it is heavily descriptive and makes little effort to analyse; and it devotes so excessive a proportion of its space to the years since 1945, as to make it patently unbalanced as a piece of history.

Professor Musgrave is altogether more sophisticated than Mr

Morrish. Thus, for example, he invites his readers to reflect on the permanence of some Victorian decisions, like those which led to the Dual System and to separate patterns of training for elementary and secondary teachers. He uses to very good effect statistics about such varied matters as Sunday newspapers, moneys raised in rates per scholar, and HMIs. But he writes most inelegantly and sometimes ungrammatically ('This had been set up as a direct result of the Great Exhibition of 1851 when some percipient observers noted that the techniques and the standard of design of the Continental exhibitors was catching up on those shown by British industry' and 'The problem of where the threshold of redefinition lies is difficult of solution' are unhappy specimens of his style). Like most sociologists, he generalises with more abandon than most historians about the meaning and impact of class, for example, in promoting educational change in the late nineteenth century. Yet the most serious charge to be laid against Professor Musgrave is simply that his use of the concept of 'the definition of the situation', which is central to his method, adds nothing whatever to the student's understanding of history; indeed it seems certain that many readers' grasp will be hindered by its artificiality. The elaborate introduction from time to time of sociological terminology, together with the stiff framework into which he forces his argument, tells us no more than that the Acts of 1870, 1902 and 1944 were important turning-points, that they were produced by various social causes, and that they had various social results. Neither Professor Musgrave's causes nor his results are novel; it would be unreasonable to expect them to be.

Mr Wardle's book is the most engaging of the three. He recognises the need to throw ideas at students, as, for example, when he talks of the self-generating power of education. He ranges widely; and, arguing that 'it is the untidy and unpredictable nature of popular education in England which makes it unrewarding to write its history around the major reports and education acts', he writes about schools and children and teachers as neither Professor Musgrave nor Mr Morrish is willing to do, and he makes most welcome use of good local material from Nottingham. By this book at least a student might be sparked into

interest and thought. But it has serious limitations. Mr Wardle
rambles about in time in a most confusing way; despite his frequent
and justified emphasis on the continuing factors which have affected
English education through modern times, he leaves the reader with
very muddled impressions of chronological development. There is
altogether too much 'non-education' in so short a book: it is quaint,
if agreeable, to find in these 160 pages Hegel, W. S. Gilbert and Calvin,
not to mention 'Saint' Monday and Godfrey's Cordial. Then Mr
Wardle hardly ever gives the source of his quotations, which is unfortunate as well as unscholarly, for some of them are rather good.
And he is a man of strong but conventional prejudices, hostile to
'amateurs', educational administrators, grammar schools, and public
schools.

These are lightweight books, even when one allows for the fact that
it is, notoriously, far more difficult to write a good short book than a
good long book on a major historical theme. Our students deserve
something better. What we badly need in this field, to take two comparable examples at random, is someone who can write as authori-
tatively and incisively as T. S. Ashton did nearly a quarter of a century
ago on *The Industrial Revolution*, or as clearly and coolly as Richard
Storry did in 1960 in his model Pelican, *A History of Modern Japan*.
Yet, to be fair to the three authors under review, we must admit that
there are some serious obstacles to the writing of convincing short
general books about the history of English education. One of these,
plainly, is the unbalanced nature of the materials, both primary resources and monographs, available to the potential author. Thus we
know, for instance, a great deal about the nineteenth-century public
schools but, as Professor Roach has once again noted in his admirable
study of *Public Examinations in England, 1850–1900*, far less relatively
about what the Victorians called 'middle-class education'. Recent work
by Dr Sutherland, Dr Johnson and Dr Bishop, among others, is
beginning to clarify the historical role of the central government in
English education during the last 150 years; but we know staggeringly
little, at any depth of analysis, about the activities of local education
authorities since 1902. We badly need substantial accounts of the

earlier colleges of education, of the evolution of the secondary school-master, and of the relationship between education and the press.

Yet the gaps in our knowledge are perhaps the least of the obstacles. Two others, very different in kind, deserve more attention. The first of these arises from the circumstances in which we teach the history of education: it reflects the widespread readiness among educationists to assume that the past existed in order to produce the present and, as a result, the custom of teaching only those parts of it which seem overtly relevant to present needs and demands. Logically these attitudes are no doubt familiar to all who teach history of any kind at any level: in practice they may be at their most dangerous and extreme in colleges and departments of education, where the history of education is, for nearly all, solely a background study, where the students are overwhelmingly concerned with the daily problems of their craft, and where the teachers are professionally passionate to be 'with it' and therefore contemptuous or neglectful of the past. As Mr Morrish's and, to smaller extent, Mr Wardle's books (but not Professor Musgrave's) show, the temptation to devote far too much space to the nearly contemporary or to treat the past as simply so many steps on the road of progress to the present, is often almost irresistible in the context of education. We cannot avoid seeing the past through the spectacles of the present, but this gives us no right to see only what we want to find there. More than most students of history, those of us concerned with the history of education must heed Professor Elton's austere warning: 'The task of history is to understand the past, and if the past is to be understood it must be given full respect in its own right. And unless it is properly understood, any use of it in the present must be suspect and can be dangerous.'*

A second sort of difficulty faced by writers of general books on the history of education is at least hinted at by the curious fact that none of our three authors, each of whom deals at some length with the Balfour Act, appears to refer in bibliography or elsewhere to the remarkable chapters written on this subject by Elie Halévy forty-five years ago in the epilogue to his *History of the English People in the*

* G. R. Elton, *The Practice of History* (1967), pp 47–8.

Nineteenth Century. No doubt Halévy's work has been corrected in detail by the research of Professor Eaglesham: it remains nevertheless far and away the best discussion of any major English educational statute, written by a scholar of liberal and pellucid mind, who was one of the great European historians of this century. Now Halévy was not an educationist, and most of the history of education, in this country at least, has been written by educationists. Few professional historians have ventured into the field. Why this is so is not clear; they may simply be discouraged by what they find going on, or feel that there is no adequate professional audience for their work. The technical difficulties are scarcely a serious barrier: education indeed is a technical subject, but no more so than, for example, many aspects of economic history, whose practitioners are not normally expected to be bankers or entrepreneurs or steel technologists. It is also a difficult one, in historical terms: the development of education, we are beginning to realise, is the result of so varied a range of factors social and economic, religious and political and biographical, that its analysis and grasp present a formidable challenge. Those who are best equipped to re-spond to this challenge by their training and their studies are the professional historians. The few who have seriously entered the lists, like Professor Perkin, Mr David Newsome (whose transfer of allegiance to the practice of education has not, one hopes, permanently deprived history of a distinguished practitioner) and now Dr Sutherland, have shown what could be achieved. It is to be hoped that before long there may be many more like them. Otherwise the gulf in the study of the history of education between educationists and historians will remain wide and little crossed, and the standard of work in this rich and socially highly significant field of study will remain far poorer than it ought to be. And for the students' sake, in particular, one prays that some day, not too far off, one of the professionals will give us a book, perhaps called *The Educational Revolution*, comparable with Ashton's masterpiece.

University of Exeter   C. P. Hill

Juan Luis Vives, by Carlos G. Noreña, MARTINUS NIJHOFF, The
   Hague, 1971, 45 guilders.

This important work is based on the whole corpus of Vives' writings, and shows at the same time an enviable mastery of the secondary
literature in English, French, Spanish, Italian, German and Dutch.
For the first time students will be able, in a systematic and detailed
way, to see Vives' educational writings in their theological and philosophical setting and to see them, too, as part of a general attack on the
social and political problems of the early sixteenth century, of the state
of the poor, of the role of the family, as well as of nationalism and
peace.

The work opens with a biographical section in which the relationship
between Vives and Erasmus is studied in detail. The author concludes
that Vives has for too long been thought of merely as a disciple of
Erasmus in whose shadow his reputation has been formed, as one
who merely transmitted Erasmian ideals as they stood. In fact, as the
author shows, there was a good deal of tension between the two men,
even though his contact with Erasmus may rightly be counted as a
point of departure for Vives, after Erasmus's criticisms of Parisian
philosophical and theological conservatism.

But during the period of their acquaintance—Vives first met Erasmus in 1516 and his last letter to him was dated 1534, two years before
Erasmus's death—there was not only a decided cooling-off period
but also a marked shift towards independence of thought on the part
of Vives, exemplified particularly in a greater emphasis on secular
problems, with correspondingly fewer references to the salvational
aspect of morality. From 1530 Vives was personally and intellectually
independent of Erasmus, having produced a body of writings which
transcended the predominant fideism of Erasmus. Like Erasmus, but
more so, Vives was more interested in the ethical dimension of religion
than its revelatory or institutional concerns, which presumably is why
Vives' reputation is not so high in Spain, whose writers emphasise
his Catholic orthodoxy at the expense of almost everything else in his
work and thought.

The growing secularisation of Vives' thought is particularly apparent in his playing down of Christian revelation and his emphasis on the importance of a knowledge of man's history, man's past experience ('the nurse of Prudence'), in solving such problems of the day as peace, nationalism and sectarianism. The long analytical sections on each of Vives' major works in these areas, and especially the chapters on 'The Range and Purpose of Human Knowledge' and 'The Process of Knowledge', are of the utmost importance to the understanding of Vives' educational thought. For example, history becomes an instrument of moral education, wisdom without virtue a total impossibility. In his far-reaching eclecticism Vives insists that it is more important to use the natural resources of the world well than to attempt a conceptual elucidation of the universe, if the bigoted sectarianism and exaggerated nationalism which all too often are started in the early stages of a child's education are to be countered. This, of course, makes a teacher's task more difficult, for it is always easier to serve a master than to make up one's mind after serious comparative study.

Students of Renaissance education, and readers of this journal in particular, will naturally ask how far the present work takes them beyond W. H. Woodward's *Studies*, Foster Watson's translations and his important paper on Vives' contribution to educational psychology. With this question in mind, it must be admitted that the chapter on education is rather disappointing; for despite the claim that 'Vives' pedagogical wisdom was firmly based upon his own ethical, religious and epistemological principles', the chapter appears to be juxtaposed alongside the others rather than fully integrated with them.

The student of the history of education will have to do much of his own work in relating Vives, the educational thinker, to Vives, the social reformer and philosopher. Nevertheless, the materials for such work are now for the first time available to him within the covers of one book, and for this we have every reason to be thankful. No exaggerated claims are made on Vives' behalf: 'his genius was not to invent but to give an eloquent and judicious expression to the concerns and goals of his generation, and to embody them in a practical programme of general education'. But by drawing the reader's attention to Vives' insistence on the social function of knowledge, the author is able to pin-point Vives' chief contribution to the history of ideas and to the history of education, his 'vision of a unified Europe, linked together not by Church or Empire but by natural tolerance, mutual respect and enlightened self-interest', a vision which is not without relevance to this day.

University of Birmingham   Kenneth Charlton

Education in Industrial Wales 1700-1900, A Study of the Works Schools System, by Leslie Wynne Evans, AVALON BOOKS, Cardiff, 1971, pp viii + 362, £3.75.

It was a distinctive feature of Welsh education in the nineteenth century that collieries, quarries and metalworks frequently set up their own schools for the education of their child workers and the children of their adult employees. So extensive did this practice become that it made a very significant contribution to the total provision of education in the Principality, especially between 1833 and 1870. Dr Leslie Wynne Evans has here drawn together the results of many years of his own research and performed a valuable service by setting forth this underestimated theme.

He traces the early development of such schools from the Society of Mineral and Battery Works in the sixteenth century, through the charity schools first established by Sir Humphrey Mackworth at Esgair Hir mines in the eighteenth century, as a prelude to their main expansion in the nineteenth. Then he traces the formation of such schools region by region in iron working (paying particular attention to the Dowlais schools of Sir John and Lady Guest), collieries, tinplate and other metal working industries of South Wales and the slate quarries of the north. Moving slightly aside from his main theme he contributes an interesting analysis of the varied reception of Sunday Schools in different areas of Wales, demonstrating their major importance in the rougher iron areas and in the coal fields and their relatively slighter importance among the more well-to-do, less turbulent and 'superior' workpeople of the copper region of Swansea. Both these areas he contrasts with Sunday Schools in the slate districts, where sixty per cent of the population of all ages attended such schools as virtually the only centres of working-class culture. Chapter 9, on Nonconformity and the Sunday Schools, is both the most analytical and also the most interesting in the whole book.

The various virtues of the work-school system are stressed. Since they were financed by generous gifts from the firms and maintained by a levy on workmen's wages they tended to be financially strong. Hence teachers' salaries were higher than in other day schools. This in turn meant that they could give advanced instruction and, since they did not need to apply for state capitation grants, they remained outside the curricular restrictions of the Code. They also ran evening classes and contributed to the higher education of their region and also aided the emergence of local democracy, with workers' representatives serving on the boards of management. Finally, they frequently showed the way to religious compromise in education. Since the employers were usually Anglican and the employees Dissenters, a common solution was often the formation after 1850 of works schools as neutral or undenominational British Schools to satisfy both sides. The chief drawback that the schools experienced was the early withdrawal of children even by respectable working-class families; most children being withdrawn after a year's schooling. This was attributed to the lack of need for literacy for their future work, the necessity of acquiring 'knack' skills early at work and the opportunities for further education in later life which diminished the finality of school leaving.

Dr Evans finds that in 1870 there were 88 works schools compared with 288 other National and British Schools in Wales but that the works schools contained about 16,000 pupils compared with the 17,000 of each of the two religious societies. After 1850 most works schools affiliated themselves to one or other of the two voluntary societies in order to qualify for government building grants and then, after the 1870 Act, they were gradually taken over by the School

Boards. But during their heyday from the 1830s to the 1870s they were a most important element in the total educational provision in Wales.

Valuable as this study is, it does lend itself to some criticism. Firstly one would have welcomed an early explanatory chapter indicating clearly the factory legislation provisions about the position of children in these various industries and the types of work they performed at what ages. It is not always clear whether works schools were for children actually working in the works, or for children of adult workers employed there. Also some early discussion of motivation would have been desirable. Pieces of evidence emerge about some industries being concerned 'to train those acute engineers and miners' and others being more concerned with 'the wise moral government of a large assemblage of workpeople'. But it would have been interesting to see, from an analysis of literacy samples in relation to occupations, which of these various industries really needed literate workers (hence justifying schools on those grounds) and which did not. This would also have given greater meaning to the other scattered comments about the lack of parental interest in prolonged day schooling because it was not necessary for work. Secondly the treatment of chapters 3 to 8 in which each individual industry is treated region by region and almost school by school, while most painstaking, does somewhat lack an interpretative form. These chapters become slightly tedious for the reader not intimately acquainted with the terrain; they lack by their nature an inherent narrative line or sequential argument, and the reader would have been helped by a summary of the main comparative points to emerge from this treatment of regions, periods and industries. This defect is most successfully avoided in chapter 9. Dr Evans' meticulous research and use of scattered unpublished sources is one of the great virtues of the book, but since several of these schools seem to be attached to the National Society, some use of their files in Great Peter Street would have been of added interest. Dr Evans may care to correct two small faults in any future edition. Faraday was not, of course, a knight (p 125) and the adjective 'climactic' is used erroneously (pp 110, 247) as a noun. Also non-bilingual historians would welcome the translations of various passages in Welsh, which could, indeed, have been put in his capacious appendices.

However, these criticisms do not detract from appreciation for what has clearly been a long-term project, based on genuinely original research, that has succeeded in adding considerably to our knowledge of a neglected area of educational history. Dr Evans has written an illuminating book on an important subject.

University of East Anglia   Michael Sanderson

Index

225

Sylvester, D. W., ed, *Educational Documents 800–1816* (C. R. Batho), 90–6
Wardle, David, *English Popular Education, 1780–1970* (C. P. Hill), 214–18
Rex, John, 17–18, 19
Robbins Report 1963, 207
Roberts, R. D., 43
Rochdale, 43, 55
von Rochow, 87
Roman Catholic school policy today, 208–10, 211
Rotherham, 16–17
Ruskin Hall, 53, 54f
Russell, Earl, 162–3, 170
Ryland, John, 143–6

Scholarships, county council, 181
School Board inspectors, 16–17
School boards, 11, 23–42, 174, 190–6, 200
School meals, 59, 62–3
School medical service, 59, 63–6
Schools Inquiry Commission Report 1867, 171
Science and Art Department, 161, 165f
Science publications 18c, 144, 145
Science teaching 18c, 139–57
Scotland, educational provision early 19c, 13
Select Committee 1865, 25
Shaw, G. B., 174, 176f, 187ff
Shaw, Hudson, 53, 54f
Sheffield:
  condition of children 1909 and 1910, 60ff
  open air schools, 60–77
Shipley, William, 147
Simon, Brian, 195
Smithfield, tutorial class at, 43
Social Democratic Federation, 175, 190

Socialism in England, Webb, S., 175
Society and Education in England since 1800, Musgrave, P. W., 14
Sociology and history, 14
Special schools 19c, 58–9
Specialisation, dangers of, 5, 8–9
Spleiss, Stefan, 118
Springvale House, Sheffield, 70
Staffordshire, North:
  Adult Education Society, 45
  Council for the Extension of Higher Education, 47
  extension and tutorial classes in, 44–53
  Miners' Higher Education Movement, 44
  proposed university college, 46–7, 49, 50–1
Stamer, Sir Lovelace Tomlinson, 45–6
Stanley, Lord, 166
State aid proposed 1868, 167
Statistical inquiries, societies, 13, 28
Stewart, Michael, 203
Stoke-upon-Trent, 48

Taunton Commission, 15
Tawney, R. H., 9–10, 15, 43–56 passim
Teacher training, 47f, 49–53, 82–9 (Belgium), 183, 207–8
Teaching methods 18c, 143–5
Technical Education Board LCC, 179–82
Technical Instruction Act 1889, 180f, 183, 191
Temple, Frederick, 32
Titmuss, R. M., 16
de Tocqueville, 10
Townshend, Charlotte Payne-, 184, 189
Toynbee Hall, 43, 44
Training colleges, 67, 183, 207–8
Trentham, 51, 52
Tuberculosis in schoolchildren, 61, 67, 72